Secrets, Silences & Betrayals

Edited by
Bill F. Ndi

Langaa Research & Publishing CIG
Mankon, Bamenda

Publisher:
Langaa RPCIG
Langaa Research & Publishing Common Initiative Group
P.O. Box 902 Mankon
Bamenda
North West Region
Cameroon
Langaagrp@gmail.com
www.langaa-rpcig.net

Distributed in and outside N. America by African Books Collective
orders@africanbookscollective.com
www.africanbookscollective.com

ISBN: 9956-762-98-9

© Bill F. Ndi 2015

All rights reserved.
No part of this book may be reproduced or transmitted in any form or by any means, mechanical or electronic, including photocopying and recording, or be stored in any information storage or retrieval system, without written permission from the publisher

Notes on Contributors

The Editor

Bill F. Ndi, Associate Professor of English and Foreign Languages at Tuskegee University, Tuskegee, Alabama, USA, earned his Doctorate from the University of Cergy-Pontoise in 2001. He is a poet, playwright, storyteller, literary critic, translator, historian of ideas and mentalities as well as an academic who has held teaching positions in several universities in Australia, France and elsewhere. His areas of teaching and research comprise among others English Languages and literatures, French, Professional, Technical and Creative Writing, World Literatures, Applied/Historical Linguistics, Literary History, Media and Communication Studies, Peace/Quaker Studies and Conflict Resolution, History of Internationalism, History of Ideas and Mentalities, Translation & Translatology, 17th Century and Contemporary Cultural Studies. He has published extensively in these areas. His publications include numerous scholarly works on Early Quakerism and translation of Early Quaker writings. He has also published poetry and plays in both the French and the English languages. Professor Bill F. Ndi has 16 published volumes of poetry of which 4 are in French, a play and 4 works in translation. He is co-editor of *Outward Evil, Inward Battle: Human Memory in Literature* with Adaku T. Ankumah, Benjamin Hart Fishkin, and Festus Fru Ndeh as well as co-editor of *Fears, Doubts, and Joys of not Belonging* with Adaku T. Ankumah and Benjamin Hart Fishkin. Also, he has served as a National Endowment for the Humanities' scholar.

Contributors

Eleanor J. Blount is Assistant Professor of English at Tuskegee University in Alabama. She specializes in the literature of African Americans, especially of the slave era, and also researches the history of antebellum America. The nineteenth century Transcendentalist writers of New England and fiction by and about diasporic Africans comprise some of her related scholarly interests. Dr. Blount studied history, journalism, professional writing, and creative writing at Paine College, Kennesaw State University, and at the University of Georgia where she composed neo-slave narratives as part of her Ph.D. work in English and creative writing. She was at one time a news reporter, and has taught English at Georgia Perimeter College and Gainesville State College among other places.

Rebecca A. Carte's research examines indigenous and African representation in Colonial and Modern discourses from Latin America. Her work has been published in *Latin American Literary Review*, *Journal of the Southwest*, and *Studies in Latin American Popular Culture*. Her latest publication with The University of Arizona Press, *Capturing the Landscape of New Spain: Baltasar Obregón and the 1564 Ibarra Expedition,* examines indigenous representation in the discourses of landscape in Baltasar Obregón´s narrative report of explorations from the northern borderlands of New Spain into New Mexico between 1564 and 1584. Other significant publications include "Mapping an Occidental History: Taking Place in Baltasar Obregón's *Historia de los descubrimientos de Nueva España* (1584)" in *Journal of the Southwest* 53 (2011). Carte earned her Ph.D. from Ohio State University in Columbus, Ohio in 2008 and currently teaches at Cuyahoga Community College in her hometown of Cleveland, Ohio.

Richard Evans is assistant professor of English at Tuskegee University in Tuskegee, Alabama. Educated in classics at the University of South Carolina, the American School of Classical Studies at Athens and Columbia University, Dr. Evans holds a Ph.D. in comparative literature with research interests in ancient and medieval literatures, theories of translation and linguistic relativity. He has published numerous academic book reviews, essays promoting the study of Classical Greek in schools, and articles on Greek and Roman authors in the Dictionary of Literary Biography and articles on various topics in classical literature.

Benjamin Hart Fishkin, Assistant Professor of English at Tuskegee University specializes in teaching Nineteenth Century British Literature. He holds a Ph.D. from the University of Alabama where he served as a Junior Fellow in The Blount Undergraduate Initiative. In his research, he has emphasized Nineteenth Century British Literature through each phase of his education. Prior to earning his Doctorate from the University of Alabama in May of 2009, he obtained a BA in English and Film from the University of Michigan, Ann Arbor, and an MA from Miami University, Oxford, Ohio where he examined the interest of Charles Dickens in the theatre and how the stage influenced his novel writing. He has published *The Undependable Bonds of Blood: The Unanticipated Problems of Parenthood in the Novels of Henry James*. He co-edited *Outward Evil Inward Battle: Human Memory in Literature* with Adaku T. Ankumah, Bill F. Ndi, and Festus Fru Ndeh, and *Fears, Doubts and Joys of not Belonging* with Adaku T. Ankumah and Bill F. Ndi. His recent research interest now include, besides his growing interest in Anglophone Cameroon literature, the problems of marriage and the American family, and the relationship between the Blues and the single-parent home in the works of William Faulkner, August Wilson, and F. Scott Fitzgerald.

Blossom N. Fondo holds a PhD in English specialized in Commonwealth and Postcolonial Literatures. Her current areas of interest are Anglophone African and Caribbean Literatures, postcolonial theory, Ecocriticism and feminism. She teaches literature and critical theory at the Higher Teacher Training College of the University of Maroua. She has been a visiting scholar to New York University in the USA and Karl Frazens University of Graz in Austria. Her publications have appeared in national and international journals.

Worth Kamili Hayes is an Assistant Professor of History at Tuskegee University. Prior to joining Tuskegee he served as an Assistant Professor of History and Chair of the Department of Social Sciences and Criminal Justice at Benedict College. His research centers on the histories of Black education, the African diaspora, 20th century U.S. urbanization, and post-world War II Black activism. His current project illuminates "the golden age of black private education" in Chicago from 1940-1990 and reveals the critical role alternative institutions played in African Americans' pursuit of quality education.

Stephen Magu is an Assistant Professor of Politics and International Relations at Hampton University in Hampton, Virginia, and occasionally teaches for the Junior Statesmen. His publications have appeared in journals such as *Cultural Encounters, Conflicts, and Resolutions: A Journal of Border Studies*, the Journal of African Studies, *The African Journal of International Affairs and Development*, in the edited volume *Africa Yesterday, Today & Tomorrow: Exploring the Multi-dimensional Discourses on 'Development'*, the *International Journal of Political Science and Development* and in the forthcoming book, *Soft Power Strategies in US Foreign Policy: Citizen Diplomacy of the Peace Corps* by Praeger Publishers. His main research interests span US and Africa's foreign policy, democratization in post-colonial Global South, social and economic development in a globalizing world, global political economy, regionalism and cultural norms in modernity. Stephen is currently working on a second book, *The Black Man's Burdens*.

Bill F. Ndi, poet, playwright, storyteller, critic, translator, historian of ideas and mentalities as well as an academic has held several university teaching positions. He teaches at Tuskegee University. He has numerous scholarly publications on Early Quakerism and translation of Early Quaker writings. He has also published extensively in both the French and the English languages. These publications include scholarly articles and book chapters, poetry, and plays. Professor Bill F. Ndi has 16 volumes of poetry of which 4 are in French, a play and 4 works in translation.

Jennifer Ross is an Assistant Professor in the Department of Psychology and Sociology at Tuskegee University. Her research interests include attachment and caregiving behavioral systems, parenting and coparenting, and the intergenerational transmission of attachment. Her current research focuses on conflict resolution among Mexican-American coparents, the influence of coparenting and culture on maternal sensitivity and insensitive caregiving in Mexican-American mothers with a toddler, and also explores whether mother-infant attachment relationships are universal or culture-specific. Jen's work has appeared in Research in Human Development.

Table of Contents

Introduction.. 1
Bill F. Ndi

Chapter 1: "Until lions write their own history":
Secrets, Silences, and Betrayals of the African
and his history..21
Stephen M. Magu

Chapter 2: Behind the Scenes of Parent-Child
Attachment Relationships......................................53
Jennifer J. Ross.

Chapter 3: Refuge or Fortress: Howalton Day
School, the African-American Middle Class,
and the Golden Era of Black Private Education..........67
Worth Kamili Hayes

Chapter 4: *Mustard Grows* Followed by
"Pokey and Me," interview with and by
Eleanor Blount.. 85
Eleanor Blount

Chapter 5: Olaudah Equiano,
Gustavus Vassa, Negotiating Identity in a
Trans-Atlantic World..113
Rebecca Carte.

Chapter 6: *Traduttore, Traditore*:
Word-for-Word Translation as an Ideology
Secretly Silencing Original Meanings.....................129
Richard Evans

Chapter 7: Hidden Agendas: Colonial Eroticism
in J.M. Coetzee's *Waiting for the Barbarians*,
Elizabeth Nunez's *Prospero's Daughter* and
Michelle Cliff's *Abeng*...153
Blossom Fondo

Chapter 8: Chaos, Concealment, and Duress
in Human Relationships in the Mimboland of
Francis B. Nyamnjoh's *Married but Available*............173
Benjamin Hart Fishkin

Chapter 9: Gardens of Blooming Secrets,
Silences, and Betrayals: Emmanuel Fru Doh's
The Fire Within and Francis B. Nyamnjoh's
A Nose for Money 195
Bill F. Ndi

Introduction

Bill F. Ndi

Human history is fairly incompletely told. This is the case even from whence human beings have taken cognizance of the importance of documenting major happenings for posterity. There are gaps in human knowledge of humans be it in their history, politics, culture and overall social infrastructure. Multiple reasons may account for this besides the avoidance of everyday life in all its ambiguity. Yet, we all are aware that some events are only primarily transmitted orally. The histories of African societies are prime examples in this regard.

Besides the above mentioned fact, even the history of colonialism and early independence of African nations or other colonized nations has been purposely re-invented. The records and observations of such societies were based primarily on prejudgments and or prejudices held by the colonists prior to their establishing the hegemon. Such epistemology draws heavily from western thought and thinking processes, while automatically excluding all others, to construct history as it is/was deemed fit to serve the desired purpose of domination. It is therefore no surprise that one of the angular arguments in James C. Scott's *Domination and the Art of Resistance: Hidden Transcripts* highlights the fact "that dominant elites attempt to portray social action in the public transcript as metaphorically, a parade, thus denying, by omission, the possibility of autonomous social action by subordinates" (45-46). This explicitly points out to the fact that the sources of knowledge on human history, especially from the dominant epistemological perspective, are hardly objective. It is in this light that anthropologist Francis B. Nyamnjoh, distinguishing between dominant and dormant epistemologies, draws attention, in "Potted Plants in Greenhouses", to "the issue of unequal encounters between the highly-mobile dominant colonial epistemology and popular endogenous epistemologies of Africa …" such an epistemology he insists, reduces the quest for truth "to 19th and 20th century preoccupations with theories of what the universe is, much to the detriment of theories of why the universe is."

The above stated reasons among all others invite a seminal investigation of the elements of secrets, silences, and betrayals that have rendered human history incomplete. This endeavor does not claim to be representative of all that which will complete human knowledge and understanding of his/her history. It is rather an invitation to readers, scholars, researchers, etc. to consider factoring in the often discarded but useful information from the perspective of the dominated. It is in this regard that the present work points towards history to becoming a cumulative record and re-recording of every human journey as well as his/her endeavor in life. It is an attempt to bring together disparate voices around topical issues that would be or have been legated to posterity as partial or half-truths. Isn't it true as Jean Bethke Elshtain would have it that "those drawn to the pristine scenes… will highlight all in roseate hues and will disdain the clutter and bustle… because that is what they want to flee, to eliminate, to cure"? (6)

As such, the postulation goading the various analyses herein emphasizes the unacknowledged platitude that some of the greatest secrets, silences and betrayals have been buried in the pages of books: novels, poetry collections, plays, pop psychology, fiction or faction, historical, political and sociological treatises. With the contention that much has been explored about all else save these aspects, our call to explore these topical issues from an interdisciplinary perspective aimed at contributing, by giving an insight, to some facts without which human understanding in those disciplinary areas will forever remain flawed or incomplete. Also, approaching these issues from an interdisciplinary perspective constitute a means of showing the relevance of these themes in bridging the gaps between hidden and exposed knowledge in any discipline. Is it not true that history as well as all endeavors at appreciating history, art, literature, human behavior, relations between nations, etc. without a thorough exploration of secrets, silences, and betrayals will be forever partial? Again, are these not skillfully slipped into the works and into the human subconscious and would remain dormant, invisible, and imperceptible to the five senses were they never awoken? Isn't it true that if the content of a work speaks loud, that which is absent from the work speaks louder?

Our expressed concern in this volume is therefore the revisionist perspectives, most especially to histories of conquest and privilege. Our world is marked by struggle between the dominant epistemology maintaining its stranglehold on the dominated with the ultimate goal of protecting its gains acquired, to a larger extent, through violence. And adding salt to injuries, the origins of such dubious rewards are never the subject of mainstream discussion or a debate open to the wider public. This must have been what Vaclav Havel beheld in stating that,

> "society is a very mysterious animal with many faces and hidden potentialities, and … it's extremely shortsighted to believe that the face society happens to be presenting to you at a given moment is its only true face. None of us knows all the potentialities that slumber in the spirit of the population" (qtd. in Jean Bethke Elshtain, *Real Politics: At the Center of Everyday Life* 7)

Stringing "Secrets", "Silences", and "Betrayals" is born of our desire to legitimate the absentee in any work: book, scholastic, social or historical discussion, as the cornerstone of broadening and clarifying knowledge and understanding in any discipline. Also, is the aspiration to slam misinformation which, either by omission or commission, upholds official discourse while at the same time disparaging official hidden transcripts (to borrow from the subtitle of James C. Scott's book). For, what is unsaid weighs equally on the scale of semantic construction as that which is said. This assertion is consequently comforted by Heidegger's claim that, "the poet remains silent about the prize which could not become a treasure of his land, but which granted him an experience with language, the opportunity to learn the renunciation…" (69). It is as a result of this fact that the editor of this collection of scholarly essays deem it necessary to remind the readers of a well-known platitude that constant reconsideration of history is part of the normal scholarly process of writing and righting history and not "revisionism" aimed at obfuscating or distorting undeniable historical facts while pushing forward questionable agenda.

In theory, government is supposed to be transparent. Its gears, its mechanisms, and its lubricants are supposed to be easily observed by all who wish to look at the uncovered subject. However, society is not an aquarium. The people within it are not small, beautiful Japanese Fighting Fish resplendent with all sorts of uplifting hues and colors. Instead, in a gray and somber display of the way things are as opposed to the way things should be, secrets, silences and betrayals are buried deep within the collective human subconscious. They are in our police force(s), they are in our judicial and legal system(s), and they are in our financial market(s). There is no translucent membrane. This leaves the artists with the choice, as wa Thiong'o suggests, of not creating but responding to conflicts and tensions, giving them shape, form, and direction or perhaps just recording them—claim as true of African artists of the twentieth and twenty-first centuries as it is of the European Renaissance artists centuries earlier (78-79).

The above brings us to the relevance of this subject as it spills over into the things we read. It flavors our histories, our news items, our psyche, our poems, our plays, our art, and our novels. It speaks to how people are culturally controlled and how they are (unknowingly) taught to place limits upon themselves. Like a colorless gas or a tasteless poison dipped surreptitiously into our food, secrets, silences, and betrayals creep into the human subconscious like so many imperceptible distractions. They are irrevocably intertwined with what we buy and how we agree to pay for it. This is about understanding. In this light, the famous English essayist William Hazlitt once drew attention to the fact that "Books let us into their souls and lay open to us the secrets of our own" ("The Sick Chamber" qtd. in *The New Monthly Magazine*, August 1830). If society suffers because the system that rules it is purposely byzantine and intentionally opaque the beneficiary of this life insurance policy is the literature produced by this irritation. For such a social critic concerned with understanding the mind and human behavior the word "irritation" may not be sufficient to describe the troubles brought about by misapplied authority. A more appropriate characterization of social injustice and enslavement might be the word "dystopian" or the word "disorder" or again, the word "chaos". The setting of much of this sort of problem, either in an African city or in one of the major Western cities, may not be nearly as important as the universal emotional reaction that follows suit. The consequences of secrets, silences, and betrayals throw up works written because it is too painful not to write them. Repressing one's thoughts incurs immeasurable cost and creates so many spiritual problems that expressing one's conscience, even when it is unwise to do so, is the only means at people's disposal to avoid going insane. People like Hazlitt, and the other

Romantics, are concerned with what is going on inside the human mind. This is no different from what writers like Francis B. Nyamnjoh, Emmanuel Fru Doh, Edwidge Danticat, Olaudah Equiano, Eleanor Blount, J.M. Coetzee, Michelle Cliff, etc. –critiqued in the present volume–are concerned with.

Ordinary people have extraordinary capabilities, even when facing long odds. The individual need not be exceptional. The individual need feel exceptional. This was true of the Romantics of the late eighteenth and early to mid-nineteenth centuries, people that William Hazlitt knew personally such as John Keats and William Wordsworth, and it is true today. Any brave soul, even a solitary one, can be alert in his or her pointed and precise critique of society, politics, culture, and mass media. This can be seen in the events that dominate the news. James C. Scott in his exploration of the art of resistance underscores especially the fact that, "when suddenly subservience evaporates and is replaced by open defiance, we encounter one of those rare and dangerous moments in power relation" (6).

A person who questions things, and defiantly too, is surely going to find real trouble. More to the point, trouble will find the person and that right soon. Nowhere is this clearer than in the case of Brooksley Born, a woman who attempted to warn the Clinton Administration of an impending financial catastrophe only to be marginalized and angrily dismissed despite her good intentions. Born, the head of the Commodity Futures Trading Commission, urged everyone who would listen to mind and note the danger(s) of over-the-counter financial derivatives. Left unmonitored, fraud, manipulation and malfeasance could cause all sorts of problems. More than a decade later they did. Her voice of regulation, as early as 1996, went unheeded. Not only did her message not get through to the powers that be, Born was labeled dangerous and subversive. Thus we are reminded of Vaclav Havel's quote that, "words are mysterious and ambiguous, yes, and all too often humble words get translated into arrogant ones" (qtd. in Jean Bethke Elshtain 3). She was a potential obstacle with her humble word viz. regulations translated into arrogant ones, subversion and danger, during an era when everyone was profiting handsomely.

The Chairman of the Securities and Exchange Commission Arthur Levitt, in a Frontline documentary entitled "The Warning", remarked that he did not know Brooksley Born but had heard that she was "…irascible, difficult, stubborn, unreasonable…" (Web. 1 July 2015). This was the price of opposition. Such a lack of oversight, such a misappraisal or a blindfolded misreading, was not unlike a Greek Tragedy Sophocles or Euripides could have written fifteen hundred years ago. People would hear a well thought out caution, disregard it and then sail calmly or ignorant of the terrible occurrence that they were hastening and even encouraging. The problems here are universal; their consequences, and the inevitable harm caused by toxic assets, unending.

But that is not the only side of the ledger. Born's quarrel with powerful government officials, all of them men, led to the publication of many books on financial fraud. The awkward hurt and heat of her collision against Washington has produced other proposals and possibilities. This could not have happened without a well thought out and persuasively articulated argument. The very academic study of global economics has changed as a consequence. Allen Greenspan, the Federal Reserve Chairman in those indelible years, is quoted by The Washington Post to have said that "…there wasn't a need for a law against fraud because if a floor broker was committing fraud, the customer would figure it out and stop doing business with him" (Manuel Roig-Franzia). This is the difference between theory and reality. Such an observation is an anathema to a sharp legal mind. The counterargument is that there must be prohibitions for flagrant infractions. Brooksley Born's "stand" was on the side of enforcement. Her willingness to be vocal, to articulate this in a famous conference paper (called a "concept release" by the Commodity Futures Trading Commission) released in May 1998 is a sign of an impending war of ideas. This split, this tension, and this showdown is healthy—especially if one keeps in mind a long-term horizon. This battle over oversight, transparency, precision and order yields an intellectual debate studied in such books as Ron Suskind's *The Price of Loyalty*, Roger Lowenstein's *When Genius Failed*, David Wessel's *In Fed We Trust* and The United States Treasury Department's *Financial Regulatory Reform*.

If Brooksley Born is, according to Manuel Roig-Franzia, a modern day Cassandra who speaks her mind and resists the surface comfort of silence she is not alone (Washington Post 05/26/2009). The larger theme, the overarching theme of focus in the present volume, is who are these other people who speak up and why are they so important to the literature we all enjoy? In Brooksley Born, even if we have never heard of her before, do we see something of William Blake and Percy Bysshe Shelley? Is there not a commonality between her and mythological figures such as Prometheus and Icarus?

It is for this reason that well-informed individuals who have deliberated carefully can challenge institutional structures for, "the exercise of powers produces indignities of grievous proportions" (Scott 6). It is necessary if we are to have an informed public. Even more to the point it is vital if the informed within the populous are to know that there are others out there who are just like them. The significance of writing *Secrets, Silences, and Betrayals* is that it provides a platform for discussions on the absentee. Talking of the absentee brings to mind, the recollection of Dana Gioia who draws attention to the significance of "the unspoken losses that had scarred her [his mother's] life." (qtd. in Rodney Phillips et al., The Hand of the poet 1). Such a book unhesitatingly tells the reader that even if they are not welcome in the shining city on the hill that everyone there knows their name and hears their song.

In the light of the foregoing discussion, in this opening chapter, Stephen Magu argues that, the distinct path of development of the societies—particularly African societies—used oral history as the primary mechanism of recording its history. This use of orality makes it necessary for African scholars to make more concerted effort to record such history expeditiously. Further, this research makes a case that African history has suffered silences, betrayals, and is full of secrets that are occasioned by the combination of epistemology, lack of recorded i.e. written history, colonization and suppression of colonized peoples' history from the educational systems, and by the independence-era governments that favored the colonizers' version of history and national unity over reconstructing their societies' history.

While it has been argued that such gaps exist primarily because African societies transmitted their histories orally, Stephen Magu shows in this chapter that the gaps in the history of colonialism and of early independence of African nations were purposely re-invented. As such, early explorers, travelers, and colonists recorded their observations of African societies, often based on pre-existing prejudices of Africa as the "Dark Continent" – with all the attendant negative connotations therewith. As the reconstruction of African societies' history between 1000 and 1800 AD proceeds, emphasis on western-derived epistemological approaches that emphasize scientific inquiry and methods has rendered it quite difficult, nigh impossible, to develop oral history as a credible alternative in recapturing history. Herein, Stephen Magu not only adds his voice to those of several scholars who point out that the sources of knowledge on African history – such as Joseph

Conrad and T. M. Thomas' – are hardly objective but highlights how the truncation of African history comes across as a well-known, well-kept and well-guarded secret aimed at betraying African societies' participation and contribution to the human civilization. It is in this regard that Africa's pre and post-colonial histories are incompletely told for as Africa was viewed and described as the heart of darkness, no mention is made of what Ngugi wa Thiong'o subtly highlights by saying, "Thames and Brussels were the gates into the heart of Darkness where people were hunted down on account of their color and the shape of their nose" (71).This chapter does justice by drawing attention to some of the existing gaps in the knowledge of African societies, their history, politics, culture and overall social infrastructure.

The second chapter "Behind the Scenes of Parent-Child Attachment Relationships" by Jennifer Ross is a careful exploration of the relationship between parent and child that grows and develops over the course of a baby's first year of life. Ideally, this relationship ought to be open, honest, and mutually satisfying, whereas unfavorable relationships are secretive, silent, and based on betrayal. This chapter provides a behind the scenes look at how a baby becomes attached and why individual differences exist in the fundamental relationship between parent and child. The chapter opens with a brief introduction to the central tenets of attachment theory and is followed by several scenarios that illustrate the different patterns of attachment. Each scenario is explained according to attachment theory and explores how secrets, silences, and betrayals play a role in the formation and manifestation of an attachment relationship between infant and primary caregiver. The chapter thus highlights the implications of Parent-Child Attachment Relationships for social relationship functioning later in the child's adult life.

Chapter three brings to light the often forgotten history of black private education in the United States. Along with its contribution to scholarship on black educational history, it helps to situate the contemporary school reform debates in an historical context. Particularly, it interrogates if middle-class blacks, whose economic advantage has allowed them to patronize private schools, betrayed working class blacks and reform efforts in public schools. These concerns also animate contemporary debates over school reform options such as charter schools in which dissidents argue that privileged blacks pursue educational alternatives, leaving the "truly disadvantaged" in crumbling public schools. Thus, charter schools, possibly this era's most divisive issue, have recently come under intense scrutiny as a neoliberal scheme that strips traditional public schools of much needed resources. Their patrons, particularly minority families, are often accused of betraying the large number of poor students who lack adequate resources to access this educational alternative. Worth Kamili Hayes' historical appraisal of Howalton troubles this notion by showing how African-American support of private education did not preclude, but welcomed, vigorous engagement with public school reform.

Also, this chapter's examination of Howalton, a private school created in 1940s Chicago, uncovers a history of African-American school reform that saw no contradiction between exploring educational alternatives while remaining committed to traditional public schools. Worth Kamili Hayes traces the various political and economic developments in postwar America that gave rise to a Black middle class that could pursue this dual strategy. These conditions, however, proved ephemeral, as increasing deindustrialization and greater competition vanquished the city's black private schools. Though many of the institutions shuddered, this dual sensibility remained, helping to conceive the modern charter movement. Partisans on both sides of the issue should be reminded of this history which shows that reform does not have to be a zero-sum game. Consequently, the chapter offers possibilities for an open and meaningful perspective for the current debates in urban education that have far too often been mired in unproductive either/or formulations.

Chapter four consists of an excerpt from the short story entitled "Mustard Grows" which is another truncated view of what slavery was like in America in the 1850's. The illustration is made through two characters, a four-year-old black slave and the four-year-old white girl who owns him. As the two children grow, they become not merely inseparable but inextricable, sadly melded. Eleanor Blount uses these lives as a metaphor for the country's race and slavery conundrum in the multiple stories that form a work of long fiction called Pokey's Story. In addition to the excerpt of faction, there is a section in which she discusses, in a mock interview/conversation with herself (author-interviewee/critic-interviewer), these issues both as history and as literature. She sheds light on why the untold, hidden, and forgotten actions of two small antebellum children are so significant for black and white Americans today. Besides, slave narratives exploring intricate race relations such as the one explored in this chapter are thrown in the dustbin of history and are shunned and yet, a close look at such relations could pave the way for meaningful race relations in the US in particular and the world in general. Race relations have been so embittered by continuous refusal, secrecy, or silence about the possibility of any real and lasting inter-racial communion.

In the fifth chapter, "Olaudah Equiano, Gustavus Vassa, Neither, Both, or a Third: Negotiating Identity in a Trans-Atlantic World" Rebecca A. Carte applies Paul Gilroy's chronotope of the Black Atlantic ship in an attempt to transcend the binary between "national" and "diaspora" perspectives in approaching *The Interesting Narrative of the Life of*

Olaudah Equiano or Gustavus Vassa, the African, Written by Himself (1789). Carte argues for a move away from the temptation to view the work through one cultural lens or another, and the need to recognize the complex web of multiple lived spaces it represents in which "pre-modern" frontiers are more fluid and nuanced than is often considered.

Carte reminds the reader in this chapter that Olaudah Equiano's narrative presents scholars with a memoir that is all too rare: a first-hand account of a slave who reports his survival of the middle passage and his eventual manumission. While this "first-hand account" may be viewed as revelatory and informative, ironically, it seems to have generated more questions (and suspicions) than answers as scholars continue to debate who Olaudah Equiano or Gustavus Vassa, the African "truly" was. Is he "more" British or African, or is he a cultural "hybrid"? Where was he "really" born? Can we trust his account? Is he a trickster (justified or not), omitting important truths or even inventing stories? Was he the betrayed or the perpetrator of betrayal of sorts? This study considers that perhaps these questions stem from our own cultural blind spots in approaching the text.

Chapter six, "Traduttore Traditore: Word-for-Word Translation as an Ideology Secretly Silencing Original Meanings" argues that the ideology conveyed by the Roman theory and practice of ad verbum translation attempts to create a hermeneutics of trust and authority by masking instability of meaning and context between a passage in Greek from *Herodotus* (Book I. 189) and its translation into Latin by the late Roman historian Orosius. Silencing or covering up differences between languages by implying the realistic possibility of "literal" translation grows out of the traditional ancient view of language as a mirror of representation, thus suggesting the dominance of a hermeneutics of trust in translations from Greek to Latin. Ad verbum translation, in this case and generally, fosters the view that stylistic or word-order equivalence implies a much closer contextual correspondence in meaning than careful analysis will allow.

Richard Evans, in this chapter, also explains how a short passage of text moves from the Greek of Herodotus to the Latin of Orosius by developing a hermeneutical model that queries and challenges the readers' trust in the stability of tight relationship between original text and its translation regardless of the close stylistic correspondence between the original passage and target language rendition as there is no such thing as a one to one correspondence in any two dead or living languages.

The seventh chapter shows, through a close and careful examination of postcolonial fictional representation and its engagement to unveil erotic perversion—the main drive behind colonial exploitation—that the colonial system, often clad in the borrowed robes of *mission civilisatrice*, brought in its wagon the myriad of abuses that marked the colonial encounter. The examined narratives reveal the ways in which colonialism constituted a system of human, economic, and political exploitation as well as of physical and cultural displacement. Making colonialism as well as slavery to become, as Ngugi wa Thiong'o would have it, "… events of shame, of guilt." (61). The examined postcolonial fictional works, Blossom Fondo contends, follow the lives and experiences of individuals and/or communities and highlight the ways in which colonialism has affected them. Through J.M. Coetzee's *Waiting for the Barbarians* the tortures meted on the so-called Barbarians by the colonizers are chronicled. In Elizabeth Nunez's *Prospero's Daughter*, the physical and cultural displacement and the unthinkable pain exercised the colonized by the colonizer are brought to the fore while in Michelle Cliff's Abeng the focus is on the psychic fragmentation consequent upon the colonial curriculum. Also, insidiously injected into the narrative, is the idea of eroticism or sexuality. This chapter uncovers the eroticism of British colonialism as captured and portrayed in the above texts from South Africa and Jamaica.

Also, guided by postcolonial feminism, Blossom Fondo argues in this chapter that, although the postcolonial writers, under study, seemingly do not make the erotic the main thrust of their narrative, they nonetheless call attention to it by making it contribute significantly to the unfolding of the events in their novels. Albeit, colonial eroticism is not placed at the center of their narratives, it plays such an important role and by this alone draws importance unto itself. Over and above, the question of colonial eroticism, the unacknowledged role of sexuality in the imperial agenda, as well as the ways in which such sexual interactions deconstruct the myth of the unattractive, dirty, diseased, and sub-human colonized are examined and highlighted. The chapter thus injects the often muted gender question into conceptualizations of post-colonialism.

Benjamin Hart Fishkin, in the eighth chapter, exposes Francis B. Nyamjoh's *Married but Available* as a display for all the trouble brought about by modern romance. He argues that Nyamnjoh's is a primer of painful and humorous anecdotes in which the author seems to be weeping and laughing at the same time, all the while stating silently "[w]hat an avoidable mess!" In an environment which takes nineteenth century literary realism and gives it a newer twist, the critic contends the reader is privy to the clumsy, klutzy, and ill-thought-out ways in which people mismanage their affairs. They take their problems, voluntarily create new ones, and then attempt to sweep the entire confusion beneath the carpet.

In exploring Nyamnjoh's locale, Mimboland, Benjamin Hart Fishkin brings to the fore the author's illustration of the machination of adults engaged in a perpetual contest to see who can obtain and discard lovers faster than anyone else. This turns out to be very much like children playing a game of hide and seek. The result is a complicated, costly, and comical mayhem. The secrets in this fictional Cameroons, which are never ultimately concealed, are tricks and schemes that have no regard for loving and tender relationships. There is no long-term planning and this problem, and its ensuing chaos, has far reaching implications for African society. At once, without any warning, what at first seems to be harmless fun quickly becomes more than merely a series of risqué allusions.

The chapter also raises issues on the serious subtext wherein *Married but Available* becomes a deft treatment of what the author discerns to be by far a greater and wide reaching problem. The Mimbolanders who lie and cheat on their partners serve as a literary microcosm for a government and public service that subsists on graft, greed, and corruption. The chapter posits that secrets, silences and betrayals exact an imperceptible psychological cost that no one is exempt from paying. No one ever speaks of or contemplates such consequences that will surely follow. People in Mimboland, and elsewhere, seem to be in a footrace to see who will yield first to the temptation of secretly and silently betraying another. No one hesitates.

By examining *The Fire Within* and *A Nose for Money*, novels by two contemporary Anglophone Cameroonian authors, Emmanuel Fru Doh (EFD) and Francis B. Nyamnjoh (FBN), Bill F. Ndi in this final chapter exhumes secrets, silences, and betrayals while portraying them as the strife and sword that these writers use to achieve victory over the lopsided and often porous official history. Official history oftentimes is a subjective narration of convoluted facts from the perspective of the victors. It discards and buries secrets, and burning issues as well as all the backstabbing and double dealing that had led the victors to their victory.

Furthermore, the chapter contends that these Anglophone Cameroonian novelists, EFD and FBN, present ideas of secrets, silences, and betrayals. Also, it shows how the overabundance of examples of these ideas reveals the element of game in which the novelists powerfully deconstruct their novelistic spaces, serving as motifs. They point to the futility—in a system skilled at letting down its own citizens—of any endeavor aimed at planting anything meaningful in the garden wherein only secrets, silences, and betrayals are permitted to blossom. These novels become, for our authors under study, a site where they unearth and warrant the bloom of secrets, silences, and betrayals like flowers decorating tombs. Anglophone Cameroonian authors are left, the chapter concludes, with only the choice of writing, not in order to be published but also to maintain their sanity. This chapter demonstrates EFD's and FBN's keen understanding of their society immersed in a culture of corruption, treachery, and debauchery buried underneath a mountain of silence.

This chapter finally shows the painstaking and illuminating deconstructions of "post-independent East and West Cameroons" wherein the bloom of embittered secrets, silences, and betrayals prevail under adulterated conditions. This spurs the writers' commitment, resentment, and disappointment in the face of global silence. Highlighting the authors' categorical refusal to submit to this inflicted humiliation and to feel sorry for themselves, Bill F. Ndi underlines that such refusal makes of their literature, one of Power and of Knowledge. Finally the chapter offers insights, judgments, and values for understanding the power shifts encrypted by Anglophone Cameroonian authors in their novelistic spaces which otherwise would remain hidden or buried in the bones of the oppressed.

If secrets, silences, and betrayals have been and are such topics of relevance drawing our attention today and to the point that we have to dig into them in an attempt to make human history whole, the reasons abound and the respective authors in this collection have demonstrated along the lines of thinking of other scholars before them that,

> [t]he denial of loss and, hence, the lack of mourning can occur at the group level; kept in a collective crypt, the trauma can be passed on transgeneratinally as "the unfinished business of the previous generation" to haunt the future. (104)

This contention by Abraham and Torok thus underscores this attempt to draw attention to the various "untold or unspeakable, unfelt or denied pain, concealed shame, covered-up crimes or violent histories [that] continue to affect and disrupt the lives of those involved in them" (Gabriele Schwab qtd. in wa Thiong'o *Something Torn and New: An African Renaissance* 58-59). The chapters all point towards the avoidance of shutting up unwanted memories in a crypt for this can lead "to a kind of hiding in language" in Abraham and Torok's parlance, "Cryptonymy" (104). The dangers of this as Schwab further warns is that, "such crypts engender silence such as the one witnessed among her elders [in Germany after the Second World War] in their avoidance of references to what had already happened" (Op. Cit.).

This volume addresses, from an interdisciplinary point of view, the tensions and conflicts engendered by secrets, silences, and betrayals and also establishes that a careful understanding of the same can warrant peaceful and harmonious relations between individuals, nations, the dominating and the dominated, etc. etc. It is an understanding akin to what Jean Bethke Elshtain think of the Vaclav Havelian "unabashed embrace of life" as one tantamount to a "post-Babelian world in which there are wondrous varieties of human homes, identities, languages, particular possibilities, but there is as well a transparticular world framing our fragile globe, united perhaps only in its travail" (8). Included in this study is how secrets, silences, and betrayals allow people to entangle themselves with untold pain and sufferings, as well as in "those rare and dangerous moments of power relations" (Scott 6) be them victims or perpetrators of such secrets, silences, and or betrayals.

Finally, addressed are a series of questions related to the eponym and central thematic concern explored in this volume. Can secrets, silences, or betrayals be an issue in international relations? Could secrets, silences, and betrayals explicate the conscious class ideology of imperialism, and of colonialism, race, and colonial relations which today are the foundations of the modern capitalist world; even those in which clearly social, economic, and political matters often wrapped? (wa Thiong'o 110). How do they define and or illuminate parent-child relationships? Can they explain the how and why of the cover-ups in race relations? What role do secrets, silences, and betrayals play in global peace or conflict resolution? Are we able to read, through them, the various agenda set by both the dominating and the dominated? Are they just a game of hide and seek in which adults not children are involved? In navigating between languages, is it possible to avoid dominance of a hermeneutics of trust? What seems to be a constant in *Secrets, Silences, and Betrayals* is that the volume brings with it more than a handful of unpleasant surprises. These are a new set of problems that traditional analysis does not easily broach from an interdisciplinary perspective. The respective chapters have drawn their conclusions given the scope and tenor of the discipline's appreciation of secrets, silences, and betrayals.

Works Cited

Abraham & Torok, "Mourning and Melacholia" *in The Wolf Man's Magic Word: A Cryptonymy*. St Paul, U of Minnesota P. 1986. Print.

Elshtain, Jean Bethke, *Real Politics: at the Center of Everyday Life*, Baltimore, John Hopkins UP. 1997. Print.

Hazlitt, William *The Sick Chamber* in *The New Monthly Magazine*, August 1830. Print.

Heidegger, Martin. *On the Way to Language* (Trans. Peter D. Hertz), San Francisco, Harper-Collins, 1982. Print

Nyamnjoh, Francis B. "'Potted Plants in Greenhouses': A Critical Reflection on the Resilience of Colonial Education in Africa" in *Journal of Asian and African Studies*, SAGE, 47.2 (April 2012): 129-154. Print

Phillips, Rodney et al., *The Hand of the Poet*, New York, Rizzoli, 1997. Print.

Roig-Franzia, Manuel. "Brooksley Born, the Cassandra of the Derivatives Crisis" in *Washington Post* (05/26/2009). Print.

Scott, James C. *Domination and the Art of Resistance: Hidden Transcripts* New Haven, Yale UP. 1990. Print.

wa Thiongo, Ngugi. *Something Torn and New: An African Renaissance,* New York, Basic Civitas, 2009. Print.

PBS, prod. *Frontline:* 'The Warning." 20 Oct. 2009. Web. 1 July 2015.

Chapter 1

"Until lions write their own history"[1]: Secrets, Silences, and Betrayals of the African and his history

Stephen M. Magu

Introduction

The issues dealt with in this chapter reflect an effort to catalog, rethink and finally suggest new directions in the domain of the mis(re)presentation of Africa in epistemological and knowledge societies, including the application of primarily occidental theories and approaches to understand the continent, articulate its place in history and into the future, assess its contributions to the contemporary world and resolve issues arising – sometimes, ironically, from the very participation in occidental systems.

Dr. Harvey, the long-serving President of one of the oldest HBCUs in the United States, Hampton University, articulates that a people (especially African Americans) must tell their own history (and that way, it is history), otherwise to let others tell one's story becomes "his-story". This research contends that for the most part, Africa's history has been others' story, sometimes an often inaccurate and incomplete record of the African Experience. This is reflected in the first half of the title of this chapter, an African saying, which in its entirety reads: *"until lions write their own history, the tale of the hunt will always glorify the hunter."* African history has tended to articulate the story of

---

[1] "Until Lions write their own history, the tale of the hunt will always glorify the hunter" – *African proverb*

the "other" rather than that of the subjects, as told by that same 'other'. The absence of written records before the advent of colonialism, and the method by which society has adapted to the transmission of knowledge (through scientific methodology and its accompanying rigor), has especially rendered a reconstruction of African history difficult.

There are practical and functional explanans for these difficulties: the reality that African history was, for the longest time, passed down orally from generation to generation. Colonization caused an upset in the traditional systems (family, community, social, economic and political); their replacement with a western system left gaps that did not immediately capture the historical experiences during and after independence.

Further, institutional memory was lost with the gradual elimination (through colonial actions, disease, attrition and other reasons). Secondly, the changes took place under conditions of occupation (colonization). As such, there was no attempt to foster an environment that recognized the importance of historical experiences, the potential future developments and the need to reconcile the differing accounts or confront their long-term social, political, economic and historical consequences.

After independence, African governments did not engender activities to facilitate recapturing the lost history and/or narratives from the communities independently or as part of the new, emerging nation. This was, in part, because newly minted governments were primarily driven to write the narrative of independence: consolidation of the new nation and freedom from oppression. A rewrite of the history could potentially resurrect negative experiences associated with the new state and discredit the new, prevailing, pro-independence government narratives. The net effect of these actions and approaches unfortunately, were that the sources of African history that had institutional knowledge were discarded, marginalized or even actively suppressed in favor of nationalistic narratives.

Language is an important medium for the transmission of cultural knowledge; in some newly independent nations, there was an active effort to suppress indigenous languages in the name of national unity. This left significant portions of African history written in English and other occidental languages (French, Spanish), yet they were inexperienced in many of the 2600 languages, some now extinct, others not translated, therefore rendering the history unknown and unappreciated. Coupled with the fact that an occidental approach to epistemology favored knowledge derived scientifically from rigorous and written records, the absence of both within the African historical narrative rendered the history to become less favored as a credible representation of the African experience over the written version.

This chapter argues a number of issues, most pertinently, that the absence of an "African Project" to recapture alternative views of African historical experiences as an alternative source of knowledge on the African history. It also argues that without this countervailing approach, most of Africa's history remains "his-story", not history; that despite what occidental paradigms represent as African history, other approaches ought to be explored and considered alongside current history. It urges that an effort be undertaken, nationally and continentally, to capture the memories of historical experiences and treasure these alongside those of the written history with a view to achieving the best reconciliation between the occidental and the African approaches to understanding its peoples' history.

Transitions: changing meaning and understanding of ownership

The representation, recording and continuity of history of the African context was bedeviled by a confluence of history and modernity; the transition from traditional societies, to colonies, to independent nations, altered more than the boundaries and forms of governments: they also altered the way history was experienced, recorded and passed down. It was also problematic given what Fyle articulates as the oft-touted myth that "if it's not written, it did not happen" in arguing that scholars such as David Hume held the "suspicion that blacks were naturally inferior to the white" and Georg Hegel's argument that "Africa is not a historical continent; it shows neither change nor development" (1-2).

Fyle adds that the bigger problem, in addition to the absence of written records to articulate history, was the notion of "the incapacity of Africans to make any serious contribution to the progress of human society" (2), even though evidence to the North – Egypt – demonstrated that this was not the case. Fyle refers to this belief as the "Hamitic myth" – the myth that any progress in Africa was brought about by Caucasoids (2). There was thus incentive and justification for the colonial systems to suppress prior history, and elevate efforts, activities and deeds that demonstrated that colonial powers were civilizing and bringing modernity, Christianity, education and medicine to a "dark continent."

One of the major changes that occurred in African societies after the appearance of missionaries and colonizers was in the form of content, its ownership, transmission, dissemination and preservation: be it history and knowledge, culture and traditions, property, and the relationships between the governing and the governed, and the eventual introduction of the Westphalian state. In terms of history, for example,

Balandier argues that part of the transmission of societal history transpired through myths (one of the several avenues - including story-telling, wise-sayings, humor, riddles etc. - through which history, language and culture were transmitted).

Balandier continues; myth "undoubtedly has more than a conservative function. It contains, along with its particular symbolic trappings, a certain amount of knowledge" (475). Bendix equates its historical value to "a Genesis, a theory of nature...the emergence of cultures ... a substitute for archives" (475). More importantly, Bendix argues that myths are more than these cultural preservation and transmission mechanisms, suggesting conditions under which systems of political authority emerge). It comprises...*an element of ideology*" (475-6), and further, as "a social charter concerning the existing form of society with its system of distribution of power, privilege and property" (476). So, while unwritten, it is clear that the history of such societies was there to be studied.

Ownership

Even though colonial administrations, for various reasons, either failed to or purposely neglected to integrate the traditional practices and especially of property holding and ownership into the colonial (and therefore post-colonial) systems, there is ample evidence that pre-colonial African societies were governed by a collection of well-organized systems, for example, customary law. For example, Smith notes that,

> The existence of a widespread customary law was noticed by early European visitors to Africa, in particular by the Portuguese. Traders enjoyed, for example, the protection of law for the unwritten contracts, based on oaths and 'medicine', which they made with the local inhabitants. Conversely, they resented the

application of West African law under which the property of a dead colleague, or their ships gone aground along the coast, were forfeit to the local ruler. (600)

The process of ownership (of wealth) is as complex as the definition of wealth itself (for example, whether or not it included children, wives, land) or whether communally owned land was considered property divisible by the parties within the community. What is evident is that with the advent of colonialism, the notions of ownership changed, particularly with reference to land. Channock states that, "colonial administrators generally approached the law relating to land tenure as a fundamental to social and economic life" (69). By itself, land tenure was a newer concept; valid arguments can be made that communities held land in perpetuity. Frederick Lugard also articulates the land-holding practices, writing that

> Conceptions as to the tenure of land are subject to a steady evolution, side by side, with the evolution of social progress, from the most primitive stages to the organisation[sic] of the modern state. In the earliest stage the land and its produce is shared by the community as a whole; later the produce is the property of the family or individuals by whose toil it is won, and the control of the land is vested in the head of the family. When the tribal stage is reached, the control passes to the chief, who allots unoccupied lands at will, but is not justified in dispossessing any family or person who is using the land. Later still, especially when the pressure of population has given to the land an exchange value, the conception of proprietary rights in it emerges, and sale, mortgage and lease of the land, apart from its user, is recognised ...These processes of natural evolution, leading up to individual ownership, may, I believe, be traced in every civilization known to history (Lugard 280-1).

To Lugard's argument, which suggests that communal property holding – or lack of private property rights somehow equaled limited evolutionary sophistication, Channock adds that "communality implied lack of advancement; an 'early' state" (70). The net effect of this was the facilitation of appropriation of land for government use. This could more easily be argued, considering that the prevailing view was that the "uncivilized" somehow lacked individual and political rights.

While the notion of individual property ownership had taken root many centuries ago, the very proponent of private property and self-interest had noted the dangers of unregulated private property by the example of medieval Rome, writing that despite the JUGERA law (my adopted term) - (a law restricting private land-ownership quantity to about 350 acres), "the greater part of citizens had no land, and without it, the manners and customs of those times rendered it difficult for a freeman to maintain his independence" (Smith 298).

Ironically, the colonial administrations were intent on replacing a communal land system that, while not egalitarian (Channock 71), in some fashion espoused Scott's "Asian moral economy" which "claims that all should have a place, a living, not that all should be equal'. Interestingly, despite the fact that property – especially land – was communally owned, the expectation that "lack of exclusive rights produces competition for the use of the resource until its...value or net worth is zero" (667) did not materialize. It is clear then, that however structured (or unstructured, per colonial authorities) the land-ownership system was, it functioned for the societies.

It also bears mention that there was a clear and close relationship between property ownership and governance, with most of the property allocation and dispute settlement carried out under the chiefs or council of elders who, for the most part, were the guardians and or custodians of the land/property. The implications of this connectedness, however, will be explored in later continuations of this work.

Pre-colonial government and culture

Long before the arrival of western traders, missionaries and later colonizers, sovereign kingdoms, empires, chieftains and principalities existed in Sub-Saharan Africa, uninfluenced by the goings-on in Europe and North Africa (including, for example, the Hellenic, Hellenistic, Roman and Carthaginian empires). Kingdoms such as Dahomey, Asante, Mali, Songhai, Sudan, among others thrived, carried on commerce and established relations with other kingdoms, contrary to widely held view where "scholars commonly downplayed local underpinnings of (West) African polities, attributing the rise of the first cities and states across the region to the arrival of conquerors and traders from distant shores" (Monroe 1).

The richness and diversity of the African civilizations and kingdoms is articulated by Corr and Moeller (32-3), who trace Africa from Pre-historic times (fossils found in East Africa) to the subsequent migration across the Sinai to Europe and Asia, the development of agriculture about 8,000 BC to Ancient Egypt's establishment around 5,000 BC. Egypt's Old Kingdom (2700 - 2200), Middle Kingdom (2200 - 1600) and New Kingdom (1600 - 1000 BC) are fairly well known, with various landmarks including funerary pyramids, preserved mummies and complete aspects of Egyptian culture spread across different museums especially in the West available to attest to their development. Others include, for example, Kush, Axum (200 BC - 600 AD), West African Kingdoms including Ghana (300 - 1200 AD), Mali (1200 - 1400 AD) and Songhai (1400 - 1600). On the East coast of Africa, Kingdoms such as Mombasa, Pemba, Zanzibar and Kilwa were well established, with sultanates whom the Portuguese alternately negotiated with or fought against as far back as 1600 (Corr & Moeller 33-4). The establishment of African societies and their level of technological advancement was demonstrated in Gertrude Canton-Thompson's 1929 excavation; (Hall 1) writes that "archaeologists were able to collect together large amounts of information and to demonstrate, with the aid of radiocarbon dating, that the first farming communities were established in the subcontinent by 200 A. D."

The establishment of these societies led to the inevitable establishment of infrastructure definitive of organized societies and to an extent that mirrored the European societies. Stambouli and Zghal conclude that especially in North Africa, there was considerable planning for urban cities, for example (3). Although the cities functioned differently from those of the Europeans who would subsequently colonize Africa, some of the cities' establishment demonstrated the relationship between the ruler and the citizens, including development of legal institutions (such as councils of elders, judicial mechanisms), moral bonds, binding community members together and an own market-place to carry out commerce. Other aspects of such infrastructure included instruments of governing a state, particularly war.

While most interior kingdoms and societies may have been shielded from the advent and distribution of modern war technology - at least at the time - there is evidence that these states used war much as it is used today: for mercantilist as well as territorial expansion purposes. Law, for example, writes that

> the importance of slaves, both in the internal economies of West African societies and as a commodity for export, contributed to the institutionalisation of warfare: for the procuring of slaves depended upon organized violence. War, therefore, was an economic activity, by which both the labour[sic] needed for domestic purposes and the purchasing

power needed to acquire foreign imports was mobilised. (112 - 114)

Of course the many "unequal treaties" – sometimes outright trickery visited upon different kings, chiefs, and princes also alluded to the presence and recognition of some political authority and government in different areas all over Africa.

Alternate Universe: the other view of Africa (and its history)

Despite the validation of aspects of the African polity before the coming of the European, some efforts persisted, then and now, to paint the level of societal organization and other such attributes including histories as non-existent, leading to external efforts to 'produce' history. Before crafting a new approach to alternative narratives, to a new history, it is beneficial to review some prior views, concepts and conceptualizations of Africa that depart from evidentiary realities. Lack of knowledge about the African continent is articulated in a passage first reported in the 1911 edition of Encyclopedia Britannica, where Chisholm writes

> Africa, with the exception of the lower Nile valley and what is known as Roman Africa (presumably North Africa) is, so far as its native inhabitants are concerned a continent practically without a history, and possessing no records from which such a history might be reconstructed (325).

Such views, unreconciled with differing accounts, were reinforced by literature generated by some of the earliest sojourners to the African continent. For example, Thomas in his 1873 work wrote that "even that faithful adherence to his false religion, superstitions and charms, when turned to the right channel, will, doubtless, be of greatest value..." and further that "as the African has a character of his own, even in his ignorance, barbarism and sin..." (219). In a section titled "The Retreat of Barbarism, 1700-1850 AD", McNeill claims that "by 1850, sub-Saharan Africa constituted by far the largest single barbarian reservoir left in the world; yet here, too, civilized and semi-civilized societies were encroaching rapidly" (724). Joseph Conrad's infamous HEART OF DARKNESS describes how, steaming up a river, "the prehistoric man was cursing us, praying to us, welcoming us - who could tell?" (ND 96).

Other sources of literature, knowledge and history on and of Africa reflected and perpetuated this narrative: that Africa was a dark, hostile, unknown, backward place, and somehow by journeying through it, studying it and exposing it to the west, its conditions of darkness would be alleviated. For example, Hardin writes that "the attention of the whole civilized world is now directed towards the Dark Continent, Africa" (136). James Stewart, an African Missionary, in a compilation of Duff Missionary Lectures on Africa in 1902, collected in a volume that bespeaks both the "problem at hand", i.e. the dark continent and the role of the missionaries in bringing it to the dawn of civilized societies (DAWN IN THE DARK CONTINENT), inquires: "why did that wonderful civilization (Egypt) leave the remainder of the African continent untouched, unhelped, uninfluenced in any way?" (13). One of the well-known explorers to Africa, H. M. Stanley, chronicled his travels in two volumes entitled "THROUGH THE DARK CONTINENT".

These views of a "dark continent", a "barbaric people" and "pagans" supported, even necessitated the mission to bring civilization to the last bastion of barbarism that existed in the world, and opened up Africa to the dual European pursuits of civilization and colonization. "Colonisation[sic] was justified as a 'civilizing mission' in a 'dark continent'" (Ndlovu-Gatsheni 43-4). However, in Stock and Stock's view it was more the result of an historical trend and a form of "superiority complex." Consequently, they postulate that:

> Europe's colonization of Africa grew from the sense of historical destiny. Europeans' long-standing views that their continent's societies were more progressive and rational than those of people in other parts of the world were espoused with increasing conviction during the Renaissance. Other societies not only were seen as inferior, but were considered by many as subhuman. Thus, European domination of other societies was seen as natural and inevitable. (34)

There are eminently troubling implications in the description of the African continent, as well as the outcomes (or corrective prescriptions) for resolving the implied "backwardness" of the continent. First, the notion that the absence of "written records" from whence history might be reconstructed suggests that only written histories were accurate descriptors of a peoples' history. This approach, in many ways, ignores one of the central tenets of the African society and the traditions of oral history and the role of generations in passing down history and traditions through words of mouth from one generation to another. Again, the differences in cultural traditions did and still do not imply that they were/are inferior to those of societies utilizing the western alphabet.

Over and above, even when attitudes towards African seemed to have changed in the 20th century, by virtue of the occidental approach to knowledge that is premised on valuing and building existing knowledge through "normal science"[2], and given that most accounts of Africa's history were orally passed down, scholars have defaulted to basing their knowledge on existing accounts, including those that describe Africa as the "dark continent." While it is possible that scientific rigor was applied to the methods and observations made in such accounts, one wonders whether these were independent, objective accounts, given the pervading view of the role of westerners to "civilize and Christianize" "barbarians". In short, the foundation of scholarship of African affairs was built on anthropological and ethnographic sources such as those of T. M. Thomas, as White points out, "it is the use of anthropological accounts in the study of African history that is very troubling..." (141).

Further still, similar approaches continue today. Knowledge and scholarship in western societies is largely based on the notion that original research also leverages reliable sources, prior literature, utilizing the Kuhnian approach and the cumulative process that leads to a shift in paradigms, beginning with "normal science." Given that the social sciences that help us study African societies fall into the "science" category, it is inevitable then that an occidental study begins with "normal science", which Kuhn argues "means research firmly based upon one or more past scientific achievements, achievements that some particular scientific community acknowledges for a time as supplying the foundation for its further practice" (10). The problem, then, is one of prior *normal science;* should accounts such as those of T. M. Thomas be believed and taken for standards? What happens to such literature and can it be classified as objective? Would science call on the events surrounding the massacre of close to 60,000

---

[2] On how societies build up on knowledge which then becomes "normal science", see Thomas Kuhn's *Structure of Scientific Revolutions,* Chicago, IL: University of Chicago Press, 1962 (chapters 2 & 3)

Nama and Herero peoples of Namibia? (Ferguson 176, Sarkin-Hughes 22, Zimmerman 244)

Indeed, many of the colonization-era practices and the mentality that suggests some ability of the West to resolve most major problems in the West are still evident today. Stock and Stock note that

> [A]lthough missionaries in Africa lived frugally, they needed to raise substantial amounts of money in Europe and North America to carry out their work. Like fundraisers today, they sought to create both a sense of the urgency of their work and the success they were achieving through their efforts. (34)

Such practices are not far removed from the present: from the 1985 USA for Africa and similar concerts, contemporary ChildAid organizations' commercials and other "mission" trips to Africa, the helping attitudes persist without mention of the gains reaped from such missions nor is any of the treacherous antics that constitute the recipe for the survival of such organizations.

Dearth of an "African Project" and Colonial History re-write

The American Public Broadcasting Service (PBS) is a study in the development, dissemination and availability of educational and other informational content. In a country where national institutions do not do so well in maintaining national confidence, PBS as an institution consistently ranks highest in public trust, according to the National Roper Survey. One of PBS' programs, *American Experience*, follows and disseminates information on persons and events of importance to American history and the American narrative, culture and history. Anyone who has watched the shows would concur that the content is arguably well researched. It presents unique insights into American history. By chronicling aspects of the American nation, history, experience, and different aspects of the evolution, history and current goings-on in the American nation are chronicled for posterity.

This is not the case everywhere else. Debates regarding the African persons (politics, society) often focus towards the future, on conflict resolution, transition to democracy, social and economic development, Africa and the future of globalization and the role of Africa in modern world politics - including issues of continuing targeting, for example at the International Criminal Court. Yet, Africa's social, political, economic and other multiple futures are tied to its past. Some of its more pertinent issues are tied in with global events of the past 150 years. For while there clearly were ethnic conflicts, periodic droughts, manifestations of inequality, troublesome (at least to the rest of the world) cultural practices such as polygamy, child marriages and female genital mutilation (FGM), the imposition of the nation-state has in some ways exacerbated some, and brought forth new challenges that often compound Africa's challenges.

Survey of literature on Africa's historical past is remarkable in its dearth – particularly as told from the African perspective by African scholars and historians. There is no "American Experience" that captures the untold history of Africa. Where there is an engagement with the past, the history of protest (mostly of colonial, then dictatorial rule), studies insufficiently contemplate the specific experiences of the African communities that were affected by these events. Scholars have often engaged in intellectual debates over the advent, progress, termination and effects of colonialism, yet the question, for example, of restitution on account of colonialism, has not been sufficiently - if at all - addressed.

There are other intellectual, academic and practical issues that originate from the 150 year period that call for reconsideration. For instance, African state boundaries have caused significant disagreements within and between states - disagreements that are ongoing to-date. Yet, one of the first actions that the Organization of African Unity (OAU) did after its formation was to (urge) recognizing the colonial-era boundaries - even where contestation was immediate such as was the case between Somalia and Ethiopia in the early 1960's (Cf. Jacqz 12; Duiker & Spielvoge 762-3; Francis 44; Hyden 68; Mwakikagile: 200-2; Mwakikagile 196; Ngomba-Roth 121).

The non-contestation of boundaries was replicated in other areas, for example, the acceptance of political systems countries inherited from the colonial powers - primarily because they benefitted the new class of politicians. The political system(s) established by the colonial authorities, argues Ahluwalia, "was concerned with maintaining order at the lowest cost...(and) rapidly disintegrated and became weak and vicious and easily captured by factional interests," and further adds that "there is no incentive for African political elites to dismantle political systems which have served their interests" (65). It is hardly a stretch to argue then, that by capturing the apparatus of state, new elites could begin to write the narrative that favored their envisioned paths to the modern African state.

Towards Independence: actual narratives, contested narratives

Narratives on independence from colonial authorities sometimes influenced the level to which newly minted governments (which also often controlled media production, and dissemination of history) pay attention to, influence and generate narratives about the past, simultaneously reconciling these narratives with the envisioned future. Post-Independence leaders were painfully aware of their sometimes limited roles in the processes and narratives of colonial protests and resistance that culminated in independence. Funada-Classen observes that "Eduardo Mondlane, FRELIMO's first president and Samora Machel, its second president, grew up listening to the story of the anti-colonial war of Gungunhana, in which their grandfathers and relatives fought" (69) rather than about their own contributions to the independence movements.

Funada-Classen illustrates this point, further pointing out the Makonde and Yao peoples' liberation struggles and how these were both the genesis and conclusion of the resistance to colonialism in Tanzania. "The Makondes were the last to end the resistance and the first to begin the struggle for liberation - with a gap of only 47 years between the two" (ibid). Shillington observes that "seemingly less-well organized polities (the Nandi of Kenya for example) fought lengthy wars of resistance against European invaders" (981). Oppong and Oppong (41) discuss the role of Jomo Kenyatta, Kenya's founding president, in the liberation struggle and observe that "Jomo Kenyatta was in exile from 1952 to 1959. He had been arrested in 1952, tried for Mau Mau crimes, found guilty and sentenced to seven years of hard labor." During Kenyatta's imprisonment, Dedan Kimathi would go on to lead the Mau Mau.

The reconceptualization of African history was often complicated by the need for the new narrative, and the state's role in fostering or suppressing it. Atieno-Odhiambo (1) labels this the "capture of state power" which, in the case of Kenya, happened in 1963 at independence. The complexity that faced the new African state, beyond recapturing its lost history, is documented as was the case of Kenya: "demands for every-day life in Kenya's postcolonial experience involved a concern with national unity, patriotic endeavor, economic development, social and spiritual space, the valorization of the cultural heritage and the definition of Kenya's place in the world" (Atieno-Odhiambo, 1).

Yet, even though "valorization of the cultural heritage" was important, the new political elite was conscious of the interwoven nature of politics with culture, the role of history in the emerging national narrative (for example, in the fight for independence) and thus providing the impetus to pursue narratives that were consistent with the desired "new national consciousness" even where this required suppression of certain cultural narratives. Clough notes that "in his own UHURU speech that night (independence day celebrations, my emphasis) Jomo Kenyatta did not mention Mau Mau fighters at all", reflected in the further observation that "in some ways Kenyatta and his government seemed to view Mau Mau as both an embarrassment and a threat" and further, in a speech, stated that "Mau Mau was a disease which had been eradicated and must never be remembered again" (46). As would then happen in other places, societies and countries, the rewriting of the African history was firmly underway.

Harmonizing a History of Africa

The writing of African history (or a history of Africa), as Asante asserts, is quite the undertaking. Asante argues that "one can only write a history of Africa" (1). Asante notes, and I concur, that "all histories are specific and particular inasmuch as they are descriptive and interpretative narratives of the themes and chronologies of a particular reality" (1). There is ample support for this position: from the sheer number of countries (or imposed territorial boundaries) to the number of cultural groups within the different countries (for example, more than 42 in Kenya, more than 150 in Tanzania, and more than 250 in Nigeria), one has to then contend with different versions of history - even within the groups. Cohen's scholarship supports this view, suggesting that Africa is an imagined place (52). Again, history being a glorification of cultural values alluded to earlier on, there will be different recollections (oral and recorded) of cattle raids, battles and wars between for example the Kikuyus and the Masai, among others and perhaps the writing of these disparate histories potentially gives the scholar greater ability to more accurately represent the historical experiences.

It is difficult to speak of Africa (other than a geographical land-mass), in the context of historical coherence, primarily due to the structure of its communities before and after colonization, before and after independence. After all, other than the general themes: slave trade in the 17th to 18th centuries, colonization in the late 1800's, protest movements in the early to mid-1900's and the processes of independence from the late 1950's, generalization of African history leads one to an epistemological fallacy. Up to and until after the Berlin Conference in 1884, one might, perhaps, speak of a history of the Kikuyus, a history of the Masai, of the Nandi, Kipsigis, Turkana, Luo etc. Since these were distinctly separate communities, ethnicities, kingdoms, tribes, an event occurring in Berlin, 4000 miles from Nairobi, did not suddenly combine the histories of the Kikuyu with that of the Luo, Masai, Nandi, Kipsigis, Miji-Kenda and others.

The struggles and protests waged, for instance, by the Nandi *orkoiyot* Koitalel arap Samoei were driven by, among others, suspicion and hatred for foreigners, especially Europeans, prior success against the Luo, Luhya, Kisii and Masai, British perceived threats to the Nandi dominance, and Kimnyole's prophesy of a "long snake belching fire" (Kenya-Uganda Railway which began in 1899), preservation of culture, cultural misunderstanding, a history of fighting foreigners and a tradition of individualism and competitiveness (Okoth & Ndaloh 133-4; Bale & Sang 151). No credible argument has, so far, appeared to suggest that the Nandi were resisting the British on behalf of all Kenyans. Neither were the Akamba, when they resisted British rule and occupation at the turn of the 19th century (Maina, Oboka & Makong'o 50-51).

How then, did the African state become consolidated to the extent that in 1963, a mere 60 years after the fully-fledged colonization process took place, the OAU determined that keeping the boundaries in territories which united groups that, not-too-long ago, raided each other with regularity and often collaborated with the British to defeat their territorial enemies, was the best course of action? Reasons thereof are clearly articulated in the reasons given by Julius Nyerere, paraphrased: Nyerere, in 1960, "received a delegation of Masai elders from Kenya, led by an American missionary. And they came to persuade me to let the Masai invoke something called the Anglo-Masai Agreement so that that section of the Masai in Kenya should become part of Tanganyika, so that when Tanganyika becomes independent, it includes part of Masai from Kenya." However, Nyerere reasoned: "Why shouldn't Kenyatta demand that the Masai part of Tanganyika should become Masai of Kenya? It's the same logic. That was in 1960." (Mwakikagile 201).

The clearest deciding factor was Nyasaland (Malawi's) future president's visit. "So Banda comes to me with a big old book, with lots of maps in it, and tells me, 'Mwalimu, what is this, what is Mozambique? There is no such thing as Mozambique" (ibid). Banda demonstrated that Mozambique could be divided up between Malawi, Southern Rhodesia and Tanzania (Nyerere recounted that he declined to endorse the idea). However, a year later, he would move the resolution for OAU to recognize colonial boundaries, in part to alleviate problems such as Banda articulated, illustrated by the ongoing war between Somalia and Ethiopia. Mwakikagile writes that at the time, "Somalia wanted the Ogaden, a whole province of Ethiopia, saying, 'That is part of Somalia," while Ethiopia was quietly saying...that 'the whole of Somalia is part of Ethiopia'" (202).

In all likelihood, the maps that Banda was showing to Nyerere were drawn up in Europe, by Europeans. While the accuracy of the maps and boundaries might not be disputable, the implications were significant: the creation of new states, dismantling of logical units, combining of former foes into unitary, Westphalian-states, and the creation of new national narratives. Western education, and the ideas that it held, were thus instrumental in determining the future – including the future history – of the societies that the new boundaries affected.

Reconciling Western Epistemology and African History's?

Colonialism and the spread of Christianity introduced new, different manifestations of social, cultural and political infrastructure, including among others, formal education. The formal education generally followed western standards, rather than the traditional, story-telling and experiential based African variety. The idea of knowledge, what one knew, and how they knew it, also changed. History became only history based on written records, effectively disregarding and nearly wiping out millennia of African history. The culprit here was the insistence on recorded history and the way knowledge was defined: in other words, what we know.

Irele & Jeyifo define epistemology as "a philosophical investigation into the scope and nature of knowledge, whether any knowledge claim is rationally grounded or not" (340). Irele & Jeyifo contend that prevailing though suggested that "Africans were prelogical and thus beyond the pale of rationality" (340), an ideology based on notions of African inferiority - this applied too, to African "education" - the transmission of traditional values, history, knowledge and trades. Given that the epistemology and the educational systems were based on European concepts and methods, even when African thought began to take shape, it was subjected to the same epistemological conditions. Here, Wai articulates the problem with these approaches arguing that the

> emerging African historiographies would remain colonized within Eurocentric frames, so that for African history to be accepted as history, for its modalities to be accepted as worthy of consideration, it had to be first subjected to the epistemological, methodological, and conceptual gaze and scrutiny of the West and framed in ways that were acceptable to the very people who had for centuries denied African historicity and its place in history. (30)

Adeleke concurs, reiterating Walter Rodney's argument that "one of the major dilemmas inherent in the attempt by black people to break through the cultural aspects of white imperialism is that posed by the use of historical knowledge as a weapon in our struggle. We are virtually forced into the invidious position of proving our humanity by citing historical antecedents...the white man has already implanted numerous historical myths in the minds of black peoples" (86) and, I might add, into the minds of consumers of scholarship. The tradition of favoring – even such – recorded history over oral history has been cemented by the scientific rigor emphasized by western education. Yet, in lieu of dismissing oral historical accounts of African societies it is beneficial to acknowledge that while no written accounts of African history exists, but denying the use of oral history absolutely does knowledge and humanity a disservice; it invokes a Swahili saying, *heri nusu ya shari, kuliko shari kamili*.[3]

---

[3] Roughly translated: "partial evil is better than total evil"

There are, admittedly, gaps in our knowledge of, and the prized, recorded history of African societies in aspects such as government, culture, religion and other things, yet, as Monroe so clearly articulates, "[o]ral sources, therefore, become a useful window in to the origins of...communities across the Slave Coast" (32). Therefore, rather than shun and or dismiss these sources merely because they did not offer written accounts of historical occurrence, African scholars should undertake programs of the "American Experience magnitude and continue the pioneering work of the Dar es Salaam School, where African historians in Tanzania attempted to "write a history that had meaning to the people concerned and not to foreign experts" (Nabudere 132), an approach that utilized oral materials and local languages to connect the researchers with the subjects. This approach would be the logical follow-up to Walter Rodney's and the Dar es Salaam School's lead, where Rodney, by conducting oral history surveys in West Africa, found "ample solid evidence to negate the misrepresentations of Eurocentric scholarship" (316)

Historical traditions abound, that utilize the range of oral history materials such as myths, poems, epics, riddles, idioms, proverbs, dirges, panegyrics, witty sayings etc., to recreate and help understand the history of a people. After all, how does one explain the wide acceptance of such widely read epics as the *Epic of Gilgamesh*, Homer's *Iliad* or Aeneas' *Aeneid*, whose origins are similarly mythical, which were often recorded several hundred years after the events that they describe (for example, the Peloponnesian War), yet cast doubt on the validity of historical accounts of African communities that were passed down in a similar fashion over just the past 150 years? While arguments about the objectivity of the oral history gives credence to the arguments for the vetting of such memory-based history against other sources, it is clear that capturing those memories before generations that in part directly transmitted them is a worthwhile, nay, *necessary* and urgent endeavor.

It is important, indeed it is high time African historians, historiographers and students of African history stopped apologizing for the absence of recorded history, and utilized the available sources – mainly oral history that articulates the best experiences, standards, practices and knowledge of African traditions – and record them as primary sources and further, make the case for their use as primary sources, rather than continue to try to fit them into occidental epistemological, theoretical and rational frameworks of knowledge. It is also necessary for African scholars and scholarship to take note that the notion of descriptions of pre-colonial systems being described as "primitive" has not abated; for example, in the introduction to section C, Bendix et al iterate "thus, even in the primitive systems of tribal Africa, there is..." (71). Considering the advancement of knowledge about cultures, histories and biology, it is interesting that rather than utilize the experience (oral history) of the particular societies, the standard of scientific rigor continues to rely on references or texts espousing such language.

Concluding thoughts: re (thinking the) telling of Africa's History

The foregoing arguments have demonstrated the challenges that the reading and telling of African history contends with. These epistemological issues, with the scientific rigors based on a western-centric approach to knowledge, and the absence of objective, recorded accounts prior to the arrival of the missionaries and later, the colonizers. It also contended with an occupying force that had no interest in recording the oral history of the colonized, in part to provide justification for the colonization and Christianization of people described as "barbaric" or "heathens" or "uncivilized". After independence,

Westphalian states that emerged from colonization had to contend with artificial boundaries, logically making the primary duty of the republic unity (and survival). Such duty often required the suppression of individual communities' histories, histories of protests and other measures – particularly through the control of information and imposition of national languages (such as was the case in Tanzania).

The confluence of these and other factors led to a lack of concerted efforts consolidate the oral history of African communities; yet, a study of such history may show that despite the perceptions of these societies, there were systematic structures of state that allowed the societies, tribes, principalities and kingdoms to organize their affairs: education, politics, state affairs, property ownership – their collective culture and history. An interrogation of the oral history will show a strong link within and between the pre-colonial societies, which would significantly challenge the existing written accounts of history produced by the early colonists and missionaries.

African cultures, history and record-keeping (through oral history) were fundamentally changed by systems such as colonialism and the succeeding Westphalian-style state. The state, in particular often contrived to rewrite history favoring the processes of independence and suppressing individual societies' history in the name of national unity. Further, gradual consolidation of the state led to state control of information production and dissemination (including research in the academy) and fostered conditions unfavorable to retention and advancement of individual and collective societal histories – a suppression much akin to that of the colonial empires. Even with the current levels and speed of globalization, contemporary African nations have not shown purposeful, focused effort to capture and preserve in perpetuity reconciled accounts of the states as well as their constituent society (tribes, kingdoms).

Such effort may serve the dual purpose of not only preserving history, but also of contesting, correcting or challenging accounts of explorers, missionaries and later, colonialists, including David Livingstone, H. M. Stanley, Joseph Conrad, Frederick Lugard and T. M. Thomas, among others. This omission is adequately captured by an online (social media) contributor's comment– which also reflects the truth among many modern African societies and their school systems: "I can tell you all about Louis XIV, Socrates, and the Magna Carta, but I always wondered when we would finally learn about African history (beyond Pharaohs and pyramids). The subject never came up" (Hennick, 2014). The continuing superficiality of African history and the contributions of Africans to civilization and modernity continue to be limited to Pharaohs and Pyramids, the source of slaves in the Trans-Atlantic trade, backwardness/darkness, and colonialism and now to intractable war.

Moreover, it is important to continue challenging the assumptions that have been made regarding Africa: from the acceptance of western-driven epistemological approaches applied to communities and societies that had or have different *methods* of generating, preserving and disseminating knowledge, and making the reading of that particular history in the context of its production, to making a more robust case for the use of oral history and traditions as a true record of what transpired in African societies. By doing so, the silence that is often imposed on African history simply because it does not meet the western-centric standards of scientific rigor will be challenged. Further, the betrayal of African oral history and its perpetuation, which have been perpetuated by colonialists and subsequently by independent African governments might be challenged, and the secrets of Christianity, colonialism, collusion and suppression of the heritage of a billion people might be given voice.

Works Cited

Adeleke, Tunde. "Africa in the Black Diaspora Struggle: Paradigms & Perspectives." *in* Jacob U. Gordon, Ed. *The African Presence in Black America*. Trenton, NJ: Africa World Press, 2004. Print.

──────── . *The Case Against Afrocentrism*. Jackson, MS: University Press of Mississippi, 2009. Print.

Ahluwalia, D. Pal S. *Politics and Post-colonial Theory: African Inflections*. Commack, NY: 1996. Print.

Asante, Molefi K. *The History of Africa: The Quest for Eternal Harmony*. New York, NY: Routledge, 2007. Print.

Atieno-Odhiambo, E. S. "The Invention of Kenya." Bethwell A. Ogot and William Robert Ochieng', Eds. *Decolonization and Independence in Kenya, 1940-93*. Nairobi, Kenya: 1995. Print.

Bale, John and Joe Sang. *Kenyan Running: Movement Culture, Geography and Global Change*. London: Frank Cass, 1996. Print.

Balandier, Georges. "Political Myths of Colonization and Decolonization in Africa." In Reinhard Bendix, et al, Eds. *State and Society: A Reader in Comparative Political Sociology*. Berkeley, CA: University of California Press, 1973. Print.

Bendix, Reinhard, et al. "Introduction". In Reinhard Bendix, et al., Eds. *State and Society: A Reader in Comparative Political Sociology*. Berkeley, CA: University of California Press, 1973. Print.

Channock, Martin. "A Peculiar Sharpness: An Essay on Property in the History of Customary Law in Colonial Africa. *The Journal of African History*, 32, No. 1 (1991): 65-88.

URL: http://www.jstor.org/stable/182579. Accessed: 26/12/2014 19:36

Chisholm, Hugh. *The Encyclopedia Britannica: A Dictionary of Arts, Sciences and General Information*, 11th Edition, Vol. 1. New York, NY: The Encyclopedia Britannica Company, 1910. Print.

Clough, Marshall S. *Mau Mau Memoirs: History, Memory, and Politics*. Boulder, CO: Lynne Rienner Publishers, Inc.: 1998. Print.

Cohen, David William. *The Combing of History*. Chicago, IL: University of Chicago Press, 1994. Print.

Conrad, Joseph. *Heart of Darkness*. Google Digital Books. (Web).

Corr, Kendra & Wendy Moeller. *World History Lessons for the Stuff That's Hard to Teach: Theme Schemes*. Culver City, CA: Social Studies School Service, 2005. Print.

Duiker, William J. and Jackson Spielvoge. *The Essential World History*. Boston, MA: Wadsworth, 2014. Print.

Evans, E. W. and David Richardson. "Hunting for Rents: The Economics of Slaving in Pre-Colonial Africa." *The Economic History Review, New Series*, 48, No. 4 (Nov., 1995): 665-686. URL: http://www.jstor.org/stable/2598129. Accessed: 26/12/2014 20:06

Ferguson, Niall. *Civilization: The West and the Rest*. New York, NY: The Penguin Press, 2011. Print.

Francis, David J.*Uniting Africa: Building Regional Peace and Security Systems*. Hampshire, England: Ashgate Publishing Ltd, 2006. Print.

Funada-Classen, Sayaka. *The Origins of War in Mozambique: A History of Unity and Division*. Somerset West, South Africa: 2012. Print.

Fyle, C. Magbaily. *Introduction to the History of African Civilization: Precolonial Africa*. Lanham, MD: University Press of America, 1999. Print.

Hall, Martin. "Archaeology and Modes of Production in Pre-Colonial Southern Africa." *Journal of Southern African Studies,* 14, No. 1 (Oct., 1987): 1-17. Stable URL: http://www.jstor.org/stable/2636694. Accessed: 26/12/2014 22:39

Hardin, William. *War in South Africa and the Dark Continent from Savagery to Civilization* ... Chicago, IL: Dominion Company, 1899. Print.

Hennick, Calvin. "7 Things I Can Do That My Black Son Can't." (Web). October 27, 2014. Accessed from: https://www.yahoo.com/parenting/7-things-i-can-do-that-my-black-son-cant-99408985077.html on 12/27/2014

Hyden, Goran. *African Politics in Comparative Perspective*. New York, NY: Cambridge University Press, 2014. Print.

Irele, Abiola and Biodun Jeyifo. *The Oxford Encyclopedia of African Thought, Volume 2*. New York: Oxford University Press, 2010. Print.

Jacqz, Jane Wilder. *Africa Policy Update*. Report 1977 African-American Conference, Williamsburg, VA. ND.

Kuhn, Thomas S. *The structure of scientific revolutions*. Chicago, IL: University of Chicago Press, 1996. Print.

Law, Robin. "Horses, Firearms, and Political Power in Pre-Colonial West Africa." *Past & Present,* No. 72 (Aug., 1976), pp. 112-132. URL: http://www.jstor.org/stable/650330. Accessed: 26/12/2014 22:39

Lugard, Lord Frederick J.D. *The Dual Mandate in British Tropical Africa*. Oxon, UK: Frank Cass & Co. Ltd., 1922 (Google digital version: 2005)

Maina, Ephalina A. Wycliffe A. Oboka and Julius Makong'o. *History and Government Form 2*. Nairobi, Kenya: EAEP, 2004. Print.

McNeill, William H. *The Rise of the West: A History of the Human Community*. London, UK: The University of Chicago Press, 199. Print.1

Monroe, J. Cameron. *The Precolonial State in West Africa: Building Power in Dahomey.* New York: Cambridge University Press, 2014. Print.

Mwakikagile, Godfrey. *Africa 1960 - 1970: Chronicle and Analysis.* Dar es Salaam, Tanzania: New Africa Press, 2014. Print.

_____ *Africa in The Sixties.* Dar es Salaam, Tanzania: New Africa Press, 2014. Print.

Nabudere, D. Wadada. *Afrikology and Transdisciplinarity: A Restorative Epistemology.* Pretoria, South Africa: Africa Institute of South Africa, 2012. Print.

Ndlovu-Gatsheni, Sabelo J. "Mapping Cultural and Colonial Encounters, 1880's-1930's." In Brian Raftopoulos and Alois Mlambo, Eds. *Becoming Zimbabwe: A History from the Pre-colonial Period.* Harare, Zimbabwe: Weaver Press, 2009. Print.

Ngomba-Roth, Rose. *The Challenges of Conflict Resolution in Africa: The Case of Cameroon.* Berlin, Germany: Lit Verlag, 2008. Print.

Okoth, Assah & Agumba Ndaloh. *PTE Revision Social Studies for Primary Education.* Nairobi, Kenya: EAEP, 2008. Print.

Oppong. Joseph R. and Esther D. Oppong. *Kenya.* New York, NY: 2004. Print.

PBS. "About PBS." (Web). Accessed on 12/21/2014 from: http://www.pbs.org/aboutpbs/news/20090213_pbsropersurvey.html

Sarkin-Hughes, Jeremy. *Germany's Genocide of the Herero: Kaiser Wilhelm II, His General, His Soldiers.* Cape Town, South Africa: University of Cape Town Press, 2010. Print.

Scott, James C. T*he Moral Economy of the Peasant: Rebellion and Subsistence in Southeast Asia.* New Haven, CT: Yale University Press, 1976. Print.

Shillington, Kevin (Ed). *Encyclopedia of African history.* New York, NY: Fitzroy Dearborn, 2004. Print.

Smith, Adam. *The Wealth of Nations*. (Pt. 2). New York, NY: P. F. Collier & Son, 1902 (Google Digital Edition)

Smith, Robert. "Peace and Palaver: International Relations in Pre-Colonial West Africa." *The Journal of African History*, 14, No. 4 (1973), pp. 599-621. Stable URL: http://www.jstor.org/stable/180903. Accessed: 26/12/2014 20:19

Stambouli, F. and A. Zghal. "Urban Life in Pre-Colonial North Africa." *The British Journal of Sociology,* 27, No. 1 (Mar., 1976): 1-20. URL: http://www.jstor.org/stable/589557. Accessed: 26/12/2014 22:39.

Stanley, Henry Morton. *Through the Dark Continent, Or, The Sources of the Nile Around the Continent in Two Volumes.* Mineola, NY: Dover Publications, 1988. Print.

Stewart, James. *Dawn in the Dark Continent, or, Africa and its missions.* Edinburgh, Scotland: Oliphant Anderson & Ferrier, 1903. Print.

Stock, Robert and Robert F. Stock. *Africa South of the Sahara: A Geographical Interpretation.* New York, NY: Guilford Press, 2013. Print.

Thomas, T. M. *Eleven years in Central South Africa.* London, UK: John Snow & Co, 1873 (accessed on Google Books).

Wai, Zubairu. *Epistemologies of African Conflicts: Violence, Evolutionism, and the War in Sierra Leone.* New York, NY: Palgrave MacMillan, 2012. Print.

White, Frances. *Dark Continent of Our Bodies: Black Feminism & Politics Of Respectability.* Philadelphia, PA: Temple University, 2001. Print.

Zimmerman, Andrew. *Anthropology and Antihumanism in Imperial Germany.* London, UK: University of Chicago Press, 2001. Print.

Chapter 2

Behind the Scenes of Parent-Child Attachment Relationships

Jennifer J. Ross

Humans are social beings. We begin to form our first and most fundamental social relationship shortly after birth. The relationship between infant and primary caregiver grows and develops over course of the child's first year of life. Ideally, this relationship is open, honest, and mutually satisfying, whereas unfavorable relationships are secretive, silent, and based on betrayal. This chapter provides a behind the scenes look at how a baby becomes attached and why individual differences exist in the fundamental relationship between parent and child. The essay begins with a brief introduction to the central tenets of attachment theory and is followed by several scenarios that illustrate the different patterns of attachment. Each scenario is explained according to attachment theory and explores how secrets, silences, and betrayals play a role in the formation and manifestation of an attachment relationship between infant and primary caregiver. The chapter concludes with implications for social relationship functioning later in the child's life.

According to attachment theory (Bowlby, 1969), infants are innately predisposed to develop an attachment relationship with a caregiver and to use that attachment figure as a haven of safety and as a secure base from which to explore the environment. The quality of the relationship and the effectiveness of a caregiver as a source of comfort when needed, however, differ across infant-caregiver dyads. These individual differences in attachment relationships reflect a history of bids for interaction from the baby and responses from the caregiver. Caregiver responses can be sensitive to, or betray, the child's needs. Through repeated bid-response exchanges over time, infants begin to anticipate the behavior from their primary caregiver and develop distinct patterns of interaction that reflect the presence or absence of secrets, silences, and betrayals in the relationship between parent and child.

Individual differences in infant-caregiver attachment relationships are most easily seen in a baby's balance between exploration and seeking proximity to the caregiver when the environment is challenging or threatening (Ainsworth, Blehar, Waters, & Wall, 1978; Bowlby, 1982; Weinfield, Sroufe, Egeland, & Carlson, 2008) as demonstrated in the following scenario.

Michael, a 14-month-old toddler, enters an unfamiliar room with his mother. Michael heads straight for the pile of toys on the floor by a mirror while his mom sits and reads a magazine. The toy airplane is particularly fun, so Michael excitedly shows his mom. She smiles and verbalizes her encouragement of his exploration. Michael continues to play until a stranger walks in the room and sits in a chair across from his mom. Michael looks to his mother and she smiles her reassurance that it is okay for him to continue playing. Michael checks out the toys while his mom and the stranger talk. Then the stranger joins Michael on the floor and plays with him before his mom leaves the room. Michael sees his mom leave, fusses, and goes to the closed door his mom just left from. The stranger coaxes Michael back over to the toys and settles him back into playing.

When his mom returns, Michael greets her brightly with a smile and approaches her for a hug. Michael's mom picks him up for an embrace and carries him back over to the toys. She reminds him how much he liked the toy airplane by zooming it around before landing it in his lap. Michael accepts the toy and his mom sits back down to read her magazine while he plays. Minutes later, Michael's mom leaves the room a second time. Michael does not like being separated from his mom. He stops playing and looks at the door. When his mom doesn't come right back in the room, Michael starts fussing and goes to the door. Michael is disappointed and feels betrayed when the stranger comes back into the room without his mom. She tries to comfort him, but it doesn't work and Michael starts to cry. When his mom returns, Michael quickly forgives the minor betrayal of being left alone and approaches her with raised arms. She immediately picks him up and pulls him into a close embrace. Michael gets the comfort he needs and turns to point at the toys indicating he wants to go back to playing. She takes Michael to the toys and gets him back into playing with airplane.

This scenario involving Michael, his mom, and a stranger in an unfamiliar room is called the Strange Situation (Ainsworth et al., 1978). The Strange Situation is a measure developed by Mary Ainsworth to assess the infant-caregiver attachment relationship. The Strange Situation procedure consists of eight episodes presented in a standard order. The episodes expected to be least stressful for the infant occur first and then the stressors gradually increase with each episode. Ainsworth found this sequence of episodes to be very powerful in eliciting attachment behaviors that were plainly observable and in highlighting individual differences in infant-caregiver relationships. These differences are broadly characterized as secure or insecure and expose the presence or absence of secrets, silences, and betrayals in the relationship between parent and child.

Security or insecurity in the attachment relationship reflects an infant's perceived availability of their caregiver if needed for comfort or protection. Attachment security indicates that a baby is able to rely on their caregiver as a haven of safety.

Securely attached infants have not experienced repeated hurt and betrayal by their caregiver and thus have confident expectations of the availability and responsiveness of that caregiver. Secure attachment relationships are open and honest, so there is no basis for secrets or silences to be harbored between child and parent. Securely attached infants direct attachment behaviors to their caregivers when feelings of threat or danger arise and take comfort in the reassurance provided by their caregiver. These infants learn to approach the world with confidence and are confident in their interactions with the environment.

The pattern of behavior that Michael exhibited with his mom in the Strange Situation demonstrates a secure attachment relationship. Michael used his mother as a secure base from which to explore in the pre-separation episodes demonstrating a balance between attachment and exploration. This was evident when Michael shared his enthusiasm over the toy airplane with his mom and when he checked in with her to see if the stranger was a threat. Michael showed signs of distress in the separation episodes, which is understandable, but he certainly preferred the comfort and presence of his mom over the stranger. Michael clearly demonstrated his attachment security in the reunion episodes when he immediately sought contact with his mom and her hugs provided the comfort he needed to get back to playing.

Attachment insecurity indicates that a baby cannot rely on the caregiver as a haven of safety (Ainsworth et al., 1978). Infants with an insecure attachment relationship have not experienced consistent availability and comfort from their caregiver when the environment evokes feelings of threat or danger. Babies with an insecure attachment relationship are not as confident in exploring the environment as securely attached infants. These infants have been repeatedly been betrayed by their caregiver; their bids for interaction are responded to with indifference, rebuffs, or notable inconsistency from their caregiver. A history of these betrayals over time results in the infant feeling anxious about the availability and responsiveness of their caregiver (Weinfield et al., 2008). These qualities foster secrets and silences in the relationship between parent and child as evidenced in the following scenario.

Amber, a 15-month-old toddler, enters the Strange Situation. Like Michael, Amber walks straight over to the toys by the mirror while her mom sits and picks up a magazine. Amber handles many of the toys, scattering the pile around. Her mom reads silently. Mother and child do not interact. Amber does not outwardly display any signs of concern when the stranger enters the room or when she speaks with her mom. The stranger joins Amber on the floor and shows her how to make a call with the toy phone. Amber accepts the phone and plays well with the stranger. The toddler looks up when her mom leaves and resumes playing with the phone. The stranger sits back in her chair and Amber bangs on the phone without seeming to be bothered by her mom's absence. Minutes later, Amber looks up when her mom returns, but does not offer any greeting. Her mom sits and reads, the stranger exits the room, and Amber goes back to her cursory investigation of the toys. Mother and child silently engage in their own activities.

Amber does not cry when her mom leaves the room for the second time and does not seem to be bothered by the stranger returning before her mom. When Amber is reunited with her mom, she takes a couple of steps towards her then turns back for the toys. Her mom goes back to her chair with the magazine. Amber toddles over to the stacking rings that are pretty close to her mom. She quietly sits with her back to her mom, though in proximity, and silently handles the plastic rings.

This scenario exemplifies an insecure-avoidant pattern of attachment. Amber did not seem bothered by the Strange Situation, but she was secretly anxious when separated from her mom. Cardiac arousal and cortisol levels have shown that avoidant babies are just as stressed by the Strange Situation as those that cry or show other overt signs of distress (Spangler & Grossmann, 1993). The difference is that Amber has learned to keep her anxiety a secret from her mother. Avoidant babies rarely cry in the separation episodes and exhibit their most conspicuous behavioral feature in the reunion episodes, which is avoidance of contact, proximity, or interaction with their mother. These infants may mingle proximity-seeking and avoidant behaviors or ignore her altogether, both of which Amber demonstrated in the reunion episodes.

Amber's secret anxiety is rooted in a history of betrayals. In an insecure-avoidant relationship, the caregiver rebuffs clear signals for interaction from their baby, causing the infant to signal more strongly, which results in the caregiver rebuffing more strongly. This lack of caregiver sensitivity epitomizes a repeated betrayal of the child's need for attention. Infants with a developmental history of betrayal learn not to turn to their caregiver over time. These babies do not seek contact when threatened. Instead these infants have learned that minimizing their expressions of attachment feelings creates a silence that allows them to stay in proximity to their caregiver as Amber did at the end of the Strange Situation. This silence leaves open the possibility of responsiveness should a serious threat arise (Main & Hesse, 1990).

There are two different organized manifestations of an insecure attachment relationship. Consider the difference in the next scenario involving a boy and his father and note that a child's primary caregiver does not always refer to the mother. Attachment security or insecurity is a product of the caregiver's responsiveness to or betrayal of their child's needs over time.

Fathers are just as capable as mothers at providing the basis for a secure attachment relationship.

A 15-month old boy named Joshua enters the Strange Situation with his dad. Joshua runs over to the toys while his dad sits in a chair across the room. Joshua picks up a telephone and brings it to his dad. His dad accepts the toy and shows Joshua how to make a call. Joshua goes back over to the toys, picks up the baby doll, and brings it back to his dad. His dad hugs the baby doll and gives it back to his son. Joshua again goes back to the pile of toys, picks up an airplane, and brings it over to his dad. His dad zooms the airplane around and gives the toy back to his son. Joshua plays with the airplane running it over his dad's legs until a stranger walks in the room. Joshua stops playing and looks at the stranger while holding on to his dad's legs. His dad encourages Joshua to play with the airplane again while he talks with the stranger. The stranger then gets on the floor next to the toys and tries to get Joshua to play with her. Joshua is reluctant and stays close to his dad. His dad verbalizes his encouragement, but Joshua stays by his side. The stranger demonstrates how much fun it is to play with the stacking rings, occasionally offering one of the rings to Joshua. The boy finally accepts one of the rings from the stranger and places it on the stack by the stranger.

The stranger and Joshua are playing together with the stacking rings when his dad leaves the room. Joshua immediately stops playing and goes to the door. The stranger tries to coax him back over to play, but Joshua is not interested. He feels betrayed by his father leaving him with the stranger and starts to cry. The stranger tries to comfort him, but Joshua is too upset by his father's betrayal. When his father comes back in the room, Joshua runs over to him. His dad picks him up and tries to comfort his son, but Joshua is angry and pushes his dad away. Joshua is put down by the toys and his dad offers him one of the stacking rings. Joshua bats the ring away. His dad tries another ring and gets the same reaction. Joshua's dad zooms the airplane that his son enjoyed earlier and is slowly able to calm him into playing.

Joshua isn't quite over his dad leaving him with the stranger when his dad exits the room, leaving Joshua alone. Joshua drops the airplane and runs to the door. He stands by the door crying until the stranger comes in. She tries to comfort Joshua, but it doesn't work. Joshua's dad comes back in and tries to comfort Joshua. He is terribly upset, but pushes away from his dad's embrace. His dad tries to put him down, but Joshua resists. His dad hugs and rocks his crying son. Joshua briefly accepts the embrace with a stiff back and then abruptly looks down at the toys. His dad puts Joshua down and starts for his chair, but Joshua stomps his feet and cries. His dad turns back and decides to sit on the floor next to his son. He offers the airplane, but Joshua bats it away. His dad zooms the airplane around and around until Joshua's fussing and anger subsides.

This example demonstrates an insecure-resistant pattern of attachment. Infants with an insecure-resistant relationship adopt a strategy opposite from the avoidant pattern. It was no secret that Joshua was upset by the separation from his father. Joshua also was not silent about his anger. However, there are secrets and silences in this attachment relationship that are based on betrayal. The parent in an insecure-resistant attachment relationship betrays their child's needs by providing inconsistent care. Over time, an infant with a history of unpredictable caregiving and betrayal learns to maximize their attachment behaviors, which masks a secret. These babies secretly do not have confident expectations of their caregiver's accessibility and responsiveness, so these infants frequently and strongly signal for the caregiver while keeping their truth silent.

In the Strange Situation, resistant infants are extremely distressed by separation yet they exhibit ambivalence towards their caregiver upon reunion, seeking close contact mixed with angry resistance to contact or interaction with the caregiver. Joshua exemplified these behaviors in the reunion episodes when he immediately sought contact, but then pushed his dad away or batted away the offered toys. These babies seek contact when threat is minimal, as Joshua did in the pre-separation episodes, but the contact is not effective in alleviating the infant's distress, which was evident in how long it took Joshua's dad to settle his son upon reunion. This strategy keeps the infant close to their inconsistent caregiver thereby increasing the likelihood of the parent's availability in the event of a serious threat.

These two insecure patterns of attachment are adaptations that promote proximity to caregivers, but compromise the balance between attachment and exploration due to the increased attention and focus on maintaining the coping strategies in an insecure attachment relationship. These coping strategies reveal the existence of secrets and silences harbored by the child in response to a developmental history of betrayal by their attachment figure. Avoidant and resistant babies have learned to anticipate the betrayal of their needs and organize their attachment behaviors around the predicted betrayal by their caregiver. A fourth class of infants, on the other hand, have experienced the worst betrayal of all and are unable to develop a coherent coping strategy as evidenced in the following scenario.

A 14-month-old girl named Rachel enters the Strange Situation. Much like the other scenarios, Rachel goes straight over to the toys while her mom sits and reads a magazine. Rachel picks up and puts down a few of the toys while her mom reads silently. There is no interaction between mother and child. Rachel stops handling the toys and stares fixedly at the stranger when she enters the room. Rachel remains frozen in her gaze while the stranger and her mom talk. It seems as if the toddler is in a trance until the stranger approaches her to try and play, at which point Rachel falls over from her seated position and lies prone on the floor. Her mom walks past her child with no acknowledgement as she leaves the room. Rachel sits up and looks to the door until her mom returns. Upon reunion, Rachel immediately takes an interest in the toys rather than greeting or approaching her mom. Her mom takes her seat with the magazine, the stranger exits the room, and Rachel pokes at the toy phone. Mother and child silently engage in their respective activities.

When her mom leaves the room for the second time, Rachel stops her cursory investigation of the phone, sits quietly for a moment, and then starts crying. The toddler is not comforted by the stranger when she comes back into the room before her mom. When Rachel is reunited with her mom, she approaches her with raised arms. Rachel gets partway to her mom before turning sharply to the wall where she stands still with a dazed expression. Her mom goes back to her chair with the magazine.

This scenario exemplifies an insecure-disorganized/disoriented attachment relationship. The terms *disorganized* and *disoriented* are used to describe the infant's movement and behavior patterns that lack a coherent strategy for dealing with the stress of the Strange Situation (Lyons-Ruth & Jacobvitz, 2008; Main & Solomon, 1990). These babies appear disorganized in their actions and/or disoriented with respect to the environment (Main & Solomon, 1986).

There were many indices of disorganization and disorientation in the scenario with Rachel and her mom. To begin, in the pre-separation episode, Rachel was clearly frightened by the stranger, but she did not seek contact or comfort from her mom. Rachel's inability to use her mother as a haven of safety in the event of a perceived threat is indicative of an insecure attachment relationship. Her silent stilling with a trance-like gaze at the stranger for an extended period of time and her assumption of a prone position when approached by the stranger are examples of disoriented behavior in the Strange Situation (Main & Solomon, 1990). Rachel was trapped in silence without a solution to her fear.

The lack of a coherent strategy was demonstrated when Rachel looked longingly at the door while waiting for her mom during the first separation and then exhibited avoidant behavior upon reunion. This sequential display of contradictory behavior patterns is an indicator of attachment disorganization (Main & Solomon, 1990). Avoidant babies are adept at keeping their anxiety over separation a secret by minimizing their attachment behaviors. Recall that Amber noticed her mom leave the room, but did not appear bothered by the separation. Amber maintained her insecure-avoidant strategy upon reunion by greeting her mother with indifference. Rachel was unable to maintain a single coping strategy as evidenced in her display of distress during separation followed by an attempt to secret it away with avoidance upon reunion.

A similar display of disorganization in the form of contradictory behaviors occurred during the second separation and reunion. It was no secret that Rachel was distressed when her mom left the room again, which she demonstrated by crying when separated. She then began an approach for comfort upon reunion before abruptly turning from her mom. This exhibition of avoidance was accompanied by disorientation as Rachel stood silently facing the wall with a dazed expression. She was again trapped in silence without a coherent strategy to alleviate her anxiety. This silence belies a secret dilemma; Rachel's mom is both a source of comfort and a source of fear.

Rachel demonstrated an insecure-disorganized/disoriented attachment relationship in the Strange Situation. The toddler displayed insecurity in her inability to use her mom as a haven of safety and secure base to explore the environment. She exhibited disorganization in her attempt to use contradicting coping strategies. It seemed as if Rachel was trying to adopt an avoidant strategy, but she could not keep her anxiety a secret during the separation episodes. Rachel was also quite apprehensive of the stranger during the pre-separation episodes, which is more indicative of a resistant strategy. This inability to adopt a single, coherent strategy for dealing with the stress of the Strange Situation reveals a developmental history of betrayal by the attachment figure.

The parent in an insecure-disorganized/disoriented attachment relationship betrays their child's needs by creating an irresolvable paradox where the haven of safety is also the cause for alarm (Main & Hesse, 1990). The parent may adopt threatening postures, facial expressions, or movements that seem aggressive to a baby. Conversely, the caregiver may exhibit behavior that shows the parent is inexplicably frightened of the infant (Lyons-Ruth & Jacobvitz, 2008). These unpredictably frightening or frightened behaviors provoke conflict in the infant because the attachment figure is at once the source and the solution to the child's fear (Main & Solomon, 1990). This ultimate betrayal creates opposing inclinations to approach and to flee, which results in the child's secret turmoil manifested as disorganized behavior or in silence revealed by disoriented infant behavior in the Strange Situation.

This chapter has demonstrated that secrets, silences, and betrayals contribute to the formation and manifestation of an attachment relationship between child and parent. Babies that have their needs repeatedly betrayed learn to anticipate the betrayal and form secrets or silences to mask their insecurity. Amber, Joshua, and Rachel had secrets and silences in their parent-child attachment relationships that were based on a developmental history of caregiver betrayal. Amber had a rejecting caregiver, Joshua's caregiver was inconsistent, and

Rachel had a frightened/frightening caregiver. These betrayals led to insecure parent-child attachment relationships. Michael, on the other hand, did not experience betrayal by his caregiver. He was able to confidently rely on his mother for comfort and safety when needed, which allowed Michael to explore the environment with confidence. Michael had no basis for secrets and silences because he had confident expectations of his caregiver's availability.

This behind the scenes look at how a baby becomes attached has implications on a child's later social functioning. Secure attachment in infancy forecasts open, honest, and satisfying social relationships later in the child's life. On the other hand, insecure attachment in infancy forecasts less than optimal relationships in the child's future. Insecure children will likely harbor secrets, silences, and betrayals in their adolescent or adult relationships with friends, family, co-workers, and romantic partners. However, change is always possible. Time and effort can repair the betrayals that led to the secrets and silences in an insecure attachment relationship. This worthwhile endeavor can change a child's path to healthy social and emotional development.

Works Cited

Ainsworth, M. D. S., Blehar, M. C., Waters, E., & Wall, S. (1978). *Patterns of attachment: A psychological study of the Strange Situation.* Hillsdale, NJ: Lawrence Erlbaum.

Bowlby, J. (1969). *Attachment and loss: Attachment* (Vol. 1). New York, NY: Basic Books.

Bowlby, J. (1982). *Attachment and loss: Attachment* (Vol. 1; 2nd ed.). New York, NY: Basic Books.

Lyons-Ruth, K., & Jacobvitz, D. (2008). Attachment disorganization: Genetic factors, parenting contexts, and developmental transformation from infancy to adulthood. In J. Cassidy & P. R. Shaver (Eds.), *Handbook of Attachment: Theory, research, and clinical applications* (2nd ed., pp. 666-697). New York, NY: Guilford Press.

Main, M., & Hesse, E. (1990). Parents' unresolved traumatic experiences are related to infant disorganized attachment status: Is frightened and/or frightening parental behavior the linking mechanism? In M. T. Greenberg, D. Cicchetti, & E. M. Cummings (Eds.), *Attachment in the preschool years* (pp. 161-182). Chicago, IL: University of Chicago Press.

Main, M., & Solomon, J. (1986). Discovery of a new, insecure-disorganized/disoriented attachment pattern. In T. B. Brazelton & M. Yogman (Eds.), *Affective development in infancy* (pp. 95-124). Norwood, NJ: Ablex.

Main, M., & Solomon, J. (1990). Procedures for identifying infants as disorganized/disoriented during the Ainsworth Strange Situation. In M. T. Greenberg, D. Cicchetti, & E. M. Cummings (Eds.), *Attachment in the preschool years* (pp. 121-160). Chicago, IL: University of Chicago Press.

Spangler, G., & Grossmann, K. E. (1993). Biobehavioral organization in securely and insecurely attached infants. *Child Development, 64*(5), 1439-1450.

Weinfield, N. S., Sroufe, L. A., Egeland, B., & Carlson, E. (2008). Individual differences in infant-caregiver attachment. In J. Cassidy & P. R. Shaver (Eds.), *Handbook of Attachment: Theory, research, and clinical applications* (2nd ed., pp. 78-101). New York, NY: Guilford Press.

Chapter 3

Refuge or Fortress: Howalton Day School, the African-American Middle Class, and the Golden Era of Black Private Education

Worth Kamili Hayes

To say there was pushback to Chicago Mayor Rahm Emanuel's plan to close multiple schools in 2013 would be an understatement. Protestors numbering in the tens of thousands held countless rallies and consistently packed board meetings in opposition to Emanuel's reform agenda which included closing "inefficient" schools and expanding alternatives, particularly charter schools. Along with the Chicago Teachers Union, many of the protestors came from the city's non-white and low-income communities which bore the brunt of school closings. In these neighborhoods, students would be displaced, faculty and staff would have to seek new positions, and strongly held traditions would be abruptly discontinued (Yaccino A. 20).

Emanuel may have expected middle class African-American families to be more supportive of "school choice", a controversial reform movement advocating alternatives to traditional public education in the form of charter schools, voucher options, transfer programs, and homeschooling. Critics have long held that school choice gives the middle class a safety valve to escape failing schools while lower income students are left behind (Lopez, Stuart Wells, and Jellison Holme 129-158). Simply put, economically secure African-Americans exploit their class privilege while betraying lower class blacks who disproportionately experience the negative repercussions of reforms such as school closings.

Unfortunately, this and many assumptions in school choice debates are not informed by history. To date, few studies have attempted to unearth historic examples of African-American engagement with school choice (Stulberg 1-16; Slaughter and Johnson 1-8; Jordan Irvine and Foster 1-7) Much of the historical literature centers on different educational strategies such as greater access, the struggle for integration, and/or improved facilities and curriculum within the confines of traditional public education (Anderson 148-185; Kluger 213-254; Irons 234-288). Consequently, there is an impression that African-Americans have an uncritical allegiance to public education and families who seek alternatives not only betray this tradition but also the many black and brown students still served by public schools.

Using Howalton Day School as a case study, this essay reconstructs Chicago's "golden era of black private education." From the outbreak of World War II to 1980, black Chicagoans, many of whom were middle class, successfully created and maintained a multitude of separate private schools partially in response to the city's racially discriminatory public education system. This history has been silenced by the more well-known struggle to integrate American public education. But as will be shown, patrons of black private schools such as Howalton did not see these two strategies as mutually exclusive. They crafted a strategy that negotiated the desire for expanded opportunities in the private sector while augmenting the possibilities of public education. Though initially successful and vibrant, the eventual closing of schools such as Howalton marked the end of this golden era and its alternative vision for educational reform.

Black Education in Chicago, 1940-1975

Like many other northern cities, Chicago's public school system experienced great strains in race relations following the mass migration of African-Americans from the South. From 1910 to 1960, Chicago's black population grew from 44,103 to approximately 813,000 residents. Migrants who were attracted by employment opportunities and the promise of better race relations soon faced racial discrimination as they competed with whites for decent jobs and housing (Grossman 127; Hirsch 1-39; Street 98).

Not surprisingly, black Chicagoans also faced racism in the city's public schools. Although racial prejudice existed in Chicago long before their arrival, the mass migration of African-Americans exacerbated the staunch discrimination that would characterize the experiences of black students for much of the 20th century. After World War II, studies of Chicago's public school system revealed that 91 percent of Chicago's elementary schools were de facto segregated and that black public schools were disproportionately overcrowded, received less money, and were more likely to be staffed by less experienced teachers (Homel; "De Facto Segregation in the Chicago Public Schools" 88-90; Herrick 311).

African-American activists opposed these conditions during and after World War II. In the 1940s, organizations such as the Chicago and Northern District Association of Colored Women (CNDA), the Chicago Urban League, and the Wellstown Parents' Civic Organization lobbied the Chicago school board, publicized the poor state of black schools through public tours, and initiated petition drives to transfer black students from overcrowded schools (Homel 144, 173-175).

After experiencing an ostensible lull in activism in the 1950s, widespread direct action demonstrations were employed during the 1960s. Inspired by the success of the 1954 *Brown v. Board* decision, more than 200,000 Chicago students boycotted the city's public schools at the peak of the reform movement. Activists even attracted the Southern Christian Leadership Conference and Rev. Martin Luther King Jr. who staged a suspenseful, yet unsuccessful attempt to desegregate Chicago's schools and neighborhoods. Shortly after, many Chicago activists grew disenchanted with earlier struggles for integration and launched a local community control movement. At its height, this youth-led crusade included more than 20,000 students who sought greater autonomy and a curriculum centered on black history and culture in their schools (Anderson and Pickering 182-337; Danns 61-88).

During this time, a parallel struggle of pursuing alternatives in the private sector emerged. The number of Catholic schools that opened their doors to black students grew from six in 1939 to 23 in 1960. Chicago also became a major hub of the Black Power era independent school movement. Similar to the community control struggle, these private schools grew out of frustration with racism in public education and featured a curriculum focusing on the black culture and history. By the 1980s, the metropolitan area had the largest number of such schools throughout the country (Sanders 215-219; *Fundiaha!-Teach!*).

Howalton's Beginnings, 1946-1975

With an intimate knowledge of the barriers to meaningful reform in public education, three teachers founded Howalton Day School. In 1946, Doris Allen Anderson, Charlotte Stratton, and June Howe Currin created a summer vacation school to provide pre-school to second grade students with enrichment in language arts, reading, arithmetic, and the fine arts. Though the number of enrolled students was small, probably no more than twenty-five, the school was continued the following summer in response to parental demand and then converted to a regular day school in the fall of 1947.

Starting with twenty-two students, all of whom were first-graders, the original founders agreed to add an additional grade each year if the school remained viable. Anderson became the school's director and handled publicity, recruitment, and other administrative matters. Stratton was appointed the principal and Currin worked as the registrar. During these initial years, the founders also created the name "Howalton" by combining their maiden names. "How" stood for June Howe; "Al" stood for Doris Allen; and "Ton" stood for Charlotte Stratton (*Gladly Learn and Gladly Teach,* Howalton School Archives [HSA], Box 1).

From this modest start, Howalton quickly experienced rapid growth. Less than a decade after opening, it expanded to include grades kindergarten to the eighth grade. By 1971, the school had grown to an all-time high of 217 students with a waiting list that was often larger than its actual enrollment (1971-1972 Assistant Principal's Report, HSA, Box 1; 1965-1966 Principal's Report, HSA, Box 1).

Several factors account for the school's initial growth. Most prominently, it was organized in a manner that was a direct response to the challenges black Chicagoans experienced with public education. Postwar educational activists' paramount grievance was overcrowded classrooms. Consequently Howalton made great efforts to maintain small class sizes. In 1949, the school had a 15 to 1 student to teacher ratio. And even when it experienced its peak enrollment in the late 1960s and early 1970s, class sizes were still small. The 1967 eighth grade graduating class, for example, had only fourteen students (HDS Newsletter, HSA, Box 1; Graduation Exercises and Closing Programs 1967, HSA, Box 2).

School administrators were quite deliberate in providing this contrast to public education. Much of their public relations literature often touted their small class sizes as an alternative to overcrowded public schools. As early as 1948, the school requested funds from prominent Chicagoans by positing that "Many children become frustrated and confused when placed in overcrowded classes for their first years of school. This sometimes results in retardation and unhappy school life. Our program is to fulfill this need" (Howalton, letter to Robert Cole, 17 December 1948, HSA, Box 1). This feature was not lost on parents who reported in a survey conducted in the 1960s that "individual attention and guidance" and "small classes" were the primary reasons they enrolled their children into the school (1965-1966 Principal's Report, HSA, Box 1).

While small class sizes don't ensure academic success, Howalton eventually became a top-performing school. Its students' standardized test scores were on par with the city's most prestigious private schools and consequently they had little trouble transferring to institutions such as the University of Chicago Laboratory School after graduating ("An Impossible Dream Comes True", HSA, Box 1). Howalton students' academic success even made national news in 1977 when the *New York Times* reported that the school's first graders achieved the highest reading averages of all public and private first grade students in Chicago (Culkin 14).

Howalton's Middle Class Composition

Howalton's early development coincided with the growth of Chicago's black middle class. The mid-century expansion of the city's overall black population boded well for black professionals who were in great demand. These professionals provided private schools with a sizable number of families who had enough discretionary income to be used for tuition. Just as the city's real estate market benefitted (and exploited) this demand, many black private schools profited from these advantageous circumstances (Drake and Cayton 413-414; Hirsch 100-170).

From its inception, Howalton drew much of its support base from Chicago's black middle class. Its summer enrichment program was held in the Michigan Boulevard Garden Homes, an apartment complex specifically built for middle class African-Americans (*Gladly Learn and Gladly Teach,* HSA, Box 1; Philpott 255-269). Families from the housing complex likely sent their children to the summer program and the expanded full-time school. Howalton would eventually educate the children of prominent black Chicagoans such as John Sengstacke, head of the *Chicago Defender*; heavyweight boxing champion, Joe Louis; and Olympic medalist and eventual Congressman Ralph Metcalfe. Many of the city's well known attorneys, businessmen, and other notable black professionals also enrolled their children (Howalton's Theatre Benefit Social, Financial Success" 20; Treadwell 13; Motley).

Howalton received considerable support from patrons whose children did not attend the school. Its board of directors read like a "Who's Who" among the city's African-American middle class. Noted educators such as W. Alison Davis and Oneida Cockrell advised the school in its early years. Davis, a pioneering education scholar, was the first African-American to teach at the University of Chicago. Cockrell was an elementary school teacher, consultant at University of Chicago Lab School, and was regularly featured in the *Chicago Defender* as an education commentator (HDS Brochure, HSA, Box 1; *Gladly Learn and Gladly Teach,* HSA, Box 1; Knupfer 118-119). Businessmen such as the multimillionaire hair care mogul George E. Johnson and Insurance entrepreneur Arthur Knight were also long-time board members (1976 HSD Brochure, HSA Box 1).

Howalton's ability to garner support from black Chicago's most celebrated figures partially stems from the school's spatial and chronological proximity to the Chicago Black Renaissance. This movement not only featured the works of literary luminaries such as Richard Wright, Margaret Walker, and Gwendolyn Brooks, but also the promulgation of a vibrant intellectual community, dynamic activist organizations, and robust cultural and political institutions. Many of Howalton's ardent supporters were also members of the Renaissance scene. Susan Motley, who attended Howalton from 1949-1956 lived with Howalton founder June Howe Currin. "Aunt June" as Motley affectionately remembered her, frequented social functions on Chicago's South Side where she mingled with many of the well-known figures who would become patrons of Howalton (Motley).

A Middle Class Refuge or Fortress?

Private education has a controversial history in black communities and may inform current debates about school choice. Following *Brown v. Board,* lily white private schools were established to allow white families to avoid desegregation. By 1975, 750,000 white southerners were educated in these "segregation academies" ("Segregation Academies" 54). It is easy to consider that Howalton substituted the racial exclusivity of segregation academies for intra-racial class exclusivity.

It is more difficult to ascertain the level of class consciousness among Howalton parents. If one did exist, Howalton parents surely did not publicize these views like white racists did. The clearest exposition of parents' interest in Howalton comes from a 1966 principal's report. The report included survey results from parents which noted that they patronized the school because of class size, progressive pedagogy, and the shared racial background of the children. Nothing was mentioned about class (1965-1966 Principal's Report, HSA, Box 1).

Nonetheless, some parents surely wanted their children to associate with children who shared their class status. There is evidence of a class consciousness in many of black Chicago's other institutions such as churches and social clubs (Drake and Cayton 522-715). It is also likely that relations developed outside of Howalton spilled over into the school. Howalton families likely lived in similar neighborhoods, had their children participate in the same extracurricular activities, and had mutual professional ties.

Ironically, Howalton administrators rarely identified the school as class-exclusive. A fundraising solicitation noted that "A wide range of families, varied in economic backgrounds...is served by Howalton" (Fleetwood M. McCoy, letter to unnamed recipient, HSA, Box 1). Similarly, in correspondence regarding a grant, Howalton director Doris Allen Anderson stated that "our parents are not as affluent as they are concerned about a certain quality education. In the most cases both parents are working in order to keep their children in Howalton" (Doris Allen Anderson, letter to Albert E. Cunningham, HSA, Box 3).

On the surface, both claims are circumspect. Howalton administrators sought financial support and could very well have feared reproach from potential donors. While many non-profit institutions must be careful in crafting their image, this is a particular concern for black institutions that have historically been in greater need of funds and have often relied on support from outside of the African-American community.

The administrators' statements may have also been an acknowledgement that middle class status, especially for African-Americans, is not necessarily a sign of economic security. By 1964, approximately 60% of Howalton parents were school teachers while roughly 35% worked in other white collar fields such as law, medicine, and social work (Erickson 4-71). While attorneys and doctors may have had no problem paying Howalton's tuition, many teachers likely endured great sacrifices for their children to attend the school. Chicago Public School teachers, black and white, had long fought school authorities for adequate pay. In 1960, beginning Chicago Public School teachers made $5,000.00 per year. The median family income for Chicagoans in 1960 was $6,738.00 (Herrick 404-405, 369-370, 376; Kitagawa and Taebur 246). Chicago's African-American public school teachers generally made even less than their white counterparts, partially because they tended to have less experience and more often worked as marginally paid substitutes (Herrick 404-405, 369-370, 376). The experiences of Howalton parents may have coincided with scholars' observations of the precarious status of the black middle class. Though granted greater class privilege than the black poor, they are often more economically vulnerable than the white middle class (Pattillo-McCoy 1-30).

The Howalton community's sense of their own economic vulnerability possibly fueled its commitment to helping working-class blacks. A major focus of this outreach was centered on youth, many of whom attended public schools. Several Howalton employees such as long-time director, Doris Allen Anderson, simultaneously worked for the private school and in the public school system. Anderson was also a member of several organizations that dealt specifically with inner-city youth and public education reform such as the Chicago Urban League, Urban Gateways, and Deb's Service League (Doris B. Anderson Resume, HSA, Box 1; "Founder Honored," HSA, Box 2). Howalton also encouraged its students to develop a sense of social responsibility. As part of Howalton's outreach curriculum, students regularly donated toys, music, coloring books, and personal items to children at Provident Hospital, the Chicago Child Care Society, and the *Chicago Defender* charities ("Howalton Students Play Santa for Little Chums at

Provident, HSA, Box 2; 1963 Howalton Day School Schedule of Christmas Activities, HSA, Box 2).

This relationship with black Chicagoans was not one-sided. The school received critical support from this community, particularly its public school educators. Not only did they enroll their children, but through the Parent's Council, paid dues and organized various social and fundraising activities for the school (Robert Wheatfall, letter to Howalton parents, HSA, Box 3) Howalton's list of supporters also included educators who made groundbreaking inroads into public education. Among them were Barbara Sizemore, Robert Lewis and Kenneth Smith. Sizemore became the first African-American woman to head a major city school system by becoming superintendent of the Washington D.C. schools in 1972. Robert E. Lewis was Chicago's first African-American male principal and Smith served as president of the Chicago Board of Education.

Along with increased enrollment, the reciprocal relationship between Howalton and the larger black community made the postwar period a golden age of black private education. Black Chicagoans' conceptions of reform were broad enough to include both public and private educational spheres. Rather than operating in a vacuum, Howalton was sustained through the support of the larger African-American community, particularly individuals in the Chicago Public School system. In like manner, the Howalton faculty, staff, and students maintained a sense of responsibility to this larger community. This strategy was practical, flexible, and creative enough to ameliorate some of the challenges faced by black Chicagoans. In time, however, the burdens of this community would become too heavy for black private schools like Howalton to bear.

End of an Era, 1975-1986

By the late 1970s, private education encountered formidable challenges. Structural changes such as deindustrialization and suburbanization greatly impacted Chicago's black middle class and in turn private schools. A gradual expansion of educational opportunities also presented black schools with stiffer competition for students. These factors would result in the eventual closing of Howalton in 1986.

Howalton endured its own host of several internal changes in the 1970s. The most impactful was the resignation of longtime director, Doris Allen Anderson in 1972. Anderson founded the school and anchored its growth. By the time she penned her resignation letter, she was close to 70 years old and believed Howalton needed "new leadership with the knowledge and experience necessary to implement new trends in curriculum..." (Doris Allen Anderson, letter to Fleetwood McCoy, HSA, Box 3). In this same period, other long-time Howalton members retired. Irma Johnson, who was Howalton's first teacher in 1947 and principal since 1961, left the school in 1970. Ethel B. Darden, Anderson's sister, and assistant principal resigned a year later (Doris Allen Anderson, letter to Board of Directors, HSA, Box 3). These foundational administrators were replaced by Julien D. Drayton and Ella Mae Cunningham who became director and principal respectively. Though able administrators, both left the school before the decade ended, and thus did not provide the same continuity as Anderson, Johnson, and Darden.

Drayton and Johnson faced a number of problems that likely led to their short tenures. During their time as administrators, Chicago experienced a sharp economic decline that culminated in the city's "urban crisis" of the 1970s and 1980s. In 1950, 69% of African-American males, fourteen and older in Chicago's predominantly black Bronzeville South Side neighborhoods were regularly employed. By 1990, this figure dropped to 37%. The majority of jobs that were retained or created in the metropolitan area shifted to suburbs where few working class blacks lived (Wilson 19-20, 37). The lack of economic opportunity led to chronic poverty in black neighborhoods. By 1980, the Grand Boulevard neighborhood, where Howalton was located from 1961 to 1983 was designated as an extreme poverty area. Though black neighborhoods in Chicago (including Grand Boulevard) experienced a net loss of 151,000 residents, the total number of poor families remained stable. This suggests that middle class blacks, such as families who could afford private education, were the majority of migrants (Ibid.).

Many of these families were destined for outlying areas in the city and suburbs that excluded black residents decades earlier. Metropolitan Chicago's black suburban residents grew from only 25,000 in 1940 to more than 230,000 in 1980 (Wiese 116, 212). The example of long time Howalton parent, patron, and board member R. Eugene Pincham is instructive. The former attorney and judge sent all three of his children to Howalton while he stayed on the 75th block of Chicago's South Side. However, his youngest son James left Howalton after the seventh grade in 1972. James transferred to Morgan Park Academy on the 110th block of Chicago's far South Side (Judge R. Eugene Pincham, letter to Mrs. Doris Anderson, HSA, Box 3). It is probable that other Howalton parents joined Pincham and sent their children to schools located on the city's periphery.

Judge Pincham's letter also reveals the greater competition Howalton faced in the 1970s and 1980s. By the 1970s, previously segregated schools such as Morgan Park Academy gradually admitted black students. Similarly, less than 5,000 African-Americans attended Catholic schools in Chicago in

1940. By the early 1980s, more than 29,000 black students were enrolled in archdiocesan schools (Sanders 219; Cibulka 146).

Public options such as magnet programs or traditional schools in outlying areas may have also been palatable to Howalton parents. Like lower class black Chicagoans, the city's African-American middle class was greatly impacted by the economic downturn of the 1970s and 1980s. In this period, the gap in income between black and white college graduates widened. It also became increasingly difficult for the children of the black middle class to maintain or improve on their parent's occupational status (Pattillo-McCoy21). These factors certainly made private education a luxury for some black parents, especially given the expansion of options in the public sector.

Howalton shuddered as a result of these internal and structural factors. While in its heyday Howalton easily enrolled 200 students, by 1983, only 70 students attended the school (Treadwell 13). And since tuition was the leading source of revenue, the school could not maintain many of its responsibilities. In 1986, Howalton closed its doors, almost forty years after it opened.

These challenges were not unique to Howalton. Many private schools that were filled with black students in the immediate postwar era experienced massive enrollment declines in the 1970s and 1980s. This prompted the Archdiocese of Chicago to begin a series of controversial closings that have continued to the 21st century (Fornero; Rado 1). To be sure, some private schools persisted and some were even created during this difficult period. For example, Marva Collins Preparatory School (MCPS) and New Concept Development Center, both founded in the 1970s, defied the odds for decades. However, financial problems caused MCPS to close in 2008 and New Concept to become a charter school in 1998.

Conclusion

With the closing of Howalton and similar schools, black private education's golden age came to an end. However, the desire for educational alternatives has persisted among African-Americans of all classes. African-Americans' contemporary engagement with school choice contains a partisan vitriol that was largely absent decades ago. However, alternate memories of private education may color this current debate. Charter schools in Chicago may conjure up flashbacks to Prince Edward County, Virginia and the many other white supremacist school districts that used private education to abandon public schools and the black bodies that inhabited them. Admittedly, conservative supporters of school choice do sound eerily similar to white racists of that bygone era.

Nonetheless, history speaks to us in multiple voices. The tradition of black private education, as demonstrated by Howalton, shows there are less destructive ways to pursue school choice. There can be a support of educational alternatives without destroying traditional public education. And given current political circumstances, any answers to school reform will inevitably involve both spheres. Charter schools cannot serve as a panacea for all of urban education's ills. The infrastructure, as it is currently composed, will not meet the needs of all students. However, it would be presumptuous and even paternalistic to ask all African-Americans to continue to swear their allegiance to a system of public education that has historically given them so little in return. Alternative institutions will not save us but neither will either/or formulations. Effective conceptions of school reform must be as broad and complex as the problems they are asked to solve.

Works Cited

Anderson, Alan B., and George W. Pickering. *Confronting the Color Line: The Broken Promise of the Civil Rights Movement in Chicago*. Athens, GA: University of Georgia Press, 1986. Print.

Anderson, James D. *The Education of Blacks in the South*. Chapel Hill: University of North Carolina Press, 1988. Print.

Cibulka, James G. "Catholic School Closings: Efficiency, Responsiveness, and Equality of Access for Blacks." Slaughter and Johnson 143-156. Print.

Culkin, John C. "40 Characters 40." *New York Times* 20 July 1977: 14. Print.

Danns, Dionne. *Something Better for Our Children: Black Organizing in Chicago Public Schools, 1963-1971*. New York: Routledge, 2003. Print.

"De Facto Segregation in the Chicago Public Schools."*The Crisis* 65 (1958) 88-90. Print.

Drake, St. Clair., and Horace Cayton. *Black Metropolis: A Study of Negro Life in a Northern City*. Revised and Enlarged ed. New York: Harper and Row, 1962. Print.

Erickson, Donald A. *Crisis in Illinois Nonpublic Schools: Final Research Report to the Elementary and Secondary Nonpublic Schools Commission, State of Illinois*. Springfield, IL: State of Illinois, 1971. Print.

Fornero, George. "The Expansion and Decline of Enrollment and Facilities of Secondary Schools in the Archdiocese of Chicago, 1955-1980: A Historical Study." Diss. Loyola University of Chicago, 1990. Print.

Grossman, James. *Land of Hope: Chicago, Black Southerners, and the Great Migration*. Chicago: University of Chicago Press, 1989. Print.

Fundisha! Teach! St. Louis, MO: Council of Independent Black Institutions, 1981. Print.

Herrick, Mary. *The Chicago Schools: A Social and Political History.* Beverly Hills, CA: Sage Publications, 1971. Print.

Hirsch, Arnold. *Making the Second Ghetto: Race and Housing in Chicago, 1940-1960* Cambridge: CUP, 1983. Print.

Homel, Michael. *Down From Equality: Black Chicagoans and the Public Schools, 1920-1941.* Urbana: U. of Illinois P., 1984. Print.

"Howalton's Theatre Benefit Social, Financial Success."*Chicago Defender* 2 July 1966: 20. Print.

Irons, Peter. *Jim Crow's Children: The Broken Promise of the Brown Decision.* New York: Viking, 2002.Print.

Irvine, Jacqueline Jordan., and Michéle Foster, eds. *Growing Up African American in Catholic Schools.* New York: Teachers College Press, 1996. Print.

Kitigawa, Evelyn M. , and Karl E. Taebur, eds. *Local Community Fact Book for Chicago, 1960.* Chicago: Chicago Community Inventory, University of Chicago Press, 1963. Print.

Kluger, Richard. *Simple Justice: The History of Brown v. Board of Education and Black America's Struggle for Equality.* New York: Knopf, 1976. Print.

Knupfer, Anne Meis. *The Chicago Black Renaissance and Women's Activism.* Urbana, IL: University of Illinois Press, 2006. Print.

Lopez, Alejandra, Amy Stuart Wells, and Jennifer Jellison Holme."Creating Charter School Communities: Identity Building, Diversity, and Selectivity." *Where Charter Schools Policy Fails: The Problems of Accountability and Equity.* Ed. Amy Stuart Wells. New York: Teachers College Press, 2002. Print.

Motley, Susan. Personal interview. 18 July 2011.

Pattillo-McCoy, Mary. *Black Picket Fences: Privilege and Peril Among the Black Middle Class*. Chicago: University of Chicago Press, 1999. Print.

Philpott, Thomas. *Slum and the Ghetto: Neighborhood Deterioration and Middle-Class Reform, Chicago, 1880-1930*. New York: Oxford University Press, 1978. Print.

Rado, Diane. "Catholics Fight for Their Schools." *Chicago Tribune* 27 Feb. 2007: 1. Print.

Sanders, James. *Education of an Urban Minority: Catholics in Chicago, 1833-1965*. New York: Oxford University Press, 1977. Print.

"Segregation Academies." *Time* 15 Dec. 1975: 54. Print.

Slaughter, Diane T., and Deborah J. Johnson, eds. *Visible Now: Blacks in Private Schools*. New York: Greenwood Press, 1988. Print.

Street, Paul L. *Racial Oppression in the Global Metropolis: A Living Black Chicago History*. Lanham, MD: Rowan and Littlefield, 2007. Print.

Stulberg, Lisa. *Race, Schools, and Hope. African Americans and School Choice After Brown*. New York: Teachers College Press, 2008. Print.

Treadwell, Jimmie. "Howalton—Building Character, Pride: A Look at Chicago's Oldest Black Private School." *Chicago Defender* 19 Feb. 1983: 13. Print.

Wiese, Andrew. *Places of Their Own. African American Suburbanization in the Twentieth Century*. Chicago: University of Chicago Press, 2004. Print.

Williams, William Julius. *The Truly Disadvantaged: The Inner City, The Underclass, and Public Policy*. Chicago: University of Chicago Press, 1987. Print.

Wilson, William Julius. *When Work Disappears: The World of the New Urban Poor*. New York: Knopf, 1996. Print.

Yaccino, Steven. "Protests Fail to Deter Chicago from Shuttering 49 Schools." *New York Times* 22 May 2013: A20. Print.

Chapter 4

Mustard Grows Followed by "Pokey and Me," an interview with and by Eleanor Blount

I-   Mustard Grows

"I just gonna stay here with you forever. I ain't going to that house no more. I hear 'em the whole time they be talking 'bout me, Maw. That girl, she say she don't want no nappy headed picaninny to take care of, cause she hate niggers and they stink."

He cried so much, his mother couldn't tell if his face and body were wetter from the hastily ordered bath she was giving him or from his tears. Bitty had been told to keep for herself some extra of the last batch of soap she made several days earlier. So she had already given him a bath that week, which was always a labor intensive occurrence for a slave child who had to help carry water from the creek. Even a four-year-old knows that two baths close together must mean something important, something life changing, something amiss. He didn't like how that made him feel. He didn't want to go outside the cabin to that house or to any place. He remembered when the others who lived there were given soap and bathed, and they went outside to some place called Auction the next day. And they stayed there. Forever. He was used to staying with his mother alone, now, and all he wanted, now, was for her to dry him and let him go snuggle into the mattress she made for them to share, out of rags and straw since she was not allowed any tick cloth. He would make sure he stayed there. Forever. Tonight, he decided, he wouldn't complain if he happened to get poked by some sharp straw that managed to work its way through the thin, finely stitched casing.

"Well, pretty boy, y'all both done got it all wrong. That girl don't supposed to take care of you. You be there to take care of her. And you is too going back to that house and that's where you gonna stay. That girl's papa done decided that for good. She ain't got no say so. You ain't got no say so. Me neither. And I don't believe they hates niggers no worser than everybody else hates 'em. Maybe if you was nappy headed like the rest of them picaninnies be around here, I'd hate you too. But ain't nothing nappy 'bout this pretty hair you got, naw sir.

And when I gets through soaping it up and rinsing it out and drying it off, I'm gonna take that knife I got hid and cuts me off a little piece. Then I wrap that pretty piece of hair in a rag and, soon as I can get that new wife of Massa's to gimme a needle and some thread of my own, I sew that rag under this here mattress just like I do that knife. Don't you worry; won't nobody know it's there but me and you. Lord knows I'd a been sewed me up some of this pretty hair long ago if I coulda got my own needle and thread like I used to from that first wife. This new wife wouldn'ta even a let me keep this extra soap, 'cept she wanted me to get you real clean before you goes to stay in that house.

"Well, you don't pay no mind to what that girl say. You sho nuff will not stink! Wait til she see your clean light skin and this pretty gold hair. If she ever get to see Massa Redhart's grown boys, she'll see you just as pretty as they is. Lord knows you belongs to one of them boys. Massa Redhardt knows it too. He just don't know which one, exactly. Me neither.

"But that don't make no difference. They all look alike and you look like 'em. Massa knows it, and he won't let nothing bad happen to you in that house. Naw, don't you worry 'bout that. Cause Massa sho nuf did love them boys. And he liked to died too when they left from here after they maw died. He ain't gonna love this girl and this new wife, her maw. Not like he did them boys and they maw. Don't you worry, though. Bitty won't never forget 'bout you."

He was sure that "forget about him" was exactly what his mother was trying to do a little later that evening when she had him follow behind her to the girl's house. He knew that everything he owned was on his back, that he was clean, and that his hair had been cut off just so his mother could put it in a rag. He knew that he should and would remember this day. His mother was walking too briskly. The more he tried to catch up to her, the faster she walked toward the house. It was as if she intended to keep him ten paces outside her grasp— on purpose. But he didn't know the purpose. The rag with the hair was tucked into her linsey woolsey blouse. He had seen it peeking through the garment's holes before she abruptly walked out of the cabin while hollering back to him, "Come on outa here."

It looked to him like the walk must have been a breeze for her. She moved with a speed that suggested she was enjoying what could have been a short trek— less than ten minutes— from their door to the big house's back porch. Yet, she didn't talk or sing to him like she usually did when they walked about in the low quarters. She didn't hold his hand. And instead of heading directly for the house, which was plainly visible after the first five or so minutes' walk, she took off running, around instead of through the large front yard, and led him alongside the burned out patches of dirt where Old Maw had been teaching her to fire up the big black pots for washing clothes and cooking soap. Then back behind another slave cabin, down through the sparse rows of pole beans and poke salad its occupant had been permitted to grow for his own needs. Then they passed a sizable plot that hosted many slightly raised mounds of dirt. Some were tiny, some much larger. Some of them had crossed wooden sticks on top. The little ones had tiny wooden cups, spoons or broken crockery— one had a corn husk doll, complete with teeny-weeny knitted cap. It looked so interesting, he wanted it but didn't wander over to get it, fearing a scolding. As he walked, though, he wondered why anybody would leave such a fine toy unattended. The next time he came by here, he would be sure to get it if nobody else was playing with it.

Finally they cut through the little meadow. It was not lush green like the bigger, farther away one where most of the Redharts livestock grazed, but it was grassy enough for the one, half-dead bull the slaves were allowed to keep for themselves. Bitty was nearly out of breath but able to yell back to him, "It's plenty of piles out here from where that bull been harnessed this morning. You bet not step in it to save yo life." That was the only utterance from his mother the whole time, so he didn't mind its feeble attempt at sounding threatening. He didn't mind having to be extra careful not to step in it, even though her skirt tail kept kicking up stinking black-brown clumps for him to dodge. Enough of it stuck to her skirt that by the time they reached the back porch, a child's lifetime later, she was way dirtier than he.

He was out of breath and wanted some water, too. His new white mistress, four years old just like himself, was standing on the other side of the back porch door and saw him and Bitty approach the steps. He heard the little girl say, "Mother Dear, that dirty mustard looking boy is here, and I suppose I ought to water him." Her mother answered, "Why, what a Christian gesture, Priscilla, darling. You go right ahead." The little girl opened the door, and he walked in as his mother fell down, right where she stood, mouth wide open and silent, at the foot of the steps. She did not get up. Without knowing how he knew it, he knew that it was this new arrangement that would last forever and forever and forever.

The knowing caused him to become something other than himself, yet he remembered the self he had been a long, long time ago when his warm, beautiful, loving mother had given him a bath and cut his hair. He knew it. He knew it for sure the next day, when Massa Redhart walked with him back to those mounds of dirt. There was a new one. It had crossed sticks like some of the others, but this one also had Bitty's scrap of rag, the one with his hair sewn inside, draped over the sticks. While this man, looking oddly grandfatherly, stood, for a quite a while, looking down at this new mound of dirt, the boy noticed that the behatted corn husk doll was still where it had been, waiting for its owner to come back. He didn't want it.

****

The girl, Priscilla, decided that Mustard would be his name because his skin looked to her a deep golden color instead of like everybody else's milky color. He was hers, brought there to be her own property, so she could call him whatever she wanted. She tried to teach him her name, but it kept coming out 'Silla, so she decided that would be all right. The two got along just fine from the beginning. Taking care of her was his job, explained the girl's mother, and he was to sleep in the trundle that pulled out the bottom of her bed in case she needed anything, like the chamber pot, or a cup of water during the night.

Each morning, he got up first, built a fire in the bedroom if it was cold, or stood over Silla and fanned if it was hot. His stirring around usually woke her up and that's when it was time for him to run down through the indoor kitchen that was not far from the outdoor pump to catch enough water in the crockery basin for the two of them to wash up. At first, he'd wash her teeth, face, neck, hands, and hind parts if she'd had an accident in bed that night, and then help her put on stockings, bloomers, chemise, waist, petticoat, skirt and sash, and button-up shoes, and then brush her hair and tie it down in back of her head with a piece of grosgrain ribbon. Just like the big mistress taught him. Then he'd use the leftover water to wash himself, jump into a flour sack blouse, linsey woolsey breeches and brogan shoes, and run back down to the indoor kitchen where the cook would have his cracked hominy, cornmeal cake and molasses ready. He would hurry and eat while the mistress of the house was up in the bedroom undoing the grosgrain ribbon so she could put curled finishing touches on Silla's hair and check to see that he hadn't missed any buttons on her shoes or left sleep in her eyes.

That was on days that weren't too hot to cook indoors. In the worst of the summer, after getting the two of them dressed, he'd have to run all the way to the older, bigger but farther away kitchen built onto the smokehouse for his breakfast (the consolation was that the cook usually gave him a slice of ham and some gravy in addition to the usual hominy), and still get back to the bedroom in time to take their chamber pots out to the privy, wash them and bring them back, and then dust the little wooden table and chairs where Silla's breakfast would be brought momentarily. After a few scoldings from Silla's mother about him taking too long in the mornings to get everything done before Silla was ready to eat, he figured he could save time if they washed at the same time. At first, the little girl pointed and laughed loudly when she got a clear sight of the funny little thing Mustard used to make water. When she asked her mother why he had to use a thing like that to make water, and she didn't, her mother told her the thing was just something that God didn't bother to cut off of niggers when they were born, but that since she was a sweet, precious, darling little white girl she would never have one to worry about.

Silla Marries John

Not until the two children were 12 did Silla wonder whether her mother had been completely truthful about niggers and other things God didn't bother himself with. The Redhart boys came, all three together, for a visit of several days. Silla had never met them before, but Mustard had. Whenever he thought back to the days when he and his mother lived together, before he turned four and had been summoned by the woman his mother only spoke of as "Massa's new wife" to live in and work in the house, he remembered being told that Massa would be bound to treat him well because he was the spitting image of those boys.

During their visit, the youngest boy spent a lot of time reading in his father's study and the others roamed the grounds much like Silla and Mustard did every day while playing games they made up together. On a day when she was not scheduled to be at the Female Seminary for the Womanly and Decorative Arts , and her mother had taken Mustard with her to load into a wagon the extra vegetables she needed go buy in town, Silla entertained herself outside without any particular purpose in mind. She ran from the barn to the chicken coops and back again, just for exercise, when she noticed her two stepbrothers standing over near the pig pens.

"How're y'all doing this morning?" she asked as she sauntered over. As she got closer, she heard them laughing and cussing. When they noticed her there, they got quieter.

"Well, I guess we do just fine," said one of them. "Fine as wine." He laughed again as he took a silver flask out of his pocket, turned it up for a drink but cussed some more as he discovered it was empty.

"Gimme that," said the other. "I'll go refill it. The least we can expect in our brief time in our own father's house is to avail ourselves of his magnificent selections of Madeira, don't you think? Wouldn't you say so, too, little girl?"

He must not have expected her to answer because before she could, he had started to wobble back toward the house. He had his flask in his hand, trying over and over to stick it in his pocket but he was too drunk to get it in. He staggered all the way to the porch waving it around with a drunk's weak aim and solid intention to fill that vessel to the rim and finish getting satiated as quick as he could.

"Y'all drinking wine mighty early in the morning," she said to the remaining stepbrother.

"Oh, it's a celebration," he said.

"What're you celebrating?" she asked.

"The good time these pigs are having." He blurted it out while slapping his knees and laughing so hard he almost fell over. "Go head and look at them get at it just like people. Go ahead. They aren't shy." He tickled himself with every sentence he spoke.

"People wouldn't do that like pigs." She was assertive, sure that she knew what she was talking about and surprised she had to explain it to a grown man.

"Then how do *you* suppose people make more people, missy?"

"Not like that. My mother says that at night, cabbage patches . . ." She didn't get to finish her sentence; he laughed so loud.

"Naw, naw, naw. The plug and the pocket on people don't look exactly like they do on pigs, but they're close enough. And the way you use them's the same. Come here and I'll show you." He had grabbed her wrist before she noticed him reach for her. She didn't know what to say. In fact, she discovered that she could say nothing because her mouth was wide open but no words came out. She didn't know what to think— she thought she should try to run away and she thought she should go along with him. She was starting to feel kind of stupid about the cabbages, and if the story was wrong, she wanted to learn better and be the first to tell Miss Renee and the other girls at the seminary the next day.

Laughing all the way, he pulled her so forcefully by the wrist to the barn, she never felt her feet touch the ground until they reached the back of the structure, where she hadn't intended to walk today because there was always brittle straw scattered back there, and she remembered, as something pricked her foot, that she came outside with no shoes on.

"So how about it, missy? I'll gladly show you mine if you'll show me yours," he said, still laughing like crazy while trying to unbutton his pants. It popped out suddenly and startled her more than she was already startled. She had trouble catching her breath. He was breathing hard.

"See there. What did I tell ya? I didn't lie, did I! The equipment's not all that different if you try to look at it in just the right way," he said.

She saw. She decided it looked a lot like what Mustard used to make water, only a whole lot bigger. But her mother had told her way back when that only niggers had them because God couldn't be bothered to cut them off before they were born. But her stepbrother was white; she was sure. No. She wasn't sure about anything anymore.

"What are y'all doing, boy?" The voice at the barn door startled her again. She jerked her head around too fast and got a catch in her neck, trying to see who it was, hoping, hoping, hoping it wasn't her father and at the same time wondering why she felt like she was doing something wrong that she wouldn't want him to see. She need not have worried. It was the other brother, back with the flask in his hand.

"Why don't you get on in here, brother. Little sister, here hadn't ever seen a snake, I don't believe, and I wanted to disabuse her of any foolhardy notions she might have picked up along the way." He laughed. "Why, don't you want to do your part, make your own contribution toward her education? Go head and show her your snake, boy."

The second one reached for his buttons so fast, he dropped the flask and she could smell the wine as strong as if she had bathed in it. Now they were on either side of her, both with their pants unbuttoned and "snakes" showing.

"All right, missy. I didn't lie to you and I showed you what I said I would. It's your turn now. You can't do nothing with two plugs and no pocket. Let's see what's under here," he said, making a motion to lift her skirts.

She shook her head, which made her neck hurt more, and pushed his hand off, and she thought she might faint. She was sure now that she wanted to run away.

"Aw, don't ruin the party so soon. It could be a real good time," said the first one.

"Well, if you don't want to open up," said the second, "just come over here and touch it. That can't hurt you, can it? You could at least do that much."

Silla said, "The cook will be out here calling me soon. My mother told her I could help her shell peas today since she's got so much extra work with y'all being here. I ought to go."

"Then come here and touch it, and then you can go," he said.

She had to pass him to get to the barn door. She started putting one foot in front of the other until she was real close to him, and it moved. It looked like it jumped at her. She thought about touching it, and as she held her hand out closer to it, she could swear she heard it hiss at her. She screamed, "SNAKE! SNAKE! SNAKE!" and tore off running back to the house. She could still hear them laughing when she made it to the porch.

****

Silla started to allow herself a little hope that she might still have a life after the reverend came out to pay a call on the family, to let them know he had been assigned to the town for a spell and was counting on seeing them on Sundays. These days, she couldn't move a muscle that her mother didn't notice. She hadn't decided, and it really didn't matter, whether her mother was worried and watchful because she believed her threats to poison herself with lye soap, or because she believed her when she said, first chance she got, she'd smother that ugly black thing that did nothing but bellow at the top of its lungs all day and night. "After all," she screamed, "it came out of me. I'll do what I please with it!" What mattered was that she was hardly prepared for the slap across her face she received from her mother after saying it. Nobody was acting the same these days, and Silla made up her mind to stay to herself as much as she could lest she be taken by surprise again. Her mother had never struck her before. Not for any reason. Not even when she knew full well she was being bad just because she could get away with it. Not wanting to be caught off her guard again, she put up a little resistance when Mrs. Redhart told her get out of bed and dress to receive Rev. Isaacs as a family for supper. She said she wouldn't be hungry at suppertime and preferred to get her rest.

"You'll eat supper this day, Priscilla Redhart, and I don't care if you're hungry. Do you really think I can have that jack leg come here and go back to tell the whole town that you're kept confined to your bedroom?" her mother said. "If there's a tongue left that's not wagging already about why you stopped taking needle and painting lessons with the other girls at the female seminary, it sure would have a tale to tell once news got out that you were being hidden right here in our own house."

"But I look so big and terrible," Silla argued. "And isn't that why you said I couldn't go to the seminary anymore? That's why I can't finish my silk sampler or the French handwork that Miss Renee was designing for me to stitch, isn't it? Mother Dear you know how much I loved learning the needle and the music lessons and how to paint flowers on the chinaware. Why did I have to stop all my lessons if it wasn't that you were ashamed of me getting so fat and ugly?"

"Child. Child. Child." Mrs. Redhart kept repeating the word. She had to convince herself that this conversation was really taking place, and that the woman she was trying to talk to was none other than her own precious baby, the baby she had kept clean and pure and apart from the debasement that came from consortium with men, but who despite the cloistering provided by a devoted southern mother, had become pregnant at 12 years of age and given birth at 13.

Mrs. Redhart would have fainted if there had been time, but it would be supper time soon and the preacher was coming. She decided that the time to die of apoplexy brought on by the shock and shame of the pregnancy had passed. She had missed her chance to die honorably in the throes of dishonor. Why God had not taken her, as he should have, in front of witnesses who could later testify to the penetrating magnitude of her womanly southern dignity that caused her to breathe her last, right there on the spot, when learning of the disgrace—why? She did not know. She had served God to the highest degree, had she not?! Why would he turn from her now, she wondered, at a time when scandal was potentially even more costly than 13 years ago when she, herself, had cause to leave home with a newborn in tow? At least *she* had had an ample inheritance, coming from such an aristocratic planting family as she had. She set up housekeeping in a neighboring state where her people were not well known, and told everyone who would listen in her new community that she was recently widowed and starting life afresh, away from the gripping memories of her true and dearly departed "husband." Keeping that up for the whole year it took her to find and latch onto a much older man and "remarry" was no small feat, and *she* had an inheritance to comfort her. She gratefully transferred every penny of it to her new husband just like she promised she would within minutes after they were pronounced man and wife. And she counted it a bargain. She was unsure as to whether he intended to settle any money on his stepdaughter. He had been good to Priscilla and was the only father she would ever know. But under the circumstances, one should not expect. Oh, what she would give to spare her sweet darling the onus that she, herself, had adeptly evaded.

But who had time now for all that reminiscent falderal? Certainly not Mrs. Redhart. The preacher was on his way and her husband had told her the man might have a connection to someone who could prove to be their salvation. She had to get that ignorant girl's hind parts up out of bed and down to the dining room in time to make a good impression. Well, as good an impression as could be expected under the circumstances.

"Priscilla, my own dearest," she started, "I don't want you thinking your Mother Dear believes you are fat and ugly. Child, no. That's not it at all. What's wrong is, we cannot continue telling people any longer that you have been ill with the grippe. It'll be a tricky thing, but we want you up and about but without anybody knowing about that . . . that . . . Oh, Priscilla, by rights, you can't even call that a woods colt. It's a picaninny! But you are *not* to smother it. Do you understand me, girl? Whatever it is and for whatever reason God visited its shame on us, God made it and sent it here and you can't kill it. Lord have mercy if word of a half white picaninny being murdered in this house ever got out around town!

"Then you mean I can to go back to the seminary and finish learning to be a good and proper lady like you, Mother Dear?"

"Child. Child, you must listen and understand quickly. You can never go back to the female seminary. That's for girls who can still look forward to debut parties and pretty weddings. You are forever ruined and have no time to spend painting flowers on chinaware and stitching samplers with some tacky, foreign old maid. The best we can hope for, darling, is that a man will come along who doesn't know that you've endured the martyrdom already. Lord help us, at 12 years old you should not have had to go through it. It saddens me that you had to. But when you told me what your father's boys had been doing to you when they were here, well, what was I to do? I couldn't go to him with anything so sordid as that. After all, hasn't he been a good provider and a blessing to you and me? Would you want to see him hurt over those boys of his? He loves those boys more than a little, and he'd believe whatever they chose to tell him. So it looked like it was better to keep still about it. Until, well, until it came out of you looking so . . . dark. If ever I had dreamed that you and that Mustard . . ."

"But, Mother Dear," Priscilla interrupted. Mustard didn't hurt me, and you said somebody must have hurt me or I wouldn't have gotten that old woods colt. All Mustard and me used to do was play like we were animals sometimes. It was just for fun, doing just what we saw the pigs in the pen doing all the time when we would be outside playing. And one time we saw the horses doing it too in the barn, but the slave driver and two of his darkies were having to coax the horses to do it, not like the pigs, and then they saw me and Mustard standing there and they yelled at us to go away. That hurt my feelings. I yelled back that I was the little mistress of this plantation and that I could stand on it anywhere I pleased without being yelled at by slaves and a hired man. But that didn't hurt me so bad that I cared any more about it the next day. No m'am. The only time it hurt was with those boys my father loves so much."

II- *Pokey and Me:* Interview with & by Eleanor J. Blount, Ph.D.

The black French Caribbean intellectual, Frantz Fanon says, "Every dialect, every language is a way of thinking. To speak means to assume a culture."[4] His assertion is that one cannot utilize a language without making a statement about the cultural significance of voice in addition to the content of the message being conveyed.

Pokey's story (*Pokey's Story: A Work of Long Fiction*) is a saga of the slave era. It illuminates the characteristics of African American servitude and of white American supremacy as it follows the lives of people from both groups. In order to create a portrait that depicts what I believe life must have been like then, I needed a cadre of people, alive as far as I was concerned, to assume the culture. Since cultural mores become inculcated early in life, some of the people had to be children. In fact, the longer I allowed the people to show me, silently explain to me, how it was possible that one racial group could betray humanity so consistently over so many centuries by not only oppressing but savagely denigrating another group, the more obvious it became that children's lives would best serve as examples of the ways in which inequitable cultures take root.

Were I to attempt some elucidation of the process by which such a portrait had been rendered by one of the masters—let us say Toni Morrison or Alice Walker—I would have undertaken an interview with her of the kind published in books of the *Conversations With* series. Were I to do so with the author (self) of the Pokey pieces, it would look like this:

Interviewer Me (IM): What, exactly, are Pokey's stories?

Author Me (AM): They are chapters in a book, *Pokey's Story: A Work of Long Fiction,* and they stand alone as short

---

[4] Frantz Fanon in *The Negro and Language– Black Skin, White Masks.* New York: Grove Press Inc, 1967

stories as well. The full text of the book is a fictional account of an enslaved black boy, the white girl who owned him as her personal dower property from the time they were both four years old, and their families. Two different characters in the book are named Pokey. The one who is several years older does not appear through as much of it as does the younger one, but her existence sets crucial groundwork for events that occur after her exit. The word, Pokey, operates as an extended metaphor for slavery and its dehumanization of black people. In one of the stories not excerpted for you in this article, a 1950's-era, 100-year-old Miss Pokey speaks to an overly inquisitive 4-year-old girl named Sugar:

After the hug, "Is Miss Pokey your first name or your last name?"

"Honey, hits the only name I got. People of the old time didn't need no last names and white folk didn't fool with givin 'em none. The fambly I belonged to did own another Pokey, but we jes call her yella Pokey and me black Pokey. But she dead, so now I jes Pokey."

Sugar's mouth could not close. She was frightened and fascinated at the same time, even though she really had no idea what the old woman was talking about. But she knew, just the same. She knew that she had just heard something important that she did not understand. She wanted to keep thinking about it. Maybe she would figure it all out all by herself, later after she was at home. But she sensed it would be hard.

Names are important to the young Sugar. She has discovered that they are what give people identity. At the age of four, one's identity is newly found but fully ignited in its process of growing robust. Sugar has recently learned to write and likes to practice the skill by spelling other people's names on paper with pencil. For some time she has been worried that Miss Pokey's name has a severely ignoble ring to it, and she risks being chided by her parents for the impertinence and goes ahead anyway and asks the antiquated friend to explain the moniker. Sugar is African American but has never heard of Negro slavery. Her parents have kept it a secret, preferring the delusion that in the 1950's New South they could escape ever having to mention it to their offspring. But Pokey and slavery have survived a long time, even into the twentieth century, and no one, regardless the race, can avoid dealing with them forever.

IM: What do the stories say about the nature of slavery in the southern United States?

AM: They say so many things about what slavery was because slavery was so many things. When they spoke to me, though, what each one of these characters said so often was that lying (not to mention secrecy, silence, and betrayal) was at the base of it all. Certainly by the immediate antebellum period if not well before, white perpetrators of slavery could not help but know that the only way total racial oppression could be sustained was for closely protected and systematized lies about racial inferiority to be maintained. From the time of the Middle Passage, but increasingly up to the onset of the Civil War, purveyors of slaves and the accoutrements of slavery concocted a mythology of African inferiority which helped them justify to themselves not only the rape of the continent they were set on perpetrating, but more perniciously, the exponential growth of cultural Eurocentrism in the so called New World. By the time of emancipation, people's binary codes of conduct, based on race, had existed and been sharpened for so long that everyone accepted the original mythology nearly all of the time, and few people seemed to recognize that there was a grand lie in the first place. Knowing that one was part of the better or worse group was so ingrained in his/her sense of self that any competing self-images were secondary, at best, but more practically, useless.

Silla and Mustard show us that blacks and whites alike were forced to act inside tightly prescribed racial norms and that breaking out of such molds was always catastrophic. As these children who were similar in many aspects of life reached maturity inside the vicious binary, the disparate roles dictated to them by the racist society became weightier and the consequences for stepping outside them became more serious, more personally painful. As they get older and draw additional people into their sphere, the web created by the grand lie also grows and tangles. Mustard does not grow alone. Pokey (slavery) is his descendent as well as Silla's, and when it (slavery) leaves the landscape another comes to replace and perpetuate itself. It never stops growing, not even when we see it having turned extremely elderly in the twentieth century.

As a trend emerged in the United States in the twenty-first century to rationalize slavery as *simply* a socioeconomic system that worked well enough for a time until it simply (yet violently?!) ended, descriptions of the peculiar institution started to sound more benign, suggesting a less damaging and less perpetual impact from the past. Accompanying this trend, a new term, post-racial, appears so as to suggest a weakening of racism's impact in the present day. My own suggestion is that it makes sense to consult the historians who have documented much of the routine practice and community procedures of the slaveholding states to get as accurate as possible a glimpse into what the daily lives of the residents, especially the enslaved ones, were really like. There is a long but too short list of authors whose nonfiction foci are exactly that. Some are:

Slave Testimony: Two Centuries of Letters, Speeches, Interviews, and Autobiographies, John W. Blassingame ed.

From Slavery to Freedom: A History of African Americans, John Hope Franklin

Slavery in the Colonial Chesapeake, David Brion Davis

Slave Counterpoint: Black Culture in the Eighteenth-Century Chesapeake and Lowcountry, Philip D. Morgan

American Slavery 1619-1877, Peter Kolchin

Soul by Soul: Life Inside the Antebellum Slave Market, Walter Johnson

Life in Black and White: Family and Community in the Slave South, Brenda E. Stevenson

Many Thousands Gone: The First Two Centuries of Slavery in North America, Ira Berlin

Roll, Jordan, Roll: The World Slaves Made, Eugene D. Genovese

Within the Plantation Household: Black and White Women of the Old South, Elizabeth Fox-Genovese

The Plantation Mistress: Woman's World in the Old South, Catherine Clinton

The Devil's Lane: Sex and Race in the Early South, Catherine Clinton

Fanny (Frances) *Kemble's Civil Wars,* Catherine Clinton

Tara Revisited: Women, War, and the Plantation Legend, Catherine Clinton

Ar'n't I a Woman?: Female Slaves in the Plantation South, Deborah Gray White

Everyday Life in the 1800s, Marc McCutcheon

Passageways: An Interpretive History of Black America Volumes I and II, Colin A. Palmer

An Evening When Alone: Four Journals of Single Women in the South 1827-67, Michael O'Brien ed.

A Diary from Dixie (Diary of Mary Chesnut), Mary Chesnut

Journal of a Residence on a Georgian Plantation in 1838-1839, Frances Anne Kemble

Slaves in the Family, Edward Ball

History of American Slavery, Duncan Clarke

IM: Why was secrecy so important?

AM: Lies nor societies built upon lies can thrive in the bright light which is truth. Therefore, part of the careful binary codifying that was necessary to keep slavery functional was the insistence on secrecy when it came to those areas of daily—DAILY—life in which blacks and whites comingled against the supposedly accepted practice. It was actually quite common for black and white children to interact as friends during their very young years. A popular, smaller genre within children's literature of the 1920's and 1930's nostalgically praised those good old days. White authors Emma Gelders Sterne, Lucy Fitch Perkins, Hildegarde Hoyt Swift, and Lucy Sprague Mitchell were women dedicated to the improved education of America's small children and were, for the most part, considered politically left leaning in their time. Yet when attempting to place attention on African Americans and include them as cultural entities worthy of examination by grade schoolers, they invariably employed stereotypical images of raggedy "pickaninnies" who were always happy to serve their white playmates or aid and abet them in their white exploits, especially when the adventures were mischievous. Their children's books, *The Pickaninny Twins* by Perkins, for instance, express sadness that modern times prevent blacks and whites from interacting so beautifully as they once had, lamenting that such interactions from a young age could be key factors in establishing more successful race relations.

These books do not emphasize that the African American children were no mere playmates, that instead, they were frequently working at their jobs which required them to stay close to, look out for, and generally take care of white children and which carried stiff punishments for the black child whose work was less than diligent. Mustard and William Faulkner's

Versh and Luster from *The Sound and the Fury* are examples of young black children who must work and work hard for white people during and after slavery. Neither do these books emphasize that the fairly genial mixed-race relationships between the children were disrupted precipitously by their elders as soon as it became apparent that the children were reaching an age at which they might exhibit more adult mixed-race genialities, especially insofar as potential sexual relationships were concerned. Disapproval of this kind of interaction would be swift and heavy handed. Nevertheless, mixed-race pregnancies have always been a fact of segregated southern life, and speaking openly about them was avoided by both racial groups. They usually resulted from liaisons, consensual and coerced, between white men and black women. While the liaisons may have been secret at the time they occurred, nothing could conceal them once the babies were born with characteristics that were obviously both Negroid and Caucasian. To be revealed as one who begets bastards seriously tarnished a white man's standing in southern society. It was especially damning to have done the deed across racial barriers, but, perhaps curiously, it was so common a practice that antebellum white men were all but expected to have African American children, and they were only chastised or ostracized for it if pretenses toward secrecy were openly ridiculed or the offending sexual activity flaunted.

This was not the case for the smaller number of white women who gave birth to mixed-race children. Gender disparities were such that illegitimate births placed far worse stigmas on mothers than on fathers, and a southern white woman whose child was African American would receive brutal repercussions before being dismissed from the protection and camaraderie of her community. Infanticide would have been out of the question for the Redhart family but that was not true of all families. As there is no way to permanently keep incognito the existence of a bouncing baby human, one born under these circumstances might be a secret for a time, but eventually something would have to be done with it, such as sending it away with some black woman to live as a slave if it were not to be murdered. However, the woman who bore the child must keep to herself not only the secret of the birth, but the pain of it and the irreversible, depressing changes to her life it prompts.

IM: What else do the stories say about gender roles of the region and time period?

AM: Women, even white women (maybe especially white women, given that black women were not considered women but chattel), lived under gender oppression in the nineteenth century that had the power to crush soul, spirit, and creativity. Priscilla is a white female who feels the impositions of sexism keenly. The excerpts here provide brief hints that, as a child, she begins to recognize the shortfall under which she lives. Later stories in the saga show her in the adult fullness of her bitterness over it and the many cruelties she employs as outlet for her frustration. As is so often true of one's lies and secrets, when the affected person (Priscilla in this case) reaches a point at which the guilt, sadness, resentment--pain of any kind--that accompanies the clandestine event can no longer be borne stoically, she becomes unpredictable and breaks the silence, at least inwardly, by spewing the pent-up venom onto the person she perceives to be the cause of all her misery. It never occurs to Priscilla to think of her bastard child as an innocent. Instead, she simply equates it with loss.

Women and girls of this era could rarely expect to be educated in the same manner as their male counterparts. Especially in southern parts of the United States, serious, formal schooling was unbecoming for the females from families of good breeding, high standing in society. Families of financial means might keep on retainer a tutor for their daughters, but a rigorous academic curriculum would be avoided. Rather, there may have been some cursory lessons in literacy so that a girl would be capable of light Bible study. She would learn enough arithmetic so as to be able to economically maintain her family's supply of household goods once she married and became mistress of her own home. More importantly, her most stressed areas of study would have been in the so called female arts. This set of skills consisted of what we would today consider the decorative arts and of a highly refined code of manners that marked a young female as someone who could be counted upon to set the atmosphere of her future husband's home to a level of decorum and exclusivity that was not common. Of the decorative arts, needlework was privileged as the activity that should consume the greatest amount of a young woman's time not devoted to truly urgent needs.

Therefore, a family looking for a suitable tutor for a girl would try hard to find a woman with verifiable prowess with her needle and possibly even with the talent to design. Perhaps the family would live in an area that could actually support a school, of a sort, that was established solely for this kind of training of girls called "finishing." Those schools, which they referred to as female seminaries, had nothing to do with preparation for the clergy, but with preparation for the objectified roles they would ultimately assume as wives appropriate for upper class or upwardly striving men. This refined tone is what a painstaking prospective husband would seek when choosing a wife he would rely on to set that same tenor in his household as he proceeded through his own skills and talents to establish himself as a meaningful presence in his community. In this respect, the prospective bride becomes an object of empowerment for him. The female is objectified in genteel fashion, but objectified nevertheless. In addition, women knew they were seen as sexual objects much of the time, but they hoped the treatment they received as such would be as nonviolent as possible. That slave women were objects of white rape so much of the time is well documented. In the Pokey stories, Priscilla illustrates how easily white females could be raped as well.

She also shows us how fixated one can become on any slight shred of opportunity for creative expression when the oppression of sexism is the order of the day. She lovingly attends to her needlework instructions at the seminary. She has reached the age at which a grand finale should be attempted. Girls frequently were expected to have stitched some master project, bigger and more complex than their usual needlepoint or cross-stitch patterns, within the last several years of schooling. Called Fancy Work, a piece such as this was usually a large framed sampler which was displayed prominently in the girl's home for visitors to see. I see Priscilla as one of those girls who gladly gives herself to the practice of stitching hour after hour, as if to an addiction, because the sampler is uniquely hers while nothing else is. She finds the practice expressive in an environment in which she is frequently told to keep her thoughts to herself and to demure to boys' and men's thoughts. At her age, there is little else to do, much less to brag about doing, and she finds that she has an affinity for it. She knows as a pre-teen that these hours may well represent the happiest she will ever be. Then pregnancy and maternity, before she has had these terms adequately explained to her, swoop down on the child and take the happiness away. She is not equipped with the maturity to place the blame for her predicament onto those who really created it. She can only see the newborn, which she finds unpleasant on its own merit, and associate it with her growing sense of depression when her mother informs her that girls with babies cannot go to school and stitch samplers in polite company. This is no small slight to her, and throughout the rest of her life she experiences less and less joy while imposing more and more discomfort on anything and or anyone she dislikes.

IM: What about the cultural legacy?

AM: In stories not excerpted for you in this article, Sugar and Jennifer are characters who represent African Americans living presently with the racism that is slavery's bequest. Sugar was a child in the 1950's and old enough to have actually met and befriended a former slave, Pokey. In her adulthood she encounters some of the same troublesome issues of race and gender that Pokey did at her age. As she works through them she realizes that, surprisingly, she is equally compelled to resolve problems that were directed more toward the white Silla than to Pokey in antebellum days. This shows her that in the late twentieth century, a black woman lives under sexism's as much as racism's oppression, and she embraces the feminist movement. Alice Walker would say that this young woman is rising to the challenge of what she terms womanism, the confluence of African American women's difficulties of expression due to the simultaneous drowning of their voices by race and gender. Jennifer is Sugar's goddaughter who, at the beginning of the twenty-first century wonders whether she ought to look to any movements at all. She expresses much of the same dissatisfaction that plagued the characters who came before her, but she believes her time in history makes her issues new and unique, and she is distrustful of anyone who claims to have suffered likewise, until her godmother shares some of Pokey's old stories with her.

IM: In whose voice are the stories told? Why?

AM: An author who writes as exercise in the manipulation of characters and their thoughts can gravitate toward god-like story telling. *Per se*, there is nothing wrong with an omniscient point of view in fiction, but there are drawbacks. It is a voice, that though meant to evoke authority, can assert a dominance that overshadows other facets of the story. It is less popular in contemporary American fiction than it was in the nineteenth century. Joyce Carol Oates once said that this is due to the populace's not having had an unequivocal belief in God since the nineteenth century. But I relish a little authorial godliness, which should be all right if not applied rabidly.

The stories excerpted here are works of pure fiction, yet they are illustrative of *my own self*, and I am very real. I never met any of the people you will meet here, not just because most of them existed a century before I was born, but because, technically, they never existed at all. So why is it that I know them so intimately, know exactly what each one would say in a given situation? Partly, it is because I am god. That is one of the few pleasant aspects of the taxing job of being a self that channels other selves.

I say I channeled them because I am reluctant to say I created them. They appeared to me as if flesh and blood, with contrary minds of their own, begging to be adapted to ink and paper. Remembering that I was the one in charge lightened the load a little. Though my omniscient voice is softer in some sections than in others, yet *I* speak whenever the characters open their mouths.

But the work is a simulcast. Not only do I speak through them, they represent people who, denied the right to expression during their lives, recount themselves through me in modernity. The characters all have composite traits of long gone elders (one believed born in the 1850s) and young friends, all of whom have survived in my memory since my childhood, and possibly a spirit or two that were known to me on some strange level even before then! And, of course, there are the historical prototypes who recurred along my journey to become a scholar of the African American experience during the antebellum and Civil War era.

Somehow, the historical personalities never revealed enough personality as I studied. I think this is true mostly because so large a portion of their stories was recorded by voices not their own. Since slaves were not allowed literacy, much of the "factual" documentation of their lives, to the extent that documentation was undertaken at all, was left to those who enslaved. I, for one, harbor a healthy suspicion of ostensibly true stories told about a subject by his/her nemesis. Fiction about black slaves by white writers has even greater potential for fallacy, so I decided to conjure up some fully flourished personae, instead of stock actors, based on what could be gleaned from the annals, and apply my African American, twenty-first century hand to their articulation. Also, I discovered they need a longer work than a single short story. Even when fictionalized, their story is built on so very, very large an amount of fact.

I strive, as a matter of respect for the humanity embedded in every character (including the not-so-nice ones), to allow each one to speak individually. I don't want children to sound like adults even if they've been forced into grownup behavior prematurely. Blacks and whites, women and men, have different points of view of the central conflict, and their language patterns should help convey those points without having to rely excessively on declarative statement. This does not mean that the people don't get to exhibit a range of behavior. In the various stories, Pokey, for instance, is both naive and sage in childhood and reiterates those qualities in old age. Priscilla is often impervious to the cruelty she inflicts, but villains seek and give love in peculiar ways. I want them all to have the opportunity to comment on life as they believed it to be, as they would have if the social constraints of the period had not vanquished their voices.

Until mid-twentieth century, readers were more likely to have derived their visions of slave life from Margaret Mitchell than from Margaret Walker. But steadily, a stream of black novelists has poured out a wealth of believable, though fictional, accounts. Edward P. Jones, Toni Morrison, and Octavia Butler are my current idols (the list grows daily), and even though their works all have some element of magical realism, they are far more plausible than the Tara tale which visits the supernatural in its portrayal of happy, singing slaves.

Benjamin Franklin extolled the virtue of authorship as a means to immortality:

> *If you would not be forgotten*
> *As soon as you are dead and rotten,*
> *Either write things worthy reading,*
> *Or do things worth the writing.*

I doubt it was a terribly unimaginable thing for him to do. Easy for him to say, I say. In his own time, people were rapt to listen to anything he said, and in subsequent centuries his writing is consulted as the memorialization of the American ideal. During and since the Revolution, African Americans were, in the main, denied that virtue. I believe many, many slaves performed feats worth the writing on a routine basis, and as I long to write the song of myself, *myself*, I'm sure they wanted that as well. Telling one's own story with one's own voice is so recognizable a human need, there is little wonder that this primordial pleasure was prohibited for those who were officially deemed inhuman.

For most of us, having our voices waft unrecognized is a seldom and innocuous event. But it's a different thing, a more sinister thing, when you come to accept that the world– the known world, anyway– has no intention of listening to you or any of your ilk for any reason, any time. People who were born into slavery's brutality– people who looked like me and would have talked and written as I do except for the accident of chronology– once had their tongues cut out, metaphorically speaking, and sometimes in their too graphic, too real lives. Agreeing with Fanon, I endeavor to highlight subcultures because the commonly held descriptions of antebellum southern culture in America's fiction and nonfiction have been disastrously monolingual though the truth is that multiple voices spoke and comprised the culture in their own ways. For one thing, we now have a totally different master narrative without all the necessarily diverse voices, but for sure, when everyone speaks we see more truth than secrets and lies.

Chapter 5

Olaudah Equiano, Gustavus Vassa, Negotiating Identity in a Trans-Atlantic World[5]

Rebecca A. Carte

First published in 1789, *The Interesting Narrative of the Life of Olaudah Equiano or Gustavus Vassa, the African, Written by Himself* presents scholars with a unique memoir; one of only a few penned by an individual who not only survived enslavement and procured his own manumission, but moreover was later able to write about his experience and manage to have it published.[6] Additionally, for over two centuries readers have been fascinated by the extent of his travels, both forced and voluntary, which took Equiano from Africa to the Caribbean, the British colonies to the Iberian Peninsula, and England to the North Pole. Indeed his life stands out as unique in many ways and the narrative, part socio-economic and political treatise; part spiritual autobiography, and part travel memoir has been well studied over the centuries. Upon its publication the text was well circulated in both the New World and the Old, meriting no less than eight editions and translation into Dutch, Russian and German before Equiano died in 1797. Since its republication in the 1960's the text has been studied extensively by literary and historical scholars alike. In fact, Janelle Collins proclaims in her 2006 article, "Passage to

---

[5] This article is based on a paper originally presented on June 19, 2013 as a part of my participation with Georgia College & State University in collaboration with the University of Hassan II at the conference, *Land, Culture, and People: The Atlantic and Mediterranean Spaces* in Marrakesh, Morocco.

[6] Olaudah Equiano (c. 1745- March, 1797). From here forward I will refer to the subject as Olaudah or Equiano.

Slavery, Passage to Freedom": "The international scholarly attention focused on Equiano has been so extensive and varied in the past two decades that 'Equiano Studies' has become a veritable subcategory within the slave narrative genre" (210).

What drives this fascination with Olaudah Equiano's narrative? Of course, in the first place, his exceptional circumstances have no doubt fueled interest in his narrative, circumstances shrouded in secrets, silences and betrayals to be sure. By his own account, Olaudah Equiano was betrayed time and time again, first when he was kidnapped from his Igbo village in present-day Nigeria as a little boy of only about ten years-old. Before his capture, Olaudah had, in his own words, "never heard of white men or Europeans, nor of the sea," but he would be at the mercy of both for much of his life (20). Indeed, Equiano would be bought and sold at least seven times by the age of twelve and would spend most of his youth at sea. After enduring the Middle Passage and spending a brief stint on a Virginia plantation, Olaudah was purchased by Captain Michael Henry Pascal who took the boy to England with him, but then took to the seas again to fight in the Seven Years War (1756-1763). After the war Equiano continued to sail with his master and captain, distinguishing his experience from that of most enslaved Africans who suffered the fate of the plantation. To the young boy's dismay, Pascal abruptly sold Equiano in 1763 and the latter ultimately fell into the hands of his last owner, Robert King, from whom he finally manumitted himself in 1776. All of his years of experience aboard ships afforded him the opportunity to learn English reading and writing, mathematics, navigation, and commerce. Once a freeman, Equiano managed to return to England, only to again travel to the West Indies and throughout the world. Ultimately, he would play a significant role in the abolitionist movement and his narrative would be read on both sides of the Atlantic. In brief, one reason to be fascinated by Equiano is his incredibly unique life, a life that makes for interesting and entertaining reading for scholars and students alike.

In the second place, the text defies genres and consequently begs myriad points of analytical departure. While Equiano obsequiously writes in his cover letter to the British Parliament: "I ought to entreat your pardon for addressing to you a work so wholly devoid of literary merit" this is far from the case. All be it at times erroneously, he quotes from memory the Bible, various theological and abolitionist texts, an array of travel and historical accounts, and literary works that include Daniel Defoe's *Robinson Crusoe* [(whom he echoes in the very title (Caldwell 270)], Jonathan Swift's *Gulliver's Travels*, Milton's *Paradise Lost*, Homer's *Iliad*, and Shakespeare's *Macbeth*, to name but a few. He adeptly employs rhetorical strategy and argument and demonstrates a worldly understanding of economics and politics.

Finally, what many view as his hybrid, English-African/Vassa-Equiano identity continues to be debated. Most studies have tended to presuppose the "duality" of Equiano/Vassa's experience, a duality that the same title of his narrative bespeaks. Renamed "Gustavus Vassa" by his captain and owner, Pascal, and most well-known by that moniker at the time of the text's publication, the author nonetheless elected to list first his Igbo name, Olaudah Equiano, in the title. The resultant question that scholars have debated for decades has been (despite his stating *the African* in the title): Is he culturally African or English, both or neither?[7] For decades scholars have debated what reading between the lines of the text may reveal about Equiano's incredibly complex identity. Recently the

---

[7] Jaros underscores that there is nothing playful about Equiano/Vassa's treatment of the play of names. "Theories of slave narrative and onomastics often neglect the importance accorded by these authors to establishing the legitimacy of their names —notwithstanding the violence and dispossession encrypted in them—in the various discursive and legal frameworks they occupy" (7).

mystery surrounding Equiano's identity intensified when, in his 2005 biography of Equiano, Vincent Carretta argued that Equiano was born in the Carolinas rather than Africa as Equiano claims in the *Interesting Narrative*. At the other end of the spectrum, Catherine Onianju Acholonu has demonstrated that Olaudah Equiano and Olaude Ekweauluo, a boy born in Isseke, Nigeria, are one and the same person.

These [spelling] discrepancies notwithstanding, the closeness between Isseke's customs and those described by Equiano, the existence of a family by the name of Ekwealuo in one of Isseke's ruling kindred, the little boy from this family who had been sold, the resemblance between Equiano in the portrait and Bright Ekwealuo, all accumulate as evidence that Olaudah Equiano was none other than Olaude Ekwealuo from Isseke in Anambra State of Nigeria, and Igbo from the Eastern hinterland. (361)

Who was Olaudah Equiano or Gustavo Vassa, the African? Where was he born? Is he more British than African or more African than American?

I would argue that it is precisely this issue of identity that has driven our fascination with Olaudah Equiano more than any other aspect of his narrative, as scholars analyze his Africanness, his Brithishness or his hybridity. By applying Paul Gilroy's chronotope of the Black Atlantic ship and focusing on the microcosm of the ships where he spent the majority of his life, however, we find that Equiano's narrative is even more complex than this African/British/American hybridity might suggest. Paul Gilroy postulates the image of the ship as "a living micro-cultural, micro-political system in motion" (ref.) in an attempt to move away from the binary between "national" and "diaspora" perspectives in Black Studies.

I have settled on the image of ships in motion across the spaces between Europe, America, Africa, and the Caribbean as a central organizing symbol for this enterprise and as my starting point. The image of the ship – a living, micro-cultural, micro-political system in motion – is especially important for historical and theoretical reasons [...] Ships immediately focus attention on the middle passage, on the various projects for redemptive return to an African homeland, on the circulation of ideas and activists as well as the key cultural and political artefacts: tracts, books, gramophone records, and choirs. (Gilroy 4)

Much like the ships he sailed on, both as a slave and a freeman, Equiano's text is a complex web in which multiple lived spaces present the reader with identities that are constantly up for grabs, and in which "pre-modern" frontiers may be more fluid than they seem. By approaching the text from the space of the ship, I believe we can gain a deeper understanding of an increasingly transatlantic world in which identity was highly dynamic and influenced by an array of Europeans of various ethnicities, Africans of different nations, and myriad indigenous groups, and all of varying social status, age, and gender. Put another way, I would like to abandon the binaries that have fueled the debate about Equiano's identity in which the text's narrator has been identified as culturally English or Igbo; geographically American or African-born; chronologically boy or man; racially white or black; economically slave or slaveholder and morally victim or trickster. I would like to suggest a reading that recognizes a triangulated convergence, one that is geographical to be sure: Europe, Africa and the Americas, but also a *bricolage* of overlapping triangulations: ethics, economics and politics; technological progress, exploration and tradition; spiritual salvation, physical violence and psychological depression; base survival, social mobility and imperial oppression, and not least obvious, race, class and gender.

Ships take on a primary importance in Equiano's life and consequently his narrative because he spends most of his life on a ship or in some port of call in between journeys. An old salt with a lifetime of sailing experience at the time of his writing, Equiano uses a great variety of names for vessels, among them wherry, punt, dragger, hoy, sloop, frigate, snow, privateer, schooner, man of war, and fire ship (45). It is not an exaggeration to state that ships dominated his world from the time he was ten until his death and, in fact, ships defined his life in countless and immeasurable ways. Collins expounds upon the ways in which the historical context provides pragmatic reasons for Equiano's continual desire to return to the sea even after he has been manumitted since black seamen enjoyed greater access to privileges and opportunity (both for escape and wealth) than most other slaves. In Equiano's case it is precisely that access that allows him to earn the funds to buy his freedom. "The irony, of course, is obvious: utilizing the economic system that underpinned the slave trade, Equiano accumulated enough capital to buy himself, thereby participating in the system in order to free himself from it" (220). Yet, while Collins examines "how sea imagery functions as a rhetorical mirror of the fluidity represented in Equiano's identity" contending that "*the sea* [...] exists as both a site of enslavement and a medium to liberty" I would add that it is not the sea alone per se, so much the *ship* (213, my emphasis).

Frank Kelleter addresses the importance of the ship as a cultural space in the *Interesting Narrative* in his 2004 article, "Ethnic Self-Dramatization and Technologies of Travel":

> It is of some significance [...] that Equiano spends his period of apprenticeship mainly on boats and ships, "moving" as Paul Gilroy writes, "to and fro between nations crossing borders in modern machines that were themselves micro-systems of linguistic and political hybridity." Equiano here literally moves *between* cultures, yet as the postcolonial hero par excellence – not as homeless wanderer and transcultural crossover artist – but as

an incorporated subject who is adaptable enough to play the role of a free (and national) individual with amazing conviction and persuasiveness. (75)

We must constantly bear in mind that from the tender age of ten, it is in a ship- its own moving, socio-economic, political, lived space associated with, but apart from the fixed places of Africa, Europe and America – that Equiano spends the majority of his life. Yet, to date we have tended to discuss Equiano's identity in terms of fixed geographical place: his Africaness, Americaness and/or his Englishness.

For the most part, studies that recognize Equiano as a transcultural subject have viewed the text through a Western lens or have couched the analysis in terms of the degree of his Westernization. In a 1994 study, Geraldine Murphy recognizes Equiano's narrative as a transcultural, hybrid product "written within and against the terms of the dominant culture," arguing that Equiano performs a sort of "dissident colonialism" by utilizing a Western genre—the travelogue—to align himself as bourgeois subject (376).[8] Terry Bozeman likens him to the trickster using cultural values to his benefit to "play the system against itself" (66). Kelleter, while advancing the conception of Equiano's hybrid subjectivity, denies this "strategic" or "subversive" aspect and posits Equiano's ethnic identity in terms of his own assimilation and emancipation, arguing that "assimilation" in the case of Equiano is a "bona fide acceptance and reproduction of dominant doctrines and practices by dominated people" (70):

> Just how much this colonial education turns him into a masterly- indeed imperial- individual becomes evident in Equiano's self-understanding as an English seafarer who, like

---

[8] Geraldine Murphy also notes the importance of the pronoun shift when Equiano addresses Igbo religion

most English sailors of the time, never thinks it necessary to learn how to swim. (Kelleter 75)

Tanya Caldwell takes the Westernization of Equiano the farthest with the idea that he "views himself as fundamentally white" (266).

That the mind behind the work is wholly that of a European – not of an African in European dress – is revealed not only in the details and the rhetorical structures of the Narrative, but, more importantly, in the recognition of and conviction in the social, political, and economic imperatives that shaped individual lives and writing in the late eighteenth century. For Equiano this necessarily involves a self-alignment not with but against the "African brethren" whose liberty he defines entirely upon the terms of eighteenth-century British economic imperatives and whose origins and identity he reconstructs rather than represents. (267)

On the other end of the spectrum, critics recognize the foundational experience of his Igbo childhood and his continued contact with Igbo people in the West Indies and Africa in Equiano's writing.[9] Paul Edwards and Rosalind Shaw argue for an African worldview in their 1989 article, "The Invisible *Chi* in Equiano's 'Interesting Narrative.'" They underscore the Igbo conception of *chi*, a sort of personal god responsible for an individual's destiny, as informing Equiano's notion of Providence, a concept that largely informs Equiano's religious views (146). Similarly, Robin Sabino and Jennifer Hall contend that Equiano's "world view remained Igbo throughout this life span" and "his acculturation to Anglo-Christian values was highly selective" (5). Babacar M'Baye, brilliantly employs an African-centered approach by pointing out the influences of African and New World Igbo trickster folktales in the narrative, concluding, "While he is occasionally ambivalent

---

[9] See Acholonu, Catherine Obianju.

toward certain parts of his Igbo customs and the participation of some Africans in the enslavement of other blacks, he never shatters the core of his Igbo identity and his respect for the customs and values of his homeland" (143). Finally, in her 2009 study, "'Excepting Himself': Olaudah Equiano, Native Americans, and the Civilizing Mission" Emily Field argues for the inclusion of Native Americans in the identity discussion, bringing attention to the "black-white axis" that has ignored the non-European and non-African people and moments in the narrative that "complicate dichotomous readings" (16). Citing Equiano's experiences in Nova Scotia with the Mi'kmaq during the war and his efforts to establish a plantation among the Miskito of Nicaragua, Field makes the case for the triangulation of the narrative that includes Native Americans.

While English, African, and Amerindian cultures doubtless inform Equiano's worldview as all of these studies convincingly demonstrate, what I would like to address is that regardless these interpretations are rooted in geographic locations despite the reality that Equiano spent so much of his life on ships. In fact, it is on the ship that Equiano's "hybrid character of his ethnic self-dramatization," to borrow Kelleter's phraseology, is realized, a point that Kelleter himself acknowledges: "[A]s soon as he is incorporated in the transatlantic trade network, he acquires an impressive cosmopolitan knowledge [...] He masters languages, sociolects, accounting, navigation, buying, and selling" (74).

Of course, Equiano's initial perception of a ship occurs in Africa when he is taken on board a slave ship headed for Barbados. The sight instills astonishment upon him "which was soon converted into terror" and he tell us, "I was now persuaded that I had gotten into a world of bad spirits, and that they were going to kill me" (38). The description that follows is one laden with violence, fear, inhumanity and a psychological and spiritual upheaval. If one were to stop reading here, s/he would never imagine that Equiano would ever board a ship of his own volition after surviving the Middle Passage. However, as the narrative continues the depictions of ships demonstrate an ever evolving relationship with the lived space of the sea vessel. For example, Equiano is still a terrified boy who views the white world as one of bad spirits and magical instruments when Pascal comes to the Virginia plantation and buys him for thirty or forty pounds sterling. Equiano is taken by horse to the merchant ship, the Industrious Bee.

When I arrived I was carried on board a fine large ship, loaded with tobacco, etc. and just ready to sail for England. I now thought my condition much mended; I had sails to lie on, and plenty of food victuals to eat; and every body [sic] on board used me very kindly, quite contrary to what I had seen of any white people before; I therefore began to think that they were not all of the same disposition. (45)

Sails, once an object of fear, now bring comfort to the boy's weary body and soul, and it is on the Industrious Bee that he first develops relationships with white people. He makes his first friend, Richard Baker, a highly educated fifteen year-old white boy from America.

We at length became inseparable; and for the space of two years he was of very great use to me, and was my constant companion. Although this dear youth had many slaves of his own, yet he and I have gone through many sufferings together on shipboard; and we have many nights lain in each other's bosoms when we were in great distress. (46)

Here, the role of the ship is that of the great equalizer, for although Richard is white, older, and a slave owner, he is a companion; although he assumes the "power" role of tutor, he suffers the distresses of sea voyage alongside his pupil; although one boy is black and the other white, they embrace and comfort one another. In fact, it is worth noting that Equiano's first memory of feeling shame about his complexion occurs not within his first two years on a ship, but only once he is on land in England.[10]

The next ship Equiano boards with his master, the Roebuck, leaves from England during the Seven Years War (1756-1763). It is through this experience that the lived space of the ship will become like home to the young Equiano and he begins to ally himself as a part of the "we" of the crew and writes,

When I went on board this large ship, I was amazed indeed to see the quantity of men and the guns. However my surprise began to diminish as my knowledge increased; and I ceased to feel those apprehensions and alarms which had taken such strong possession of me when I first came among the Europeans, and for some time after. I began now to pass to an opposite extreme; I was so far from being afraid of any thing [sic] new which I saw, that, after I had been some time in this ship, I even began to long for a battle. (50)

Clearly, by age twelve Equiano has already seen quite a lot and his worldliness has increased. During his time on the Roebuck he has more interactions with boys of his age, learns new skills, and sees Holland and Scotland. He reports, "There were a number of boys on board, which still made it more agreeable; for we were always together, and a great portion of our time was spent in play" (51). He explains that for the "diversion of the gentlemen" on board, the boys are paired according to their physicality and made to fight, "after which the gentlemen gave the combatants from five to nine shillings each" (50). Consequently Equiano is made to fight a white boy,

---

[10] The oft-quoted passage occurs when Equiano is Guernsey lodging with a mate of his master's. "This mate had a little daughter, aged about five or six years, with whom I used to be much delighted. I had often observed that when her mother washed her face it looked very rosy; but when she washed mine it did not look so: I therefore tried oftentimes myself if I could not by washing make my face of the same colour[sic] as my little playmate (Mary), but it was all in vain; and I now began to be mortified at the difference in our complexions." (49)

which he does for over an hour, and from that point on the captain and the ship's company "used very much to encourage him" in the sport. Additionally, during this time, Equiano learns the maneuvers of the ship and how to fire the guns all of which, in my view, make this period a sort of coming-of-age for the young boy.

While Equiano does not go into detail about the Roebuck's stops in Holland or Scotland, the international nature of such expeditions is established thereafter when he boards The Royal George. This marks the beginning of Equiano's extensive travels from port to port and his continual movement through the sea as he comes of age inside vessels that are microcosms of global interaction.

The Royal George was the largest ship I had ever seen; so that when I came on board of her I was surprised at the number of people, men, women and children, of every denomination. And the largest of the guns, many of them also of brass, which I had never seen before. Here were also shops or stalls of every kind of goods, and people crying their different commodities about the ship as in a town. To me it appeared a little world, into which I was again cast without a friend, for I had no longer my dear companion Dick. (52)

This largest of little worlds exposes Equiano to an entirely new crew, without the help of his friend and instructor. He fairs well despite this, and when the crew of the Royal George is transferred to the Namur and sails to Nova Scotia, Equiano truly becomes one of the boys, referring to "our troops" fighting against the French. He develops a sense of solidarity among his shipmates and no longer fears his new environs.

It was now between two and three years since I first came to England, a great part of which I had spent at sea; so that I became inured to that service, and began to consider myself as happily situated [...] From the various scenes I had beheld on ship-board, I soon grew a stranger to terror of every kind, and was, in that respect at least, almost an Englishman [...] I now not only felt myself quite easy with these new countrymen, but relished their society and manners. I no longer looked upon them as spirits, but as men superior to us; and therefore I had the stronger desire to resemble them; to imbibe their spirit, and imitate their manners (56).

As the passage elucidates, Equiano's narrative now abounds with pronoun shifts, which are often cited as examples of his hybrid English/Igbo identity. I am not dismissing these shifts as evidence of that in any way because clearly both African and English culture play dominant roles in shaping his worldview, rather I am bringing attention to the importance of the fact that by this point, Equiano has spent a large portion of his formative years (ages 10-14 or 15) on board ships. He is "happily situated," less fearful, worldlier, and clearly more comfortable with English culture because of his on-board experiences. Ships, with their own cultural norms, have been his home far more than any other place for at least four years. Furthermore, Equiano will return to ships again and again throughout his lifetime. Once he at last buys his freedom he continues to work tirelessly so that he may leave the West Indies – a part of the world he loathes for having suffered endlessly there-- so that he may return to "Old England," the place he has longed for more than any other, even Africa, during his years as a slave. Yet, although he finds work as a hairdresser in England, he remains in London for only brief stints - at most a little over a year and more frequently for stays of two, six, or ten months - only to sail off again. He even returns to the West Indies and at one point tells us, "I was again determined to go to Turkey, and resolved, at that time, never more to return to England" (137). Equiano now seems unable or unwilling to settle in one place; a man with no other country than that of the ship he occupies.

To be clear, it would be erroneous to assume that ships are always a welcoming home. Equiano is duped, abused, betrayed, mistreated, and even kidnapped during his travels. He learns the hard way that in the West Indies the life of a freeman is as precarious as that of slave, even more so. Shipmates and captains may be cruel and untrustworthy, and often Equiano does not respect them. However, at the same time he forms relationships on board ships in which he feels at times like a son, a peer, a brother, and even a mentor. Moreover, there is a clearly well defined "we" forged of a space not wholly European, African, or American on these vessels and Equiano is arguably as much a product of that milieu as any other. Despite the hardships, tenuous hierarchy, and injustices of these largest of little worlds then, Equiano returns to ships throughout his lifetime. Although initially by violent force, ultimately it is by choice that Equiano returns to what appears to be his preferred home.

Paul Gilroy invites cultural historians to "take the Atlantic as one single, complex unit of analysis in their discussions of the modern world and use it to produce an explicitly transnational and intercultural perspective" (Gilroy 15) and in which ships are thought of as "cultural and political units" and "possibly a distinct mode of cultural production" (Gilroy 17). While the hybrid nature of Equiano's narrative identity has been viewed largely in the geo-cultural terms of England and Africa, and less so America, the reality of the ships aboard which he came of age was significantly more complex. On ships and in the ports of call to which they carry him, Equiano meets, dialogues and negotiates (at times for his very life) with sailors, scientists, princes, musicians, plantation owners, slaves, priests, hairdressers and governors who are culturally Igbo, Akan, Aro, Senegambian, British, Spanish, Dutch, Portuguese, French, Greek, Turkish, Scottish, Mi'kmac, Miskito and religiously Quaker, Atheist, Catholic, and Methodist. These interactions are distinct and independent from their respective cultural norms creating, I believe, the distinct mode of cultural production to which Gilroy refers.

For over two centuries Olaudah Equiano/Gustavus Vassa and his life's travels, hardships and spirituality; his historical, political and socio-economic circumstances; his cross-genre narrative style, and perhaps above all else his hybrid identity have all generated fascination, discussion and debate. The mysteries surrounding his birth and the passion with which his readers ally themselves with aspects of his identity have only fueled this debate further. *The Interesting Narrative* offers nearly inexhaustible discussion and simply put, one can read Equiano/Vassa as one likes. He can be whomever his reader wants him to be. The result, to my mind, has been that scholars have made convincing arguments regarding his identity from the perspective of one side of the Atlantic or the other, with the caveat of limiting our reading to ethnic binaries that may not consider the whole of his work and his identity. I warrant that if we approach the narrative in the context of the black Atlantic world in which the ship is Equiano's cultural talisman we might avoid troubling ethnic absolutisms and recognize the complicated interactions that blur our imposition of contemporary conceptions of race, culture, nation, and ethnicity. Perhaps it is best, then, to shift our approach from that of reading the text through the Western lens or the African lens and instead accept that we need a kaleidoscope.

Works Cited

Acholonu, Catherine Obianju. "The Home of Olaudah Equiano – A Linguistic and Anthropological Search." *The Journal of Commonwealth Literature* 22.1 (1987): 5-16. In Sollors.

Bozeman, Terry S. "Interstices, Hybridity, and Identity: Olaudah Equiano and the Discourse of the African Slave Trade." *Studies in the Literary Imagination* 36:2 (2003): 61-70.

Caldwell, Tanya. "Talking Too Much English: Languages of Economy and Politics in Equiano's *The Interesting Narrative.*" *Early American Literature* 34 (1999): 263-282.

Carreta, Vincent. *Equiano, the African: Biography of a Self-Made Man*. Athens, Georgia: 2005.

Collins, Janelle. "Passage to Slavery, Passage to Freedom: Olaudah Equiano and the Sea." *The Midwest Quarterly* 47.3 (2006): 209-223.

Edwards, Paul and Rosaland Shaw. "The Invisible *Chi* in Equiano's *Interesting Narrative*" *Journal of Religion in Africa* 19 (1989): 146-156.

Equiano, Olaudah. *The Interesting Narrative of the Life of Gustavus Vassa, the African, Written by Himself*. [1789] Ed. Werner Sollors. New York and London: Norton & Company, 2001.

Field, Emily Donaldson. "'Excepting Himself': Olaudah Equiano, Native Americans, and the Civilizing Mission." *MELUS* 34 (2009):15-38.

Gilroy, Paul. *The Black Atlantic: Modernity and Double Consciousness*. London: Verso, 1993.

Jaros, Peter. "Good Names: Olaudah Equiano or Gustavus Vassa." *Eighteenth Century: Theory & Interpretation* 54 (2013): 2-24.

Kelleter, Frank. "Ethnic Self-Dramatization and Technologies of Travel in *The Interesting Narrative of the Life of Olaudah Equiano, or Gustavus Vassa, the African, Written by Himself* (1789)." *Early American Literature* 39 (2004): 67-84.

M'Baye. Babacar. *The Trickster Comes West: The Pan-African Influence in Early Black Diaspora Narratives*. Jackson: UP of Mississippi, 2009.

Murphy, Geraldine. "Olaudah Equiano, Accidental Tourist," *Eighteenth-Century Studies* 27 (1994): 551-68. In Sollors.

Sabino, Robin and Jennifer Hall. "The Path Not Taken: Cultural Identity in the Interesting Life of Olaudah Equiano." *MELUS* 24 (1999): 5-19.

Sollors, Werner, ed. *The Interesting Narrative of the Life of Olaudah Equiano, or Gustavus Vassa, the African, Written by Himself*. New York and London: Norton & Company, 2001.

Chapter 6

Traduttore, Traditore: Word-for-Word Translation as an Ideology Secretly Silencing Original Meanings[1]

Richard Evans

Andre Lefevere, reviewing the history of translation in the West in an article, "Introduction: Comparative Literature and Translation," comments on the persistence of the ideology of fidelity in translation based implicitly on a commitment to language as an instrument of representation. Speaking of academic considerations about translation theory in the mid-twentieth century, he reports: "Many of the questions asked bore on whether a text is a translation, an imitation, a version, a paraphrase, or what have you, unfortunately crowding out other questions of a more fundamental nature..." (8). This academic issue of what label to place on a given translation which reports the original in any other way than what is easily recognized, within an ideology of representational language, as a mirror recapitulates the Western civilization's persistent and "fanatical devotion to the word, both in translating (word for word) and in thinking about translation" (Lefevere 3).

The pretense of word-for-word translation as a realistic possibility within the nature of natural languages dissolves in the face of an understanding of linguistic relativity or, perhaps

---

[1] This chapter is curled from a 2002 University of South Carolina dissertation by Richard Evans, "From Greek & Latin to the *Old English Orosius:* Contexts for Translation and Reception." Although much of the original wording is preserved, the text has been reconfigured to suit a different context and serve a different purpose.

better formulated, linguistic particularity. Of course, certain exceptions to translatability have long held popular currency such as the old saw that poetry is what get lost in translation, a trope also active in Anglo-Saxon England. A special defense mounted for non-literal translation (really an assertion of the impossibility of literal translation) is the remark that follows the Old English translator's rendering of Caedmon's hymn. In the *Historia Ecclesiastica Gentis Anglorum,* Bede explains how "poetry" gets lost in translation when the word order of one language cannot be truly reproduced in another:

> Hic est sensus, non autem ordo ipse verborum...neque enim possunt carmina,quamvis optime conposita, ex alia in aliam linguam ad verbum sine detrimento sui decoris ac dignitatis transferri. (IV. xxiv)

> This is the sense, but not the exact order of the words...for it is not possible to translate poems, however excellently executed in their original language, into another language without damage to their beauty and worthiness. (my translation)

Bede's concern about the deformation of the aesthetic form and effect of the poem, its essential style, reveals a strong awareness of the limits of translation from Old English into Latin for capturing the unique properties of Germanic verse. Bede's remark that some aspects of language are not *translatable* at all further privileges Old English poetry as something unique with its own *decor* and *dignitas*, poetic language on an equal footing with Latin. Thus, this defense of non-literal translation is really a challenge to the possibility of the very sort of translation that is implied by a conservative, word-for-word rendering that supports the implication that *ad verbum* translation somehow constructs meaning exactly faithful to the original text:

The common denominator is an almost fanatical devotion to the word, both in translation (word for word) and in thinking about translation. That devotion to the word was enshrined early on in the development of Western tradition, when translators in Akkad and Sumer drew up bilingual word lists, making the word both a unit of translation and the limit of translation thinking for thirty centuries.... Finally, the devotion to the word was made enforceable and enforced during the long reign of Christianity in its several variants. Since the Bible was the word of God, it should not be changed, and it should be translated word-for-word. (Lefevere 3)

More broadly, casting a hermeneutics of suspicion on the entire project of translation is the well-known Italian phrase, *traduttore, traditore*, playing on the slight change of one vowel sound within one language as illustrative of the larger issues of lost meanings across languages (Danto 1). The *Old English Orosius* provides a memorable and remarkable illustration of betrayal of original meaning, even in what appears as a deliberately literal, *ad verbum* style translation, with a passage the origin of which is Herodotus' *Histories*. 1300 years separate the Old English passage from its ancient Greek source, and about 830 years stand between the Herodotean passage and its translation in the Latin Orosius, the intermediary between the Greek and the Old English versions of the narrative. The passage that will be the focus of the following examination is found in Herodotus A, 189.1-2; Orosius, Book II, 6, 3-4; and *Old English Orosius,* Book II. iiii. The Latin text will be presented first as it both looks back (as an apparent *ad verbum* translation according to traditional terminology) to its Greek source and itself is transposed into the Old English:

> **3** Nam unum regiorum equorum candore formaque excellentem, transmeandi fiducia persuasum qua per rapacem alveum offensi vado vertices attollebantur, abreptum

praecipitatumque merserunt. 4 Rex iratus ulcisci in amnem statuit, contestans eum qui nunc praeclarum equitem voravisset feminis vix genua tinguentibus permeabilem relinquendum....

For whirlpools submerged and swept down headlong one of the royal horses, outstanding in dazzling whiteness and appearance, as it relying on its strength for swimming across (went in) where the eddies, opposing a crossing, arise in the swift channel. The king, enraged at the river, determined to get vengeance and announced that the one who now had devoured his famous horseman (*equum* changes to *equitem* in the Latin text) must be left scarcely wetting the knees of the women. (my translation)

This passage is taken from Herodotus, whether directly translated by Orosius himself or from the translation of another is not known for sure (*Orose,* Arnaud-Lindet, Tome I, XXVII-XXVIII with associated notes). Whatever the source, the close replication of content elements and narrative order in Latin with respect to the Greek source imply that the translator here was trying for a word-for-word translation. Because of the close parallel in progression of the narrative order of events of the Greek reflected by the Latin translation, the Latin passage might be called in the terminology of traditional stylistic discussions of translation, derivative, not a creative, literary translation. Herodotus, A.189 at the end of section 1 and all of 2:

...ἐνθαῦτά οἱ τῶν τις ἱρῶν ἵππων τῶν λευκῶν ὑπὸ ὕβριος

ἐσβὰς ἐς τὸν ποταμόν διαβαίνειν ἐπειρᾶτο, ὁ δέ μιν συμψήσας ὑποβρύχιον οἰχώκεε φέρων. κάρτα τε δή ἐχαλέπαινε τῷ ποταμῷ ὁ Κῦρος τοῦτο ὑβρίσαντι καὶ οἱ ἐπηπείλησε οὕτω δή μιν ἀσθενέα ποιήσειν ὥστε τοῦ λοιποῦ καὶ γυναῖκας μιν εὐπετέως τὸ γόνυ οὐ βρεχούσας διαβήσεσθαι.

>...at that time, one of his glorious, white horses because of its restiveness tried to cross over the river, but the river snatched the horse, pushed under and swept on, carrying it off. Cyrus was greatly angered at the river for doing this violence, and he threatened that he would make it so insignificant that for the future even women would easily cross it without wetting their knee. (my translation)

This short narrative about the loss of one of Cyrus' horses falls into two sentences in Greek. The first sentence, in turn, divides into two sections: section one describes the horse, its high spiritedness and its attempt to cross the river; the second part relates how the horse was swept away in the river. The Latin translation follows the same sentence structure, first describing the horse and its self-confidence; second, the ending of the sentence relates how the horse was submerged and swept away. The Latin, however, contains some words, perhaps a gloss, for which there is not counterpart in Greek, *qua per rapacem alveum offensi vado vertices attollebantur*. The Greek makes no mention of dangerous whirlpools or eddies in the river as the direct cause of the disaster. But with the exception of this additional element of content, the movement of the Latin translation parallels the narrative order of the original Greek sentence.

More specifically in the first sentence, Herodotus uses the adjectives ἱρός and λευκός to describe the physical aspects of the horse, splendid and white. Orosius matches the Greek with the adjectival expression *candore formaque excellens*, royal and excellent in whiteness and shape. The adjective *regius*, royal, is implicit in the Greek by the identification of the horse as one of those belonging to Cyrus through the pronoun οἱ. Herodotus discloses the character of the horse and the reason for his rush into the river with the telling and fateful phrase ὑπὸ ὕβριος. Again, Orosius parallels this phrase in Greek with *fiducia persuasum* in Latin and collapses the entire idea of the Herodotean ἐσβὰς ἐς τὸν ποταμόν διαβαίνειν ἐπειρᾶτο (having entered the river tried to cross) into the one Latin gerund *transmeandi*, of crossing over. Orosius, or his Latin translation, next introduces an apparent aside that has no real counterpart in the Greek, *qua ... attollebantur.* This gloss or additional comment does not deform the narrative progression of the Orosian sentence that ends with the same basic actions in Latin as it does in Greek: (1) snatched, *abreptum*, συμψήσας; (2) in Latin: submerged him, cast down headlong, *praecititumque merserunt*; and in Greek: (the river) swept on, carrying him off submerged, ὑποβρύχιον οἰχώκεε φέρων. So far the Latin seems to be aiming at a very close, direct report of the Greek content elements and their narrative order or progression, in traditional terms, an *ad verbum* translation.

The second sentence in Herodotus also conveys two major points, first, the rage of Cyrus toward the river's violent action and, second, the type of punishment that the king planned to impose as revenge for his horse. The Orosian translation basically follows the Herodotean narrative order of the sentence, but several modifications in the Latin do require notice.

The first part of the second Herodotean sentence reports that the king is angry and will punish the river: κάρτα τε δή ἐχαλέπαινε τῷ ποταμῷ ὁ Κῦρος τοῦτο ὑβρίσαντι καί οἱ ἐπηπείλησε οὕτω δή μιν ἀσθενέα ποιήσειν .... The Latin develops this idea declaring: *rex iratus ulisci ...statuit, contestans*, the enraged king determined to get revenge, stating that.... The Greek, on the other hand, asserts the king's anger directly with the verb, ἐχαλέπαινε, he was angry, but leaves implicit the notion of revenge (*ulisci*) in another verb, ἐπηπείλησε, he threatened. Further, Orosius slightly alters the syntactical order of his translation in respect to the Greek by moving the idea, expressed by the Greek participle ὑβρίσαντι, doing violence, after the verb of saying in Latin, *contestans,* whereas the reference to the river's violence had occurred before the verb of verbal action in Greek, ἐπηπείλησε. The word, ὑβρίσαντι, meaning *to act violently* in Greek, is refocused in Latin directly into a metaphor appropriate to the river's sucking the horse/horseman under and expanded syntactically into a clause, *qui nunc praeclarum equitem voravisset,* (the river) which *had* just now *devoured* his famous horseman. Although by specifying the type of violence of the river with the word, *voravisse,* Orosius does not seem to shift away from the essential idea of violence found in, ὑβρίσαντι, the change from *equum* to *equitem,* from horse to horseman, does seem to be an interesting leap. Since *equitem* is the reading of the majority of manuscripts and the *lectio difficilior,* (*Orose,* Arnaud-Lindet, Tome I, 96 with textual notes), it may be best to suppose that the translator wrote *equitem,* simply imposing his own personal view that a king would not be so upset because of losing a horse but because of losing its rider. Clearly the substitution of *equitem* as a translation for the Greek, τις ... ἵππων, departs from a word-for-word translation in this particular instance, changing the semantic meaning while holding to the same stylistic and narrative pattern of the original text.

The final idea of the second sentence in Latin is reported very directly from the Greek original: οὕτω δή μιν ἀσθενέα ποιήσειν ὥστε τοῦ λοιποῦ καί γυναῖκας μιν εὐπετέως τὸ γόνυ οὐ βρεχούσας διαβήσεσθαι.

The Greek phrase, οὕτω δή μιν ἀσθενέα ποιήσειν ὥστε τοῦ λοιποῦ, to make it (the river) so weak that for the future, is managed by the Latin, *eum ...reliquendum,* a passive periphrastic denoting necessity for the future. The word, ἀσθενέα, weak, is omitted from the Latin; however, γυναῖκας μιν εὐπετέως τὸ γόνυ οὐ βρεχούσας διαβήσεσθαι, that women will cross over easily, not wetting the knee, is executed with the Latin words, *feminis vix genua tinguentibus permeabile,* scarcely damp for women touching their knees (in it).

Overall, the Latin Orosius carefully and directly transposes this short two-sentence narrative from Herodotus. With the exception of two editorial changes, one of which may be explained away by as a textual issue, the Latin text fairly follows the Greek in narrative order and accounts for most of the specific content elements of the story. With the exception of the limited editorializing, a strong argument may be raised for classifying the Latin translation in traditional terms as *ad verbum*, word-for-word, keeping the verbal style of the Greek. Surely, the Latin translation appears closer to an attempted literal translation in respect to the repetition of the basic content and narrative order of the Greek story in the Latin version.

This demonstration that Orosius tried for and produced a fairly literal translation would be a sufficient analysis if one accepts, even implicitly, that the primary tendency in language is representation and that a translator's task is faithful reproduction of the source text in some formal way. Based on such a representationalist ideology of language as that of the literalist translator, it is possible to recapitulate and define even more precisely what the features of literal translation are by applying the four criteria that are laid out by E.D. Hirsch in "Appendix I: Objective Interpretation" of *Validity in Interpretation*. Although these criteria are put forward as a means for verifying the author's intended meaning in textual interpretation, they work well as parameters for defining literal translation. The four criteria, linked to a hermeneutics of trust and authority, (that establish an interpretation as a match to authorial intent) are *legitimacy, correspondence, generic appropriateness and coherence*. Legitimacy requires that "the reading be permissible within the public norms of the *langue* in which the text was composed" (236). Correspondence requires that "the reading must account for each linguistic component of the text" (236). Generic appropriateness demands that the generic history of the text must be part of its meaning, that one would not read a serious scientific article as an informal conversation, for example (236). Finally, the governing and ultimate criterion of coherence demands that the text make sense as a whole in conformity with its specific context (236-37).

These criteria for judging the probability of an interpretation as one that matches authorial intent connect obviously and immediately to Hirsch's project of authoritarian hermeneutics, "to impose those (meanings) of the author" on the text (236). The justification for the so-called literal translation makes a similar move, to establish faithfully in the target language the originally intended meaning of the text undergoing translation. Hirsch believes that this project of establishing authorial intent, the original meaning of the *Ur Text*, is possible because of his commitment to a representational view of language. Likewise, Hirsch's four criteria for verification of the probability of a reading can be transferred as a sound framework for establishing a definitional frame for literal translation within the representationalist ideology of translation.

Within this moralistic and authoritarian ideology that emphasizes stability of linguistic meaning, legitimacy speaks to translating through obvious, public norms in the target language that are viewed as consistent with the norms of the language of the original text. Clearly, if a translation should be perceived as linguistically deformed or deviant in reference to the original, the very referential meaning of the original comes into question through translation.

For the literal *ad verbum,* translation, the notion of close correspondence suggests that the basic content and verbal elements of the original text need to be accounted for obviously and clearly in the translated text. In the example of the translation from Herodotus to Orosius above, it was easy to spot an added idea because of the close correspondence of both content elements and order of the narrative pattern in the Greek and the Latin sentences.

Generic appropriateness suggests an appropriate stylistic placement of the generic type of the translated within the speech genres of the target language. In the case of Greek into Latin, the matter is easier because of the influence of Greek on Latin literary history and style. The story of Cyrus' horse both in Herodotus and in Orosius conforms to accepted historical narrative prose in both Greek, where, of course, Herodotus was a pioneer, and in Latin, where Orosius comes at the end of a long tradition of historical writing. This stylistic issue might be murkier if an historical text was transferred into a linguistic system that had no generic tradition or style developed for historical writing.

Finally, overall coherence demands that the passage or text make sense in terms of being a closely reported utterance that can be accepted as authoritative in respect to referential meaning (content) as well as clearly comprehensible in linguistic construction. A comparison between the Greek text and Orosius' translation of story of Cyrus' horse/horseman meets all these criteria reasonably well. Thus, a believer in the efficacy of literal translation might argue that, prima facie, Orosius had found and replicated in Latin the content and even paralleled the generic style of Herodotus. Hirsch's criteria based on a hermeneutics of trust will privilege the idea of the ethical superiority of reproduction and word-for-word matching, as well as generic or stylistic correspondence and, indeed, claim them as the very measure of faithful, honest translation. When these similarities and correspondences have been duly noted, the commentator's job has been done and analysis has confirmed that the literal, ideational meaning of the original has been transferred to the translation: readers can be confident that they have an authoritative translation, fulfilling the moral standard of truth.

Literal translation as an antidote against slippage in referential meaning (falsification of meaning) has a continuous history from the word-matching lists of Babylonian scribes to contemporary schoolroom translations. The fact that Western translation ideology has been bound to the word-for-word matching since the bilingual Sumerian-Akkadian word lists implicitly acknowledges an underlying intuition that translation does tamper somehow with referential meaning. To affirm just the opposite, that referential meaning is, in fact, safe from significant change through translation, the ideology of Western translation has spent much effort supporting a façade, the conservative powers of literal translation:

> That devotion to the word was enshrined early in the development of the Western tradition, when translators in Sumer and Akkad drew up bilingual word lists, making the word into both the unit of translation and the limit of thinking about translation for thirty centuries…Finally the devotion to the word was made enforceable and enforced during the long reign of Christianity in its several variants. Since the Bible was the word of God it should not be changed, and should therefore be translated word-for-word. (Lefevere 3)

At this point in the argument, the suspicious side of a dialogic hermeneutics must come strongly into play where notable and complicated distinctions arise in the ideology of the Herodotean and Orosian world views that will puncture the façade of literal translation as we move from fifth-century Greece to Christian Late Antiquity.

The following analysis will focus on the reception of this early fifth-century Greek text by a later Latin historian, and a contrastive analysis of the Latin passage to its Greek source will evince cardinal distinctions in historico-cultural contexts between Herodotus and Orosius. Despite the similarity of progression in the narrative pattern of events in both the Greek source and its Latin translation, the application of a dialogic hermeneutics (of suspicion) will reveal how different languages tell a story in their unique ways by virtue of the ideological traditions of each language. In the Homeric example of reported speech, the changes in the contexts surrounding quoted words were easy to designate, and the simplicity of this model helps set up the principle that even when words seem alike, there are inevitable differences.

Within various natural languages such as Greek, Latin or Old English, that themselves are composed of numerous, special competing micro-languages (the languages of law, religion, history, government, heroic poetry, satire, comedy, high oratory, etc.), each ideologically driven from disparate social motivations, it is difficult to discover, specify and analyze the inter-orientation of these various languages of heteroglossia at a given historical time. The difficulty, moreover, of finding and delineating the tension and ideological inter-orientation between two or among three distinct natural languages at different historical periods is immense, and the very acknowledgment that any natural language is "heteroglot from top to bottom" (*Dialogic Imagination* 291) precludes a belief in the stabilizing notion of exact correspondence between any two natural languages. It is true, however, that the literary forms of Latin developed through deliberate transposition and imitation of stylistic and generic correspondences with Greek. Thus, many of the languages of heteroglossia in Latin are, in fact, formed with reference to languages of heteroglossia in Greek. Latin literature, regardless of its creative use of Greek generic and stylistic resources, is nonetheless unique and much ink has been spilled to demonstrate this particularity of Latin literature in reference to its Greek sources (*Dialogic Imagination* 62-63).

Further, within any natural language "at any given moment languages of various epochs and periods of socio-ideological life cohabit with one another" (*Dialogic Imagination* 291). Some of the languages enjoy a continuity of hundreds of years, for example, the special *Kunstsprache* of Homer throughout Greek Antiquity or the Liturgy of St. John Chrysostom in current Greek. Since particular languages of heteroglossia are unique in the history of each natural language, it is high unlikely that any two natural languages could ever match up in a one-to-one correspondence even after deliberate imitation. (Ennius, for example, tried to create in Latin an epic-like language that would reflect the Homeric *Kunstsprache,* but this poetic language turned out as an artificial move to make up for the non-existence of an epic diction equivalent to Homer in Latin.) Each natural language, then, carries its own ideological contexts within it and these contexts will be different from the ideological mixes in any other language. Thus, It is with this understanding of the internal heteroglossic complexity, along with all sorts of other relativities, of each natural language that we must begin any analysis of much greater complications of polyglossic (inter-language) intersection and the problematic of translation.

The short, two-sentence narrative about Cyrus' horse from Herodotus A. 189 appears to be simple enough, especially in its Latin translation in Book II of Orosius' *History*. But the appearance of directness and clear simplicity raises suspicion within a framework that searches out heteroglossic and polyglossic complexity as inherent in the nature of language itself. Herodotus uses a keyword in the Greek version of the narrative; the word is used both in nominal and verbal form: the object of the preposition in the phrase ὑπὸ ὕβριος, because of *overweening pride,* and the participle with its object τοῦτο ὑβρίσαντι, doing this violence. As already discussed, the Latin translates the prepositional phrase, ὑπὸ ὕβριος, with the instrumental ablative *fiducia,* with high confidence. *Fiducia,* is related etymologically to *fides,* faith, and *fidus,* trustworthy, and does not carry a negative connotation in Latin (Lewis and Short, *A Latin Dictionary*, s.v., *fiducia*). Of course, the Greek word ὕβρις, a word well known to anyone who has studied Greek tragedy, is another matter, loaded as it is with denotations of violence and overstepping boundaries. The Greek phrase, τοῦτο ὑβρίσαντι, is picked up in the Latin by the translator's specification of the particular type of violence involved in the destruction of the horse, *voravisset,* devoured. By moving from the general idea of arrogant violence denoted by the Greek verb, ὑβρίζειν, to the specific act of *devouring,* the Latin translator subtly shifts the emphasis from the river's outrage to the type of death suffered by the horse. Translation, thus, inevitably produces such semantic modifications as it is not possible for the lexicon of one language to reproduce fully the lexicon of another. In English, we have simply borrowed the word, *hybris,* in order to maintain its particular Greek connotations and thus to avoid the problem that Orosius faced in this passage. Yet an analysis of the semantic differences between Herodotus' Greek and Orosius' translation only begin to open up the issue of ideological context that turns on the one word, ὕβρις.

The word, ὕβρις, in this Herodotean narrative connects outward in two directions: in one direction it links thematically back to the story of Croesus and later to the fate of Xerxes in the *History* of Herodotus himself. But more than this, it connects to a particular archaic Greek pattern of thinking about destiny in the world, especially developed by Athenian tragedians. Charles Beye in *Ancient Greek Literature and Society* summarizes this Greek tragic morality cycle upon which the fate of Croesus and Xerxes turn in Herodotus:

Unremitting prosperity is...dangerous in the thinking Herodotus represents...The prosperity is like getting drunk, it make you feel good, it makes you feel secure, more like your real self, able to act out the true you in otherwise generally repressed dimensions; it also make you giddy. Your success makes you successful. The Greeks talked of prosperity (*olbia*) or satiety (*koros*) when one's person was expanded, his being so high, that the natural limits of his personality and intuition were not there; this is his pride (*hybris*). At this point the intoxication is fatal, every stimulus is a seduction (*ate*)...The flushed prosperous, prideful man thinks to commit himself on the inflated terms of his successful self, he misjudges (*hamartia*), misses the mark as the Greek word implies, and is engulfed in catastrophe (*nemesis*). (214)

The key words mentioned by Beye, *olbia, koros, hybris, ate, hamartia,* and *nemesis,* are all associated in a linked nexus of ideas, but they may appear separately and still allude to his entire tragic morality cycle. Thus, when Herodotus uses the word, *hybris*, in the story about Cyrus' horse, the entire morality cycle is evoked in the mind of the fifth-century Greek audience. (Ample evidence of the pan-Hellenic appreciation of this morality pattern is found in Solon, *Elegy* 1; Aeschylus, *Persians*, 821-822; as well as Herodotus A.34.1.) The river has committed an outrage, and the audience is cued by the phrase, τοῦτο ὑβρίσαντι, to expect that the river will receive punishment for its arrogance just as the horse, ὑπὸ ὕβριος, because if its overweening confidence, was overtaken by the river.

Herodotus builds the story of Croesus, the first in his *History* around this thematic cycle of *koros, hybris, ate* and *nemesis* and closes with the repulsion and defeat of Xerxes, defeated by the fateful power of *nemesis*. Here we can see a special language of heteroglossia (in Bakhtin's terms) at work in early Greek literature. Wide spread and well understood, the ideology of this special language about the relationship of good fortune to human happiness infuses the Herodotean account of Solon's visit and conversation with Croesus in Book I. 30-34. The vocabulary of this language recurs in the short narrative of Cyrus' horse, implicitly linking punishment (*nemesis*) to overweening pride or arrogant action. Here we have a special language carrying a unique cultural perspective on mankind's relation to power, wealth and potential or actual downfall. The use of any one of the appropriate key words within a context of discussing wealth or pride will evoke allusion to or use of the special language. Herodotus uses the ideology of this language as a way to structure his historical narrative overall as well as to link history to some meaningful moral or ethical explanation of life. "Herodotus has given the story of a king's fall in brief (Croesus) and then imposed that narrative on the massively detailed and seemingly uncontrollable adventures of the Persians in their invasion of Greece" (Beye 219).

The cultural and ideological contexts for Orosius' translation and use of this Herodotean narrative were significantly different from the fifth-century Greek world of the father of history. Barbarian invasions were suggesting to pagans that Rome was under assault because of the rise of the Christian faith. Orosius was writing history with an apologetic thrust to "prove to the pagans of his day that the sack of Rome by the Goths was not owing to their desertion of the old gods" (Whitelock 90). A crisis of Roman political and cultural history, barbarian invasion, produces the ideological contestation between the language(s) of Christianity and the language(s) of paganism, the battlefield for Orosius' historical polemic:

But what Orosius did was to give a Christian view of the world history; he christianized the Roman historians' conception of the *pax Romana*, and showed how the whole of history, through the empires of Babylon, Macedon, and Carthage, had been leading to the universal empire of Rome, so that Christ should be born in the universal peace of Augustus' reign and the faith could be spread through a universal empire. (Whitelock 90)

No ideological purpose could be further removed from the historiographic orientation of the pagan pre-Christian Herodotus. Orosius attempts to reveal God's plan for human salvation in the rise and fall of great past empires, pointing out the horrors of life before the advent of Christianity. Herodotus tries to make sense of history based on a pagan Greek morality pattern. Why would anyone expect Orosius' translation to incorporate the special sense of Herodotean *hybris* in the Christian Latin of the fifth century A.D.?

Although the Orosian translation gets at the core elements of the narrative action in original Greek, the horse jumps into the river, and even offers a motivation, *fiducia persuasum*, persuaded by his self-confidence, no clue is offered in Latin to the ideology of *hybris* and *nemesis* that is clearly evoked in the Greek of Herodotus. Is the Herodotean ideological complex lost in translation or simply irrelevant to the Orosian intent and, hence, silenced? The archaic Greek morality pattern and Christian morality are distinctly different and there is no need for a Christian historian to reproduce the ideology of archaic Greece in translation even if he understood the full implications of the Herodotean text.

The probability that the *Old English Orosius* was created in Old English for those ignorant of Latin may account for some of the changes of factual elements in the Old English translation of the Cyrus passage vis-à-vis both the original Herodotean narrative and its Latin translation. Moreover, paleographic issues, in addition, beyond linguistic interpretation in the translation, point to concerns with textual and manuscript integrity. The *Old English Orosius* from Book II. iiii:

> Þa gebeotode an his ðegna þæt he mid sunde þa ea oferfaran wolde mid twam tyncenum, ac hiene se stream fordraf. Ða gebetode Cirus ðæt he his ðegn on hire swa gewrecan wolde, þa he swa grom wearð on his mode and wið þa ea gebolgen, þæt hie mehte wifmon be hiere cneowe oferwadan , þær heo ær wæs nignon mila brad þonne heo fludu wæs.

> Then one of his lords declared that he intended to cross the river by swimming with two casts, but the current drove him off course. Then Cyrus proclaimed that he intended to get such revenge on it for his (horse) man, because he was so angry in his mind and enraged against the river, which a woman could wade over it up to her knees where before it was nine miles wide when it was flooded. (my translation)

The first sentence of the Old English departs from the Latin in both its first and second part. In the first part of the Latin sentence where it describes the physical features of king's horse, *unum regiorum equorum candore formaque excellentem,* the Old English translator substitutes, *an his ðegna,* one of his soldiers, and then eliminates any reference to the physical characteristics of the horses. The Old English translator, no doubt, heard or read the Latin word, *equitum,* in place of *equorum*. This change is easy enough if the translator was reading or hearing a manuscript that presented *equitum,* and indeed three, H, Z 2 and J offer that textual reading (*Orose,* Arnaud-Lindet, Book II.6.3 with textual notes). Thus, the omission of *candore formaque excellentem* from the Old English now seems a sensible editorial adjustment if one presses the illogic of such a description aptly fitting one of the king's horse soldiers.

Further, the phrase, ὑπὸ ὕβριος, very important in the Greek, rendered in Latin by *fiducia,* does not appear in Old English at all, while *transmeandi,* the gerund dependent on *fiducia,* does come across as *þæt he mid sunde þa ea oferfaran wolde,* that he intended to cross the river by swimming. It seems that Orosius sensed that *hybris* was important enough in Greek to require reporting directly in Latin, but his choice in translating that word, *fiducia,* though catching some of the semantic range of the Greek, did not cry out to the Old English translator for such direct reporting.

After the verb, *oferfaran,* comes a singularly strange addition in Old English, *mid twam tycenum,* with two casts. This phrase does not seem related to any part of the context and simply does not make sense. Even the meaning of the word *tycenum* is obscure and not really understood in Old English (Bately, *Old English Orosius,* s.v. *tycen* in the "Glossary"). What has happened here? It is possible to explain *an his ðegna* by reference to a variant reading in the Latin text of the translator, and editorial omissions or additions are quite standard practice throughout the Old English Orosius as well as other works that were translated by Alfred himself (Whitelock 89-94), but glosses tend to add useful historical or cultural facts that would be helpful to the audience. *Mid twam tycenum* adds no useful information and does not seem to have a connection to the content of the passage.

Two possible explanations do present themselves for what must look like a case of simple misunderstanding. The translator had a corrupted copy of the Latin in front of him or, if the Latin text was being dictated to the translator orally as is a possibility (Bately, cix - cxvi), perhaps he simply misheard what the dictator spoke. The dictation theory (based on careful phonological evidence of variant spellings of proper names throughout the text of the *Old English Orosius* and accepted since the nineteenth century) offers an attractive way to save the translator and connect this translation problem both to the historico-cultural ambience of orality in ninth-century England and to the theoretical model of reported speech.

Now in returning to the analysis of the first sentence of the passage under consideration, it may be observed that the entire clause in Latin, *qua per rapacem alveum offensi vado vertices attollebantur,* (this clause was not part of the Greek passage at all), is omitted from the Old English translation by editorial compression, no doubt. The sentence ends, however, in Old English paralleling the narrative order in Latin *abreptum praecipitumque merserunt* which phrase becomes *ac hiene se stream fordraft.* In sum, this sentence comes over into Old English not as directly reported, a word-for-word attempt but more loosely, *andgit of andgiete,* sense for sense. The Old English translator does transfer three basic content ideas from Latin; (1) a horseman tries (2) to swim over the river and (3) is swept away. The translator also shows awareness, by preserving the referential core of the utterance, that he is reporting the message of another speaker, but more in the manner of indirectly reported speech than direct discourse with compression and even addition but nonetheless making the other's words the theme of the utterance

The second Latin sentence of the passage comes across more in the manner of reported direct discourse. Here, the Old English translator holds down omission and makes only one change in a factual element. The first two clauses of the Old English sentence report that Cyrus would get revenge for his knight, *ðæt he his ðegn on hire swa gewrecan wolde.* This clause covers the Latin, *ulisci* and *equitem.* The next Old English clause goes back to the head of the Latin sentence to pick up *iratus in amnem* with *þa he swa grom wearð on his mode and wið þa ea gebolgen*; thus the precise narrative order of the Latin is not preserved but all content elements are, in fact, covered. Here the rearrangement seems to be more a matter of the narrative ordering of content elements than syntactical adjustment of Old English to Latin. This sort of transposition of content elements, again, is consistent with a translator who is listening to a text being dictated in another language; after listening through a period or long phrase to the end, he transposes into the target language retrospectively, picking up all the content elements but not necessarily in the precise order of the original text.

The final part of the Latin sentence that describes what Cyrus did to the offending river, *feminis vix genua tinguentibus permeabilem reliquendum* comes across with only on minor elaboration, *þæt hie mehte wifmon be hiere cneowe oferwadan, þær heo ær wæs nignon mila brad þonne heo fludu wæs*. The remark that the river had been formerly *nine miles wide* is the rhetorical exaggeration of the Old English translator. Such embellishment cannot be construed as ignorance of Latin or mistranslation since it is keeping with the narrative direction of the story. This embellishment here fits cultural attitudes of a performance-oriented, pre-print society where rhetorical showmanship was at times more valuable than accurate authorial attribution.

The descent of this short narrative from the Fifth-century Greek Herodotus to the late Roman, Christian apologist Orosius to Anglo-Saxon King Alfred's court tells a compelling story of ideological and textual transformation through over 1200 years of history. The greatest ideological gap, between Herodotus and Orosius, seems to coincide with a real attempt to produce in Latin a direct report of the Greek. A translator who attempts to construct a literal or word-for-word translation always produces something different from the original utterance simply because of the dynamic heteroglossia within both the source and the target language. The intersection of the source and the target languages will connect the specific languages of heteroglossia within each natural language only with great difficulty, and then there are always the traditionally accepted problems of different sound, syntactical and lexical patterns. In this case of the Herodotean narrative, the ideological gap between the Classical Greek world-view of the envy of the gods, the fall of men because of *hybris*, probably did not find its way into a language of heteroglossic mix of later Latin. Perhaps Orosius excluded that pagan Greek view from his text deliberately even if he understood the full ideological import of the Herodotean use of the word, but more than likely, Orosius did not control the languages of heteroglossia in Greek well enough to fully grasp its ideological orientation and tradition.

Further in the historical descent of this story, much as a phrase at end of the parlor game, "Gossip," has become unrecognizable from its first expression, the *Old English Orosius* picks up, in the Latin text, a minor incident in Cyrus's campaign against Babylon, and relates it in an Old English narrative appropriate to the Christian era, devoid of any uniquely Greek moral or theological ideology. If, indeed, the Old English translation was intended for those hearers or readers who did not understand Latin, much less Greek, the liberties or misunderstandings of Old English translators with respect to the Latin text would count for little in the end as long as the Old English narrative made basic sense to the medieval hearer. Nonetheless, for present academic readers with historical perspective, much significant ideological meaning has been silenced by contextual shifts in cultural and ideological frames of reference. Translators' attempts to preserve word order correspondence, the basic rhetorical style, from Greek to Latin to Old English serves only to mask silencing of the ideological orientation of the original Greek text by diverting readers' attention toward style which itself has been uncoupled by translation from the essential moral meaning of the original text. Although the translations maintain, at least superficially, the style of the original text, the central moral, and ideological point of the Herodotus' story of the king's horse, that nemesis follows acts of hybris even in small matters, is betrayed and silenced.

Works Cited

Bakhtin, M.M. *The Dialogic Imagination*. Trans. Caryl Emerson and Michael Holquist. Austin: University of Texas Press, 1981. Print.

Bately, Janet, ed. *The Old English Orosius*. The Early English Text Society. London, New York, Toronto: Oxford University Press, 1980. Print.

Bede, *Venerablilis Baedae Opera Historica*. 2 vols. Ed. Charles Plummer. Oxford: Clarendon, 1896. Print.

Beye, Charles Rowan. *Ancient Greek Literature and Society*. Garden City, NJ and New York: Anchor Press/Doubleday, 1975. Print.

Danto, A.C. "Translation and betrayal." *Anthropology and Aesthetics* No. 32 (Autumn, 1997): 61-63. JSTOR: RES. Web. 15 Nov. 2014.

Evans, Richard. "From Greek & Latin to the *Old English Orosius*: Dialogic Contexts for Translation and Reception." Diss. U of SC, 2002. Print.

Herodotus. *Herodoti Historiae*. Ed. Carolus Hude. 3rd ed. Vol.1. Oxford Classical Texts. Oxford: Clarendon Press, 1927. Print.

Hirsch, E.D., Jr. *Validity in Interpretation*. New Haven: Yale University Press, 1967. Print.

Lefevere, André. "Introduction: Comparative Literature and Translation." *Comparative Literature* 47.1 (1995): 1-10. Print.

Lewis, Charlton and Charles Short. *A Latin Dictionary*. Oxford: Clarendon Press, 1870.

Orosius, Paulus. *Orose Histoires*. Ed. and trans. Marie-Pierre Arnaud-Lindet. 3 vols. Association Guillaume Bude. Paris: Les Belles Lettres, 1990. Print.

Whitelock, Dorothy. "The Prose of Alfred's Reign." *Continuations and Beginnings: Studies in Old English Literature*.

Ed. Eric Gerald Stanley. London: Nelson, 1966. 67-103. Print.

# Chapter 7

Hidden Agendas: Colonial Eroticism in J.M. Coetzee's *Waiting for the Barbarians*, Elizabeth Nunez's *Prospero's Daughter* and Michelle Cliff's *Abeng*

Blossom N. Fondo

British colonialism, like that of the other European powers involved besides the confiscation of other lands and the displacement of local cultures, languages and religions, the acquisition of "sexual territories" through the mostly forced and abusive sexual relations between the male colonizers and the local colonized women. This constitutes the sexual dimension of Western colonialism which has led some critics to opine that the driving force behind empire building was the export of surplus emotional or sexual energy, not the export of surplus capital (Hyam 240). Ronald Hyam, in his 1990 study, further iterates that "sexual dynamics crucially underpinned the whole operation of British Empire and Victorian expansion" (417). This practice witnessed the representatives of the colonial governments keeping mistresses and most often against the wishes of these women. Barbara L. Voss and Eleanor Conlin Casella have noted the following:

> Although archeological studies of the historic past have long explored the dynamics of European colonialism, broader issues of sexuality, embodiment, commemoration, reproduction, and sensuality have only recently become acknowledged as essential components of the "imperial project". [...]. Ranging from anticipated and pleasurable to strategic and even involuntary,

these intimate encounters are not mere by-products of colonial projects but are fundamental structures of colonization. (1)

This issue which constitutes one of the several less appetizing aspects of colonialism has nonetheless fueled the artistic imagination of several postcolonial writers as they pursue their cataloguing of the myriad abuses of colonialism.

This chapter is interested in examining this dimension of colonialism as represented in three postcolonial texts: J.M. Coetzee's *Waiting for the Barbarians* in which he presents the sexual relations between a magistrate and a Barbarian girl, Elizabeth Nunez's *Prospero's Daughter* which portrays such a relationship between Dr. Gardner and the local girl Ariana and Michelle Cliff's *Abeng* in which she gives an important place to the relationship between Judge Savage and the slave girl Inez. These relationships constitute some of the "secrets" of colonialism in the sense that colonial historians were less prepared to talk about this aspect than they were about other aspects of colonialism. Of the several abuses of colonialism, the sexual "exploits" represented an under-explored area. The sexual dimension of British colonialism was thus for a long time one of the dormant areas of colonial historiography. This was especially so because colonialism was at its peak during the Victorian period when the British claimed as a defining feature for themselves, their sexual restraint. Worth noting is also the fact that human sexuality has always been shrouded with secrecy and this probably due in part to the dynamics of intimacy involved. In a similar vein, the selected writers for this discussion do not make colonial sexuality the center of their oeuvres, but nonetheless accord it the necessary importance to indicate that it was a significant feature of colonialism. Secondly, the British colonizers had presented themselves in a morally superior light, which coincided with the presentation of the colonized as morally depraved beings with excessive and uncontrollable sexual drive. The colonial experience was also justified by the British claim that they were exporting the light of their moral propriety to the morally degenerate colonized. Getting openly involved with local women then belied this claim. Thirdly, the colonizers had in their representations of the colonized, portrayed them as less than human, Alastair Pennycock corroborates this when he writes that "a constant theme that runs through writing from the colonial era and beyond is one in which the colonies and their people were seen as dirty and diseased" (64). To therefore engage in such intimate relationships with them seriously questioned such representations.

The three authors under study graphically portray how such relationships were played out. Consequently, this paper builds upon the argument that colonialism was not just a question of land seizure, economic exploitation and cultural displacement, but that in which sexuality played an important role and this undermined the superior moral claim of the colonizer. It also expatiates on the fact that the colonial masters did find the local women sexually appealing and made the appropriate moves not only to get sexually involved with them but to also conquer their bodies as terrains for sexual gratification and pleasure. This is one of the reasons why Anne McClintock has noted that women and men did not experience colonialism in the same way, postulating that

> Colonized women, before the intrusions of imperial rule, were invariably disadvantaged within their societies in ways that gave the colonial reordering of their sexual and economic labor very different outcomes from those of colonized men. As slaves, agricultural workers, house servants, mothers, prostitutes and concubines of the far flung colonies of Europe, colonized women had to negotiate not only the imbalances of their relations with their own men but also the baroque and violent

array of hierarchical rules and restrictions that structured their new relations with imperial men and women. (6)

Given this state of affairs, the discussions herein are guided by postcolonial theory, specifically by postcolonial feminist theory which conceptualizes the unique oppression of the colonized woman. Through the engagement of this theory, it is seen that the colonized woman like the colonized man, suffered gross subjugation, oppression and humiliation from the colonizers. But beyond these, the sexual dimension of her subjugation gives an added burden to her plight whereby in addition, she is reduced to a sex object simply because she is a woman. The result of this is the loss of not only her dignity but even the ownership of her own body. Colonialism although piloted mostly by white men, nonetheless granted some measure of recognition to white women over non-white women. This implies that feminist theory as practiced in the West usually cannot critically and objectively engage with the unique position of colonized women who were mostly non-whites. The fact that whiteness was then a marker of privilege means that white women had more access to power than non-white women, prompting McClintock to posit that,

> the rationed privileges of race all too often put white women of decided – if borrowed – power, not only over colonized women but also over colonized men. As such, white women were not the hapless onlookers of empire but were ambiguously complicit both as colonizers and colonized, privileged and restricted, acted upon and acting (6).

This explains why a race – based feminism is necessary for a study like this that explores the position of the colonized woman from whose body sexual pleasures were exacted by the colonizers. For as Reina Lewis and Sara Mills have noted, postcolonial feminism is engaged in a two-fold project "to racialise[sic] mainstream feminist theory and to insert feminist concerns into conceptualisations[sic] of colonialism and postcolonialism[sic]" (3). This justifies why for any study of the sexual politics of colonialism, postcolonial feminist theory is the most appropriate reading practice.

As we have introduced above, the colonial undertaking largely involved the seizure and appropriation of the bodies of colonized women for the pleasure of the colonizer. This constitutes the secret and silenced dimension of colonialism which may be termed sexual colonialism and to which colonized women, were especially victims[1]. The bodies of these women thus became sexual landscapes upon which the European colonizer exercised his colonial phallic power. These colonizers established intimate relationships with colonized women either by coercion or "consent". Such relationships which came to the open especially through memoirs, *testimonios* and oral accounts have drawn some critical attention to this uncontestable fact of colonialism. Ronald Hyam was one of the first critics to profoundly engage with this aspect of British colonialism in his 1986 study *Empire and Sexuality*. He notes that historians of Empire have been slow to confront the place of sexuality in the imperial encounter which gap he set out to fill with his book. He further argues that sexuality must be accorded a significant position in the treatment of British colonialism. His later studies have continued to lend an important place to the role of sexuality in British imperial expansion. Ali Behdad's 1997 study of colonial eroticism in *Waiting for the Barbarians* is an important contribution to the field and this study builds upon and also extends his thesis that "the aim of colonial eroticism is to create a sense of political

---

[1] Documented sources have shown the ways boys were also victims of this. This was especially through sodomy and homosexual relations. These were usually frowned upon, whereas heterosexual relations between colonizer and colonized went generally unquestioned.

continuity by subjecting the colonized to a violent process of dissolution in which he or she is subsumed in the hegemony of Empire" (202). This is closely related to Michel Foucault's opinion that sexuality is an especially 'dense transfer point for relations of power between men and women" (103). Herein, however, it is further indicated that such sexual liaisons were not just geared towards conquest and dominance, but were significant sources of sexual gratification for these colonizers. So although in several documented cases this involved violence, for others it was the mere pleasure of sexual adventure and the opportunity to experience long-held fantasies that fueled colonial eroticism. This is not to deny the fact that for many of these colonized women, this was perceived as violence, whether the sexual relationships were clearly violent or not. Their position of powerlessness vis-à-vis the colonizing male meant that for many of them, there was no question of choice and this then places the relationships within the prism of violence.

The sexual perversity of the non-European is well established in European imagination. The West in its erection of rigid oppositional binarisms in conceptualizing its relation with non-Europeans has been able to represent itself as the morally pure against whom the sexual looseness of the non-European was defined. Thomas Greg concurs with this by underlining that "the specter of the savage, sensory nature and sexuality unchecked by 'higher civilization' defines race, racism and empire" (104) Hyam's studies mentioned above however deconstruct this self-representation by indicating that "colonial frontiers offered Europeans the possibility of transgressing their rigid sexual mores" (*Sexuality and Empire* 34). Foreign lands and peoples certainly spelt the possibility of new sexual experiences, which is why they became both exciting and monstrous for the European imagination. (Ania Loomba 127). Loomba has further noted that "For most European travelers and colonialists, however, the promise of sexual pleasure rested on the assumption that the darker races or non-Europeans were immoral, promiscuous, libidinous and always desired white people" (158). Such a mindset although intending to portray the non-Europeans in a negative sexually debased light, also ironically portrays the Europeans in this same light precisely because they were in part drawn to the colonies by thoughts of gratifying their libidinal instincts which belied their acclaimed sexual restraint and purity. The sexual restraint was rather a repression of innate sexual urges due to the firm societal norms, which once in the colonies were given free reign. It is this attitude towards sexuality that gave the Victorian period in England its hypocritical tendency.

The authors chosen for this study do not necessarily make these erotic relations the main focus of their work but by throwing them in, they reveal them as a significant part of empire. In fact the recurrence of such erotic relationships in postcolonial fiction shows that they were not merely an important but an inescapable element of the colonial encounter. The colonial contact zone was not just one of cultural and racial encounters but also of sexual encounters. In the selected texts for this study, the authors do not clearly make such sexual encounters the main thrust of their plots, but the reader doubtlessly gets a glimpse into this facet of empire by reading through these novels. These sexual encounters contribute significantly to the plots of the narratives and as such can only attract the reader's attention.

Waiting for the Barbarians, one of Coetzee's earlier novels allegorically presents Apartheid in South Africa shows the ways the colonizers perceived their difference from the colonized as a marker of their superiority and as an excuse for subjugation. The novel captures the colonial paranoia which is manifested in the person of colonel Joll who considering these colonized as Barbarians, continuously holds that they are planning an attack on the colonizers. This serves as reason for the brutal torture of these colonized who have been pushed to the periphery of their lands. At the side of this tale of torture and colonialist misrepresentation is imbedded the sexual exploitation of the Barbarian girl by the Magistrate.

In Coetzee's text, he closely presents the relationship between the magistrate and the Barbarian girl. Before this, Coetzee lets it be known that the magistrate is a representative of colonial authority, outlining his activities without mentioning the sexual dimension of these. He states:

> I am a country magistrate, a responsible official in the service of Empire, serving out my days on this lazy frontier, waiting to retire. I collect the tithes and taxes, administer the communal lands, see that the garrison is provided for, supervise the junior officers who are the only officers we have here, keep an eye on trade, preside over the law-court twice a week. For the rest, I watch the sun rise and set, eat and sleep and am content. (8)

This omission of the sexual dimension of his activities in the colonial outpost constitutes a silence which rather serves to draw attention to itself because his actions thereafter fill this gap. So, what the above passage reveals is the fact that the magistrate is a colonizer in this outpost, but what it does not present is that he also preys on the femaleness of the local women, but this soon comes to light. When the visiting Colonel Joll orders the arrests of several Barbarians for questioning, a Barbarian girl who has been rendered blind and lame by the torture is left behind after their interrogation. The magistrate asks that she be brought to him for questioning, and after threatening to expel her for illegally begging in town, he eventually offers her work and lodging in his house. This marks the beginning of an erotic relationship with her. This is exposed when he relates the kind of pleasure he gets from washing the girl's feet and eventually her entire body: "I begin to wash her. She raises her feet for me in turn. I knead and massage the lax toes through the soft milky soap. Soon my eyes close, my head droops. It is rapture, of a kind" (29). This metamorphoses into a more intimate relationship:

> First comes the ritual of the washing, for which she is now naked. I wash her feet, as before, her legs, her buttocks. My soapy hand travels between her thighs, incuriously, I find. She raises her arms while I wash her armpits. I wash her belly, her breasts. […]. I feed her, shelter her, use her body […]. There used to be moments when she stiffened at certain intimacies; but now her body yields when I nuzzle my face into her belly or clasp her feet between my thighs. She yields to everything. (30)

The magistrate has insidiously conquered the body of this local girl who he claims to have rescued. Her body subsequently becomes a source of constant pleasure to the magistrate, defined by his use of the word "rapture"- which carries undertones of ecstasy and in this case sexual ecstasy- to describe the feelings he had in his intimate dealings with her. The phrase "use her body" connotes the sexual service which the Barbarian girl is made to offer. Just like the colonizers captured and exploited territories for their political and economic benefits, so too does the magistrate capture this girl's body for his sexual gratification. So, although he does not explicitly indicate his sexual ventures as part of his activity in the colony, it has nonetheless been revealed through his description of what goes on between him and the so-called barbarian girl. Ali Behdad notes that "the washing of the tortured body is thematized as erotic, as the magistrate becomes engulfed in the pleasure of ablution. The body of the colonized provides the benevolent colonizer with the erotic vehicle for achieving the state of dissolution" (205).

He claims to have "relieved her of the shame of begging and installed her in the barracks of the kitchen as a scullery-maid" (32). Yet, she is more of an object of sexual pleasure; her existence has not become more dignified by her migration from the streets to the barracks. As the soldiers note, the kitchen maids are usually made to serve the sexual needs of the magistrate, hence the adage in the barracks "from the kitchen to the magistrate's bed in sixteen easy steps" (32), and these gossips are a source of irritation to the magistrate who feels that they impinge on private affairs. Although the author gives the relationship between the magistrate and the girl the most detail in the novel, he nonetheless reveals that he engages in such relationships with many other local girls. It is said for example that the other kitchen maid "ascended the sixteen stairs once or twice last years" (32). Given the magistrate's position of power, he is able to exercise control over the bodies of these local girls. Being a colonizer, he colonizes their bodies and makes them available to serve his needs whenever they arise. Thus the daily routine of this barbarian girl involves catering for among many others, the erotic impulse of the magistrate. Her activities are outlined as follows:

> In the morning after I have left, she comes to sweep and dust the apartment. Then she helps in the kitchen with the midday meal. Her afternoons are mainly her own. After the evening meal, after all the pots and pans have been scoured, the floor washed, the fire damped, she leaves her fellows and picks her way up the stairs to me. She undresses and lies down, waiting for my inexplicable attentions. (33)

This paints a life and body resigned to serving the colonial master. She has become more or less the property of the colonizer and consequently her body is dedicated to providing erotic pleasure, and she seems completely helpless to free herself from these shackles of colonial erotic desire. In one of her conversations with the magistrate, he asks her why she is with him and she replies resignedly "because there is nowhere else to go" (40). This illustrates her dilemma as a colonized female. Her people so-named barbarians by the colonizers are under constant siege from these intruders who capture and torture them violently. Her blindness and lameness are all caused by such colonial ferocity and added to this is her sexual subjugation. The magistrate does not seek to know if this erotic relationship is acceptable to her. From his colonial and patriarchal positions of power, he makes her available to serve his sexual needs.

But even while he used the body of the Barbarian girl to attenuate his sexual desires, he experiences bouts of ambivalence expressed in his ponderings on what draws him to what he terms her "alien body", yet he continues his trysts with her. His sexual dealings with her are tantamount to an exercise of power over her body. It therefore is only apt when he compares lying in bed with her and beating her up: "the girl lies in my bed, but there is no good reason why it should be a bed, I bathe her, I stroke her, I sleep beside her – but I might equally well tie her to a chair and beat her it would be no less intimate" (43). Thus both the eroticism and the imagined beating constitute important elements of colonial power. In this relationship, the magistrate constantly wonders about the lack of desire, especially from the girl and he asks in frustration "what do I have to do to move you?" (44). He however provides the answer himself when he comes to the realization that for this Barbarian girl, he and those who physically tortured and maimed her, must be one and the same. They all misuse her body, doing with it as they please. They claim unreserved ownership of her body and as such, she can experience little excitement in her erotic affairs with the magistrate. Although the magistrate holds that "there is nothing to link me with tortures", he fails to recognize that by representing the colonial powers that sanction such tortures, even if he does not execute them, he is seen as complicit. Besides, his appropriation of the femaleness of the colonized woman for his sexual pleasure is an act of torture not so dissimilar to the other forms of torture. Such sexual adventures became a defining aspect of colonialism, such that the magistrate reports that "if there was anything to be envied in a posting to the frontiers, my friends told me, it was the easy morals of the oases, the long-scented summer-evenings, the compliant sloe-eyed women" (45). Although the British in their self-presentation as the torch-bearers of moral rightness (which they were bent on exporting to their colonies), their acclaimed sexual restraint merely constituted another face of the hypocrisy of empire.

While the British very easily affirm the political and economic benefits of colonialism, the sexual domain is one area that has been understandably shrouded in secrecy, yet eroticism was an important part of colonial activity. Postcolonial fiction in its fictionalized presentation of the several abuses of colonialism has tended to address this important facet which many historians, especially colonial historians overlooked. This explains why in the magistrate's initial outline of his activities, he omits his erotic excursions, yet in the account of his life in the colony, these sexual adventures with local women occupy an important place. From the time he arrives the colony to the end of the story when he has considerably aged, the story of his life in the colony is also a story of multiple erotic adventures with local women. This only goes to confirm Hyam's assertion that "the expansion of Europe was not only a matter of 'Christianity and commerce', it was also a matter of copulation and concubinage. Sexual opportunities were seized with imperious confidence" (364). Such seizure of sexual opportunities was not always consensual but sometimes involved the use of brute force and rape. Such is the situation portrayed by Michelle Cliff in her novel *Abeng*.

Cliff's novel apparently traces the growth and education of its protagonist Clare Savage under the influence of colonialism. This has led critics to read the novel as a postcolonial variant of the bildungsroman. However, in one of the several allusions she employs in the narrative, she reveals that beyond the displacement and domination that characterized colonialism was also the sexual exploitation of the colonized woman. She suffuses her narrative with a sub-text that captures the story of Justice Savage and Inez the slave girl who is forced into becoming his mistress. Through this "side-story", Cliff highlights the sexual aspect of colonialism. The manner in which Cliff buries this story into the main narrative draws attention to it and indicates that sexuality was central to the colonial venture.

Cliff introduces this theme by stating: "Inez, the woman the justice had taken to be his mistress was bronze" (33). Her being bronze indicates that she is a local woman and the phrase "had taken" shows that theirs was not a consensual relationship but one determined and imposed on her by the justice. This is soon unveiled when Cliff recounts how Inez came to be Justice Savage's mistress. It is revealed that he had met her in court when she was brought before him on wrongful charges of the theft of a rifle and some ammunition from the Selby Plantation. For these charges, Inez would have had her hands cut off or been given a hundred strokes of the cat, "but the judge intervened and took her home, where he raped her. He raped her for six weeks until he left for one of his trips to London. She was eighteen" (34). The idea of rape, shows how the justice is brutally and inhumanly seizing sexual opportunity. Inez's body is forced to give pleasure to Justice

Savage. Just as the colonizers plundered the lands of the colonized, so too does the justice's rape of Inez carry undertones of conquest, betrayal and plundering. He sees in Inez a sexual opportunity to be seized. So, inasmuch as economic exploitation has become the defining aspect of colonialism, it is seen that sexual exploitation constituted a significant aspect of it, even if it was not usually brought out in the open. Inez as a conquered and enslaved giver of pleasure is reported to have survived two years of sexual exploitation "by planning her escape, waiting for emancipation, devising a way to avenge herself – all of these things" (39). It is because she is an unwilling participant in this relationship that she so carefully and patiently hatches a hitch-free escape. On the day she escapes, the Justice returns and moves from hut to hut on his plantation in search of her. This feverish search indicates the extent of the sexual pleasure he exacted from her. Also, it intimates on the Justice's concern for being betrayed by his source of sexual pleasure. So, even though he disparagingly refers to her as "my nigger wench", his apparently uncontrollable desire for her means that nigger wench that she is, she is desirable and able to not only arouse him sexually, but also to erotically satisfy him such that he fears betrayal and would want to have her as a permanent mistress against her wish. In this regard, Moira Ferguson, citing Frances Lanaghan, observes that 'slaves and free black females were often expected to become the mistresses of white men", or, in West Indian terminology, *housekeeper*" (40/41). This forced sexual relation exemplifies the ways in which the colonized, believing in their power to dominate, arbitrarily claimed the bodies of the colonized women. Stephen Garton has noted that "sex was both a signifier and a practice for asserting dominion over other peoples" (130). The Justice therefore asserts his dominion over Inez through forced sex. Through the forceful taking of her body alone, he manifests the extent of the power he has over her. The fact that she cannot even exercise ownership over her very body but is forcefully made available for colonial sexual consumption shows how powerless she and several other colonized women were in the face of European colonization. Behdad has intimated that

> The domain of colonial eroticism, to borrow Bataille's definition, is always the domain of violence and violation – the latter to be understood here in the French sense of "rape". The colonizer must always assume the position of the sacrificer, forcing his victim into anerotics of dissolution that involves ultimately the violation of her self-containment, her discontinuity – always by piercing. (206)

In *Abeng*, Inez stands for all the colonized women of Jamaica whose bodies had been violated by the European colonizers. This explains why Cliff writes that "the grandmothers of these people sitting in a church on a Sunday evening during mango season, had been violated again and again by the very men who whipped them" (19). So, sexual intimacies constituted a natural part of colonialism with women making up the bulk of the victims. Colonial power and sexuality are therefore intricately interwoven as illustrated in *Abeng* especially through the practice of forced 'concubinage' and rape. The forced concubinage here does not only symbolize the power and domination of the Justice over Inez as a colonized woman, but equally point to the fact that he gets sexual pleasure from her. So, whereas, power and dominance could be exercised more efficiently through other means like mental enslavement and the use of physical force, they were few available means for sexual gratification than by these dominated women who could be made to give what the colonizers needed. It is as a result of this that Pennycock concurs that "sexual relationships were a significant part of colonialism" (63). Some of these relationships articulated through rape underline an important abuse of colonialism, such that Greg intimates that for the European, "the colonies are supposed to be a site of complete sexual savagery" (104).

Elizabeth Nunez's powerful postcolonial reworking of Shakespeare's *The Tempest, Prospero's Daughter* focuses mainly on Dr. Gardner's false accusation of Carlos of having attempted to rape his daughter Virginia. The main plot is the investigation of Gardner's allegations. It is in the course of this investigation that it is revealed that Dr. Gardner has been involved in an abusive sexual relation with Ariana the servant girl from when she was nine. Gardner's displacement of Carlos from his house which he goes ahead to take over, captures the political domination, physical and cultural displacement that were defining features of colonialism. But underneath this colonial domination is hidden the story of colonial eroticism. Thus the colonial outpost served not only political and economic purposes, but sexual or erotic ones as well.

Such eroticism is captured in this text. This is first introduced when she gives the reader the idea that there is an erotic liaison between Dr. Gardner the British fugitive in Trinidad (whose actions nonetheless mark him as symbolic of the colonizers) and his servant girl Ariana. When Inspector Mumsford comes calling on Gardner's alleged attempted rape by Carlos of his daughter Virginia, it is said that "Mumsford had knocked on the door, and when there was no answer he had peered through the window. He was certain he had seen a naked woman dashing across the drawing room" (35). This naked woman is later revealed to be Ariana, his servant. Eventually when Ariana is being questioned at the police station she reveals with much bitterness that she hates Gardner because "he take advantage of me" (94). A little more probing reveals even more salacious details to the effect that Gardner had begun sexually abusing her when she was only nine.

Through this interview, Nunez unfolds a macabre tale of blackmail, treachery and gross sexual exploitation of Ariana by Gardner. Ariana details how Gardner's fondling mutated into sexual relations: "he do little bit at first. He don't do everything. But he start for real when Miss Virginia turn woman" (96). Through the exchange with the police, it is further revealed that to keep her silent and continuously give in to his sexual demands, Gardner had been blackmailing Ariana. Sylvia Codrington, Ariana's mother's employer had caught Ariana as a child wearing her clothes and Ariana had also stolen her diamonds. Sylvia had written and hidden a letter about this with threats to hand it to the police should Ariana ever wear her clothes again. After Ariana's mother dies and Dr. Gardner takes over the house, he finds this letter and uses it to blackmail Ariana into having sex with him, otherwise he would give it to the police. She recollects:

> In the night when everybody sleeping, he come on top of me with his thing. He say if I tell anybody he touch me, he show the police the letter. Every lunchtime he make me come in his room and Miss Virginia and Carlos think is message he giving me. And when my mother still living, is true is message he giving me. He telling me what to cook and how he like me to cook it. He treat me nice, nice, nice. He pretend he watching out for me and he like me. I believe him. Then my mother die. He bring me in his room after that. (98)

Ariana's tale is one of great pain, betrayal, blackmail, loss and suffering. Deprived of her childhood innocence at an incredibly young age, she spends her growing up years as the sex slave of Dr. Gardner, attending to his every sexual need. Although an unwilling participant, she seemingly gives herself to him generously in the hopes that he would not betray her to the police and would eventually love her enough to give her

her freedom. Dr. Gardner's sexual exploitation of Ariana cannot therefore be read only as a means of racial and/or colonial subjugation; although it also amounts to that. He must also be seen as deriving sensual delight and fulfilment from this relation. Gardner constitutes one of the sexually frustrated British colonists for whom the colonial outposts constituted a source of sexual pleasure.

In the above discussions, it has been seen that although grossly under-represented in discussions of colonialism, British colonialism was largely characterized by gendered violence. We have seen the ways in which the question of colonial eroticism constituted hidden agendas both for the colonizers as well as for the postcolonial writers. The colonizers were not drawn to the colonies simply by political and economic ambition, but also by sexual opportunities which resulted in the appropriation and violation of the body of the woman. This thus constitutes the hidden agenda of colonialism as few of these colonizers were ready to confess to this dimension of their colonial ventures. They made secrets of these and kept silent about probably not to betray the hidden agenda, Similarly, postcolonial writers make exposing this aspect of the colonial hidden agenda, the cornerstone of their writings. While apparently focusing on the well-known elements of colonialism, they nevertheless infuse their tales with the sexual aspect of colonialism. This can also be read as the hidden agenda of the postcolonial writer who couches his/her narrative thrust in a sub-text of voicing and exposing carefully kept secrets of betrayals. These writers show that sexuality constituted the unspoken and secret driving force of colonialism. They draw attention to this by ironically not making it the center of their narrative. It rather comes across as a kind of detour from the main narrative which leads the reader to question the apparent digression and consequently exposes this important facet of colonialism. It is therefore the task of the reader to decipher this element of colonialism from the sub-texts, detours, side-tales or allusions. The authors tactfully and artfully expose this precisely by couching it at the seeming margins of the main narrative. Since literary analysis and criticism involves close reading, leading to the deciphering of the author's meaning through style, readings of these texts, in the quest for both the surface and deeper meanings will invariably lead to an understanding of these issues. The reader is thus led to the understanding that eroticism occupied an important place in the colonial agenda. Thus colonialism, drummed up and even sugar coated as a *mission civilisatrice*, was not only a matter of political and economic exploitation. Sexual adventure also constituted an important part of it and served both as a weapon of subjugation as well as an opportunity for sexual indulgence.

Besides the annexation of physical territories, the arrogation of female bodies for sexual gratification made sexual colonies out of the colonized woman. The colonized woman's body became a terrain on which was played out the sexual politics of the empire. This sexual domination coupled with her political and economic disenfranchisement is what has rendered her doubly colonized and constitutes the unique position of postcolonial feminism which has guided the foregone discussions.

Works Cited

Cliff, Michelle. *Abeng*. New York: Plume. 1984. Print.
Coetzee, J.M. *Waiting for the Barbarians: A Novel*. New York: Penguin Books. 1980. Print.
Ferguson, Moira. *Colonialism and Gender Relations from Mary Wollstonecraft to Jamaica Kincaid: East Caribbean Connections*. New York: Columbia UP. 1993. Print.

Foucault, Michel. *The History of Sexuality Volume 1: An Introduction.*(Trans. Robert Hurley). New York: Pantheon Books. 1978. Print.

Garton, Stephen. *Histories of Sexuality: Antiquity to Sexual Revolution.* London and New York: Routledge. 2004. Print.

Greg, Thomas. *The Sexual Demon of Colonial Power: Pan-African Embodiment and Erotic Schemes of Empire.* Bloomington and Indianapolis: Indiana UP. 2007. Print.

Hyam, Ronald. *Understanding the British Empire*: Cambridge: CUP. 2010. Print.

Hyam, Ronald. *Empire and Sexuality: The British Experience.* Manchester: MUP. 1990. Print.

Lewis, Reina and Sara Mills. *Feminist Postcolonial Theory: A Reader.* New York: Routledge. 2003. Print.

Loomba, Ania. *Colonialism/Postcolonialism.* London: Routledge. 1998. Print.

McClintock, Anne. *Imperial Leather: Race, Gender and Sexuality in the Colonial Contest.* New York and Oxen: Routledge. 1995. Print.

Nunez, Elizabeth. *Prospero's Daughter.* New York: Ballantine Books. 2006. Print.

Thomas, Greg. *The Sexual Demon of Colonial Power: Pan-African Embodiment and Erotic Schemes of Empire.* Bloomington: Indiana UP. 2007. Print.

Voss, Barbara L. and Eleanor Conlin Casella (eds.). *The Archeology of Colonialism: Intimate Encounters and Sexual Effects.* Cambridge: CUP. 2012. Print.

Chapter 8

Chaos, Concealment, and Duress in Human Relationships in the Mimboland of Francis B. Nyamnjoh's *Married but Available*

Benjamin Hart Fishkin

In 1702, before he had written such famous novels as *Memoirs of a Cavalier*, *Moll Flanders*, and *Robinson Crusoe*, Daniel Defoe was betrayed by an informer and delivered to prison for a large reward. This secret, silent gruesome violation was not buried in a book; it was the causation for books and it nearly buried him. This idea relates to Francis B. Nyamnjoh's *Married but Available* where relationships are not harmonious. They are complex, they difficult, they are unstable and they are populated by irresponsible and unreliable men and women.

The satire Defoe presented in *The Shortest Way With Dissenters* was, like that of Jonathan Swift, Mark Twain, Alexander Pope and Voltaire, too good. It was too sharp, too effective, too witty and (above all else) too embarrassing a treatise on a subject that no one wanted to publicly discuss. Herein is the power of the secret on the human psyche. It is devastating. The person who is aware of a secret suffers inwardly. The person who drags it out into the light is an instant public target. It is as a result of Defoe's bright and observant criticisms that his was labeled unfaithful, disloyal, and subversive. The Queen did not mince words in her indictment of Defoe which read:

> ...being a Seditious man and of a disordered mind, and a person of bad name, reputation and Conversation, by a disgraceful felony perfidiously, mischievously and seditiously contriving, practicing and

purposing to make and Cause discord between…the Queen and her…Subjects…. (qtd. in Backsheider 104)

A naïve student just starting out would think that a novelist bent on social and economic development would be a welcome figure. This was not necessarily the case. Defoe's attempt to flex his intellectual muscles resulted in pushback. The above rhetoric is very revealing. It is the consequence of taking "street knowledge", in all of its strength, and forcefully displaying it, sparkling, for the world to see. When a secret is disinterred, and examined, we get exaggeration, contrivance, shame and bombast. The recipient shakes, stammers, and hesitates. In a moment of excitement, confusion and spasmodic repetition we get inarticulateness. The previously well-spoken jailor, who must use language to persuade and influence, becomes an incoherent mess—just like the English government under Queen Anne.

Human nature, despite more than four hundred years of history between Defoe's hurt and pain and the present, has made little progress. This is unfortunate because once secrecy is understood, why it is there and how to avoid it, its nets become easy to elude. The way people twist themselves into knots and feel compelled to maneuver and manipulate falls away once they realize that "covering one's tracks" in order to cheat and deceive requires an enormous amount of energy. Nowhere is this outflow of psychological capital more palpable or more nerve-wracking than when it comes to the issue(s) of infidelity, love affairs and faded relationships.

While presenting this term with a slightly different emphasis, authors Clive Hamilton and Richard Denniss surely have a lot to say about the connections and relationships between romantic and sexual partners. This condition, which the authors' term "intermittent husband syndrome", has the ability to travel and this can be seen in Francis B. Nyamnjoh's *Married but Available* (Hamilton and Denniss 91). The extended absence of a partner that is male creates "…higher levels of anxiety, stress and depression…" in his betrothed (Hamilton and Denniss 91). The need to part, reunite, quarrel and negotiate creates a living space that is unstable, unhealthy and expensive (if the couple splits). *Married but Available* looks at the economics of relationships and the secrets that are necessary to keep all of the necessary breakable moving parts in the air. Almost always they are torn asunder. Mrs. Lovemore, her first name is not revealed, tells us of a woman named Nicole who is married to a Mimbolander. She is from Muzunguland in this cross-cultural marriage. After having three kids with her, he decides to take a second wife. "Her husband would go so far as to sleep with his second wife and then show up in his first wife's bedroom" (Nyamnjoh 222). When she inquires as to what he wants he unhesitantly replies "Desert" (Nyamnjoh 222). This is how the broken pieces of yesterday's life hit the ground. What an avoidable mess! In an environment which takes the literary realism of the nineteenth century and gives it a brand new name we are privy to the clumsy, klutzy and ill thought out ways in which people mismanage their affairs. They take their problems, voluntarily create new ones, and then attempt to sweep the entire confusion beneath the carpet.

Like children playing a game of hide and seek, the adults in Nyamnjoh's Mimboland are engaged in a perpetual contest to see who can obtain and discard lovers faster than anyone else. The result is a complicated, costly and comical mess. The secrets in this fictional Cameroon, which are never ultimately concealed, are tricks and schemes that have no regard for loving and tender relationships. There is no long-term planning and this problem, and its ensuing chaos, has far reaching implications for African society. At once, without any warning, what at first seems to be harmless fun—with a "nudge" and a "wink" similar to *Monty Python's Flying Circus* of the late sixties and early seventies or the slap and tickle of Geoffrey Chaucer nearly seven centuries ago —quickly becomes more than merely a series of risqué allusions. *Married but Available* is a deft treatment of what the author discerns to be a far a greater problem. The Mimbolanders who lie and cheat on their partners serve as a literary microcosm for a government and public service that subsists on graft, greed and corruption. Secrets, silences and betrayals exact an imperceptible psychological cost that no one is exempt from paying.

No one escapes the consequences of infidelity and Nyamnjoh highlights this with a signpost displayed at the entrance of the club: "Lillies of the Valleys, a tropical paradise situated outside of Puttkamerstown..." The signpost reads "Hitch a colourful[sic] ride through the Garden of Eden with or without Eve" (167). When Francis B. Nyamnjoh's main character finds herself staring at this sign, roughly halfway into *Married but Available*, it is clear that this book is not a grandfather's travelogue. The scenery appears in no AAA guide, but is rather the tight provocative skin of the drinkers and would be socialites who buzz around a beach community where everyone wears as little as possible. This is a sign that encourages guests to live a little and it rests just above the entrance of Lillies of the Valley, a discreet establishment where people "...flood in for their lunchtime quickies and snacks" (Nyamnjoh 168). Lovely flowers are present, poinsettias and peonies of every shade of pink, yellow and purple surround the establishment. Nowhere, just as there are no clocks in casinos, is there a sign that indicates the consequences and the messiness that will surely follow. People in Mimboland, and elsewhere, seem to be in a footrace to see who will yield first to temptation. No one hesitates.

As Lilly Loveless, a graduate student of Social Geography, sits in this upscale bar and talks about sex, power and the things it can buy with her research assistant, Britney, the two look like patrons enjoying the colors and smells of the flora. The tropical birds are singing and the attractive young women each have a cold drink before them. Anyone in Puttkamerstown would think that they are two business associates taking a long lunch. Nothing could be farther from the truth. They are in search of other people's secrets. No one knows their sly and surreptitious purpose. They are there, like broadcasters before a heavyweight-boxing bout, to observe and analyze the sweet science. Lilly and Britney are there to work, their eyes precise and their nostrils focused with bated breath (Nyamnjoh 168). This is part of their academic study; to observe, under the cover of camouflage, the interaction between "…sugar daddies and sweat mamas…" (Nyamnjoh 14). The sex farce of *The Canterbury Tales* is now grist for the academic mill.

Nyamnjoh speaks critically, or some would say realistically, about companionship. However, he does it with humor. The style so light and so entertaining that it threatens to float off the page. It is easy to miss the subtext— relationships are unhealthy. People get into them to see what they can get out of them. It is an exchange of goods and services in the most crass, commercial and material sense. Just as Corporate Inversion is a method of reducing a tax burden by changing a company's domicile, for example the Walgreen Company chain of drugstores based in Deerfield, IL is right now rumored to be "moving" to Switzerland for tax purposes, Nyamnjoh calls any sexually charged relationship between a man and a woman (or any other gender combination) an "extractive industry" (Nyamnjoh 386). This is part of the secret, the façade, the pretense, the lie, the sleight of hand or any other synonym you would like to choose for an action that is not forthright. As the behavior changes the academic science that reports upon it must change as well to keep pace with the times. Lilly Loveless of Muzunguland delves into categories that are brand new to anthropology and ethnology. Into the debate enters "concubine syndrome" where the male in the relationship clumsily begins to see another in what the author calls a hide and seek relationship (Nyamnjoh 169). Undoubtedly this is a reference to Robert Louis Stevenson's *The Strange Case of Dr. Jekyll and Mr. Hyde*. The two alleged partners, the secret being secret no more, descend into volcanic rage plotting, scheming and being successful only at making one another miserable. The idea is to outmaneuver the other. At one time it was the opposite. This is the bitter truth that Nyamnjoh wants everyone to see. The novel is part klieg light and part a forensic pathologist's microscope.

When a couple argues, and the title *Married but Available* leaves about as little to the imagination as a French bathing suit in regard to what they are arguing about, we get an embarrassing confusion much like Defoe's battle with the Crown. A disordered condition seeps from the carouser to the government or perhaps it is the other way round where people see crooked policeman, tax collectors and administrators and rationalize why they should uphold the (moral) law when the law never works to their benefit. Why not have secrets when there is no one to protect one's own personal territory from encroachment? By keeping things hidden, the thought process changes for the worse. It could be plausibly posited that people do not realize what they are doing as they are doing it. People erect fences, just like the alleged purveyor of thinking, the university, spends money to put up a fence around a campus that has no books in the library. The University of Mimbo lacks the basics, even toilets; the local cathedral in Nyamnjoh's companion novel *Mind Searching* has no roof. This is a way of telling people, as Stephen Blackpool does in Charles Dickens' 1854 novel *Hard Times*, that something is wrong. 'Now, a' God's name…show me the law to help me!' (Dickens 74) Not only do people in Nyamnjoh's Mimboland need to learn how to make love safely they need a collective therapist to point out that the psychological cost of doing it haphazardly, I would argue, exceeds by far, the physical one.

A concubine, although you won't find her name in the yellow pages, is a proponent of a consumerist product. This is a business arrangement with all of the sentiment and emotional heft of paying one's power bill or going to the post office to mail a letter to South Dakota. Such sentiments are irrevocably linked to overconsumption or the need to buy things that are not needed. The concubine is a transaction. Why shouldn't Mr. George, the man Lilly and Britney contemplate at Lillies of the Valley, feel good if he has the wherewithal to pay for it? The fact that he and Mrs. George have lived together for more than fifteen years and have made a commitment to each other has flown out the window like one of the parrots, finches or toucans that flutters about the tropical resting place. In a wonderful remark on biology, the male parrot is nearly always more colorful in appearance than the female. Scientists call this sexual dimorphism—a colorful difference in ornamentation on the part of the male plays a role in the mating game. The money in Mr. George's cigarette case, wallet or billfold is his plumage.

Economics is more important than family structure. Relationships, like the one between Mr. and Mrs. George, are dictated by opportunity. The casualty is the stable two-parent home and this is a Western societal trend that is now, for the very first time, being exported overseas to influence Cameroonian i.e. Mimboland culture. Nyamnjoh not only sees this transformation that places relationships within the context of the marketplace, but also examines the structure of the colonialism that produces it. The French social scientist Pierre Bourdieu tells us how capital on one continent is appropriated by power brokers on another. He writes,

> When all that has been said, one still needs to rethink the question of the status of the foreigner in modern democracies, in other words of the frontiers which can legitimately be imposed on the movement of persons which, like our own, derive so much advantage from the circulation of persons and goods. (17)

In other words, how can France continue to exert her self-interest on a separate entity that has been independent since 1960? It does so by encouraging the Cameroonian to be part of a community—of a culture-- where he/she is not genuinely wanted.

Some birds, however colorful, are not meant to be caged. Bourdieu's "status of the foreigner" grapples with this schizophrenic xenophobia (17). On the one hand the French do not find foreigners to be terribly appealing. I am purposely choosing my words carefully; some would say they are downright hostile. On the other hand the French surely understand that a relationship with *these* foreigners can be extremely profitable. Therein lies the rub. The Cameroonian is indeed trapped in some sort of metaphorical no-man's-land. Whereas the finch requires a physical cage the Cameroonian rests in one not made of stainless steel and acrylic. It is a translucent cage, a secret cage, an obeyed cage that lets one exist, but only within certain parameters. The buyer can pretend to be French, but not truly be French. Once one understands this little bit of playacting it is a small and easy step to see how couples can pretend to be in love, but not truly be in love.

The desire to appear falsely and the need to deceive power *Married but Available.* Instead of a bittersweet novel of loved ones forsaken, we have a well-researched anthropological study of social mobility where no one is loved. The word Lilly Loveless uses for the sort of behavior she sees before her is "ingratitude", but I call it a form of calculation in which every step is planned not for consolation but for compensation (171). A man who works every day at the palm plantation in Puttkamerstown is able to live a reasonably satisfying life with his wife and six children. All of a sudden, through no fault of his own, his job ends "…because of impending privatisation[sic]" (Nyamnjoh 255). Now that he is no longer the income provider or "breadwinner", the wife moves out of the marital bedroom and the male is marginalized to the point where not only is he experiencing privatization at work but he is sleeping in private at home (Nyamnjoh 256). There is something deep about this. More is at play here than the plight of an unemployed palm plantation worker. It says something about Africa's economic growth in general and Cameroon's in particular. Privatization is a form of what Dow Jones publications call "Structural Adjustment Programs". Such programs reference the International Monetary Fund and the World Bank. In a book review in the *Wall Street Journal,* Richard Dowden sums up this process.

The continent was essentially handed over to the World Bank and the IMF. They imposed "structural adjustment programmes[sic]." African governments were forced to slash health, education and infrastructure budgets (laying off a generation of employees) and float their currencies in the belief that less government and more open markets would attract investment. But African currencies sank like rocks in the 1990s, and millions of people were impoverished. Aid halved as the European Union and the United States instead poured support into Eastern Europe. (Dowden in *Wall Street Journal* April 20, 2012. Web. Edition.)

At the core of these "arrangements" is currency and everyone, at every level, is out for something (Nyamnjoh 256). This is an element that comes from afar. Extreme materialism is an import from the West. Appearance and reality become antinomic because this is not the way relations between men and women are supposed to be. But it is the way relations between men and women are. All of the players lead double lives. There is no instantaneous appreciation. Just like the International Monetary Fund, high and often hidden interest rates culminate in ultimate recession. There is no harmony beneath a carefully constructed facade. There is no gratitude, or at least any lasting gratitude, hence the title *Married but Available*. What's more, and this is the subtext that Francis B. Nyamnjoh does not even have to write down, there is no stability in a world where everyone is susceptible to a higher or the highest bidder.

Mimboland is an unbalanced society with dubious contradictions. If the society were a single person that person would have a controversial psychiatric disorder. Key points are withheld and the kettle simmers. What is revealed is how savage relationships are. The world, if you look at it dead on and let the scales fall from your eyes, is not civilized. Its people are not kind. Their emotions rise and fall dramatically and they do not always act in their own best interest. One of Lilly Loveless' "patients" tells us "I have nine sisters, six brothers and three mothers…" (Nyamnjoh 208). So many family members complicate the matter. All of them have to eat. There are nineteen of them. No wonder the people are under pressure. The individual, understandably, is unnerved about the fray that he/she is in. This quickly leads to the secrets, lies and shenanigans without which human understanding is incomplete.

Perhaps this is the way it has always been. Francis B. Nyamnjoh may not have uncovered something that is new, but he has discovered and invented a fun way to talk about it. Colonialism takes the financial pressure that is already there and raises the temperature considerably. The African sees cute western cell phones, designer clothing and sleek sports cars and wants them. This has not always been the case. What is also an outlier or an aberration is not so much that sex plays a role in this material exchange, but that this role is increasingly a technological one. Broadband connections, cybercafés, webcams, Skype and Western Union have replaced chocolates, flowers and emerald earrings (Nyamnjoh 209). All of these mechanisms give rise to aliases, tricks and trapdoors. Instead of people falling in love across a crowded bar room we see facades, manipulations, ploys and counterintelligence. Often times across racial lines. No wonder Cameroon needs a shrink. There are no answers. All we have is a narrator and a receptionist at the Mountain View Hotel to explain to us the behavior of people who are psychologically stripped down to their most basic parts.

You wouldn't know it by looking at their escapades but the people who populate Nyamnjoh's sub-Saharan Africa in *Married but Available* are all afraid of intimacy. They talk about taking the time to get to know someone, to truly know someone, but they don't seem to mean it. Beneath a paper-thin veneer of nonchalance is a frightened and scared hoi polloi. The people are vulnerable and do not have the faintest idea of how to order, solve and manage the things that bother them. This is a dreadful arrangement and it carries over to their kids. The Mimbolanders of Lilly Loveless' field study live what Henry David Thoreau calls "lives of quiet desperation" yet even that term is deceptive and betrays the actual truth (*Walden*, Chapter One). They are not quiet, but they are quiet about the true quality of experience they would like us to believe they have well in hand. Instead, from a transcendentalist point of view, we have people who have failed to make the leap and fit Henry David Thoreau's stereotypical portraiture of the games and amusement of mankind when he draws attention that:

> What is called resignation is confirmed desperation. From the desperate city you go into the desperate country, and have to console yourself with the bravery of minks and muskrats. A stereotyped but unconscious despair is concealed even under what are called the games and amusements of mankind (Thoreau qtd. in Parker 1810).

Here we have only amusements. The novel is an artist's sketch in pretending. It is playacting with actors who are too careful to maintain an arm's length distance. One would think that all of the *dramatis personae* have the psychological equivalent of the Ebola virus which has created an epidemic in Sierra Leone, Guinea and Liberia. Nyamnjoh tells the reader that "Secrets are always safer in the hands of a perfect stranger…" (212). Isn't this precisely the opposite of how people should seek out one another? Could Nyamnjoh subtly be telling us that this tendency to trust strangers is at the root or kernel of Mimboland's problems with colonialism? The fantasy, the danger, and the coded language that drips with innuendo are all part of the excitement. No one, especially not the terrified, wants to give that up.

What also excites people are other people's property and wealth. Sex cannot be teased out of this equation. Love affairs are one way, but not the only way, to leap over class divisions. Nyamnjoh revels in the complications that these relationships inevitably cause. There is no utopia and people are not constrained by models of decency. The interwoven fabric of African culture is changing. Literary and social theorist Ulrich Beck points this out by saying "…traditional certainty is perishing and being replaced—if we are fortunate—by a legally sanctioned individualism for all" (qtd. in Hier 362). The rules and connections that once governed Africa are breaking and falling apart. Further, the pace of this decoupling is exacerbated by influences from Western Europe that are brought over to Africa. Colonialism and consumerism are reshaping and re-sculpting the way people meet, have relationships and the duration of those relationships.

At one time Africa was not comprised of individuals. That sounds like a physical impossibility. On the surface that was an impossibility that could never happen. The importance of society, the strength of society, lay in the community. The view was that the village was everything, i.e. the center of the world so to speak. The individual, other than as part of a broader structure, was nothing. This philosophy has spilled into the modern political debate. The village provides sustenance and raises children. People cooperate within a unifying format. People get along. The system is not perfect, but there is a rhythm to it. There are parameters and this dominated Cameroonian thought before the German's arrived with Otto von Bismarck's nephew-in-law in the Victorian Era in what was then known as Kamerun. People from the West arrived in Africa (although the Germans were more benevolent than most) and taught Africans how to be afraid. They introduced items into the lexicon that no one wanted to lack. They brought with them a new set of values that uprooted the topsoil and the continent is yet to recover. This is the seismic shift that Beck talks about. Instead of the traditional we have a Free for all. All Nyamnjoh is doing is conduct an autopsy for a culture that is in shock.

The pandemonium of Mimboland is a new way of thinking. This is a new way or a new manner of how things are put together. *Married but Available* is a collection or a gathering of a group of unrelated or discordant ideas and objects—the break between the old Africa and the modern Africa. Literary theorist Michel Foucault looks at such situations not solely as a process, but more importantly with a nod to show how the implementation of that process creates shifts in culture. This espouses Foucault's assertion that,

> [d]iscontinuity—the fact that within the space of a few years a culture sometimes ceases to think as it had been thinking up till then and begins to think other things in a new way—probably begins with

an erosion from outside, from that space which is, for thought, on the other side… (50).

The use of erosion makes one think of archaeology, geology and evolution. Almost imperceptibly Africa changed its composition. It changed its consciousness and opened its arms willingly to new ideas and recalibrated its values. But this was not evolution in the Darwinian sense where things improved, got better and people flourished. It is the opposite of that. The "other" in Foucault's quote refers to people who did not look, think, act or dress like Africans. The Germans, the French and the English all came to Cameroon and taught the African how to forget.

The consequences and resonances of this cultural amnesia are impossible to quantify. The colonial situation, rather than cause a widespread backlash, has caused a historical and sociological implosion. Abiola Irele, a Professor of African, French, and Comparative Literature, powerfully asserts that "[w]hat is however undeniable is the fact that the ascendancy of western civilization in the context of colonization did effect a distinct orientation of African minds away from the indigenous culture…" (93). The argument, according to Irele, is that the African's mindset changed, the frame of reference changed and the use of ideas to bring about this transformation was far more effective than any conquest brought about by the barrel of a gun (93).

Also, it is a hell of a lot cheaper than engaging a paid standing army. Why pay for a standing army to occupy a land that is thousands of miles from your home when you can change someone's ideas? The subject, without knowing that it is being experimented on, can colonize itself. People can be taught to forget what they were doing. Even more to the point they can be taught to forget what their grandparents were doing fifty or sixty years ago. It is so easy for two generations to lose each other. The power of colonization, I would argue, is not one of force nor is it about violence. It is about the ability to separate and isolate a culture from its past. It is about molding the subconscious of another—and profiting from it. What the French and the English, in the modern era, and the Germans and the Portuguese before that, have done is create a society where no one knows where he or she truly belong. Like a child who has two parents from two distinct races this is a potential problem of identity. It is not easily solved, it is painful and no one wants to openly confront it.

Instead of a bold and head on collision, Nyamnjoh opts for subtlety. Measure by measure he reveals another card in an allegorical study utilizing sexual exploits and gamesmanship and manipulation to reveal what colonization has wrought. People have always had sex and they have always had love affairs, but Nyamnjoh brings in an "edge" or a "hustler's mentality" which was not in Africa before the white man set foot in Africa. At first the reader feels that he/she is a privileged "insider" who gets to hear entertaining stories without being susceptible to them or paying any sort of a price. However, with money there is always a price. Even the best of us are vulnerable to the enticements of gossip and that is what the author wants the reader to feel; that he/she have before him/her harmless gossip that hurts no one. But this is a trick, a masterful ploy that ultimately reveals how bad choices have entered the environment, just like an addictive narcotic with long term ramifications enters the bloodstream via an intravenous drip or hypodermic needle. The worst is yet to come and this belies the fact that (at the moment) everything seems to be just wonderful. Lilly calls her study of how people keep company, "[a]ll is smooth sailing" but she is quickly corrected by Britney who points out that "[o]n the surface, yes, but badness has a way of playing games with goodness in this world of ours…" (Nyamnjoh 274).

Without even knowing so, the African has given up the veins and the reins with which he/she had previously defined himself/herself. What starts with a few risqué stories, ostensibly about research, ends with a litany. The sheer number of them, the volume of them, points out how Africa is suffering in a post-colonial world and this suffering is pervasive. It is homogenous. It slices through every social and economic layer of society. Independence, little more than dead paper or an official certificate that means little in practice, means nothing in a continent western and white in its buying habits. In the sixth chapter of *Married but Available* we learn that "[y]ou know someone is having an affair when they usually feel happy and light within themselves…" (Nyamnjoh 79) and this is the casual and carefree flavor that I am talking about which eventually and seductively turns like a worm into something new where Lilly Loveless says to herself that she is "…gradually turning native…" (291). Things in Mimboland acquire a heft that they did not have before at the beginning of her raw expedition. The number of escapades retold is a statement all by itself and Lilly Loveless ceases to be impartially above the fray. She sees that the relations around her cause destruction yet she is sucked into the undertow all the same.

Instead of observing Mimboland's behavioral economics, finance and psychology Lilly Loveless becomes part of the investigation she purports to study. Her own movements, functions and reactions lack discipline, planning and forethought just as the behavior of her alleged subjects lacks discipline, planning and forethought. She has yet to realize that she has the ability (and the responsibility) to separate herself objectively from the figures she writes about. The political forces, to paraphrase Eleanor Roosevelt, that kinetically travel between the two continents are incapable of harming her if she does not grant her consent. Unfortunately, she does so all too willingly. This could be naively read or interpreted as "going native" whereas it is a secret device to silently extract the information she needs to dominate Mimbolanders. This is highlighted by Ngugi wa Thiong'o in *Decolonizing the Mind,* in these words:

> But its [colonialism's] most important area of domination was the mental universe on the colonized, the control, through culture of how people perceived themselves and their relationship to the world. Economic and political control cannot be complete or effective without

mental control. To control a people's culture is to control their tools of self-definition in relation to others (16).

Lilly perceives herself as a scholar, but she is not one. The Mimbolander perceives himself or herself to be a free thinker, but he/she is not a free thinker. Both are influenced and manipulated and cajoled by other people in boardrooms far far away whose decision-making represents millions of dollars and countless jobs. That is power. That is the control of the mental universe that Ngugi Wa Thiong'o is talking about in *Decolonising the Mind: The Politics of Language in African Literature*. What's more this is all done in secret, with a relatively small number of people making choices that will impact a disproportionate number of others who have no idea that their thinking has been irrevocably changed. The acceptance of all things foreign as an almanac for how one should breathe, think, buy and plan represents more than a yielding to a dominant culture; it represents a contempt and a willingness to turn away and spurn one's own culture for a shot at a seat at someone else's banquet table.

In a sprint for the middle class Francis B. Nyamnjoh's characters have let the qualities of community and connection deteriorate, corrode and atrophy. No one, with the possible exception of the author, seems to refuse, resist or put up any sort of a defense against this rapid transformation in African society. This acceptance, without a more spirited resistance, is surprising. The collision should have some twisted metal, shattered glass and torn platinum wiring. An invading army can be fought by bullets, but ideas—and sharpened, calculated, polished and nuanced ideas at that—are far trickier. A group, even one confident in its own authenticity, cannot fight propaganda. You cannot hit back at a target you cannot see. There was as Ngugi Wa Thiong'o states that there is a,

> ...new climate of thought that the world was knowable through human experience. At long last the world of Ptolemy was being replaced by the world of Copernicus and Galileo; the world of alchemy

by that of chemistry; that of magic and divine wills by that of experience in nature and in human affairs. The Edmunds of the new world were everywhere challenging the King Lears of the old order. (65)

In the words of Ngugi Wa Thiong'o the spiritual world (I am hesitant to use the word "religious") was replaced by a world concerned with only profit and loss (Ngugi Wa Thiong'o 65). Instead of an interconnected stability we have the chaos of the marketplace; with people doing the equivalent of shouting and yelling in an exchange in a climate where no one else cares about their wellbeing.

If truth is indeed stranger than fiction we are voyeuristically tricked and treated with one shock after another. Neo-colonialism changed labor policy, censored literature, dictated the language in which that literature appeared and attempted to stifle (unsuccessfully thank God) the rise of the African novel. More to the point, it tried to muzzle "true" or "genuine" African behavior and in its place presents a far more sanitized replacement that encouraged the individual to eschew history and adopt the conventional social values that Nyamnjoh is so critical of. *Married but Available* is but an extreme example of the principle in this shift in this study of economic, social and reproductive habits of the middle class. If the past has not been actually changed it has been covered, adorned, edited, repackaged, reconstructed and (mis)represented. The scenery on a Hollywood set in Culver City is a false front; a paper-thin facade propped up by wooden beams. It is only convincing if the camera is facing the opposite side of the lack of structure. That is what is happening here where there is a red and bitter harvest to be made of what never was. The novel shows that no one has autonomy. The results of the sociological and philosophical study dictate not only that things are not the same, but also that none of those sinned against can go back. Their steps have been erased with the same ease as a cartoonist or a cartographer uses the blunt side pencil.

Into this chasm from which no one can take a backwards step we get a bifurcated culture—a hybrid which satisfies no one. A society cannot appraise itself when it doesn't know who it is. A psychiatrist might call this a mid-life crisis when dealing with an individual patient, but age has nothing to do with it. It is a problem of inner-voice or, more poignantly, the pain of not having one. In this study of social habits in Mimboland we see the consequences of being rudderless, the price paid in not having an unambiguous philosophy of how to live and the ludicrousness in thinking that someone else is trying to help without the hope of unjust enrichment. Is it any wonder that when Lilly and Britney go to the little coastal village of Munyinge-Fish they are offered, "…grilled barracuda…" while they are conducting business? (295) This says something about the temperament and the temperature. Ruby, the owner of the place, sees how focused and involved the two are in their work and sits down to throw more blood in the water (295). Barracudas are hunters. They want something and their sharp teeth and snakelike shape assure that they get it. Moreover they pursue glittering prizes and gleaming objects. This is revealing in the context of *Married but Available* given the fact that so many of Britney and Lily's interviews take place in fishing villages and on beaches. They are known for trapping their prey—for having the discipline to remain very still for hours until their target(s) is at its weakest and most vulnerable. Is this not a description of a mercenary bitch (and the men are equally culpable)? This is not a gendered argument. A barracuda is a formidable opponent; at a young age it can literally change its colors to better blend in with its surroundings. What does all of this information say about someone who eats grilled barracuda? This is why Nyamnjoh has chosen this fish out of all the species in this genus.

Only a very naïve individual would say that politics and economics have nothing to do with relationships. It is this terrible truth that is exploited by the author and turned into prurient entertainment; the sort of fun that one knows that he/she probably is not supposed to enjoy but enjoy nevertheless against his/her better judgment provided no one is watching or listening very carefully. Francis B. Nyamnjoh takes this inconsistency—this discovery of how universally weak, wretched and pitiful people really are—and channels it and funnels it into something that is unrecognizable after the transformation. At an oil refinery crude oil becomes gasoline and diesel fuel. Here personal agony becomes pleasure for the perfect stranger. The novel aims low but it hits and obliterates the target just as *The Shortest Way With Dissenters* did so long ago. Both well-played satires are so well composed and so sharp that they cannot be ignored. Their dangerous irony produces a reaction out of proportion with the original events. In both cases society is found to be, according to Nyamnjoh, "...incapable of love..." in any form (300). Twenty years after his imprisonment, when Daniel Defoe wrote *The Fortunes and Misfortunes of the Famous Moll Flanders & c. who was born at Newgate, and during a Life of continued Variety for Threescore Years, besides her Childhood, was Twelve Year a Whore, five time a Wife (whereof once to her own Brother), Twelve Year a Thief, Eight Year a Transported Felon in Virginia, at last grew rich, liv'd Honest, and died a Penitent* his heroine needs only two chapters of the novel to understand just how foolish, stupid and inarticulate men are when it comes to the subject of women and anything that has to do with sex. Almost three hundred years later we learn from history that we are in precisely the same place that we were before and that globalization is just another word for intense pain has no international borders.

Works Cited

Backscheider, Paula R. *Daniel Defoe: His Life,* Baltimore, John Hopkins UP, 1989. Print.

Bourdieu, Pierre. *Acts of Resistance: Against the Tyranny of the Market.* New York: The New Press, 1998. Print.

Dickens, Charles. *Hard Time*s. Oxford, London and New York: Oxford University Press, 1978. Print.

Dowden, Richard. "Greetings from the New Africa" in *Wall Street Journal* April 20, 2012. (Web. 05/21/2015).

Foucault, Michel. *The Order of Things: Archaeology of the Human Sciences*. New York: Vintage Books, 1994. Print.

Hier, Sean P., ed. *Contemporary Sociological Thought: Themes and Theories*. Toronto: Canadian Scholars Press Incorporated, 2005. Print.

Irele, Abiola. *The African Experience in Literature and Ideology*. Bloomington and Indianapolis: Indiana UP. 1990. Print.

Ngugi Wa Thiong'o. *Decolonising the Mind: The Politics of Language in African Literature*. Oxford, Nairobi and Portsmouth, New Hampshire: James Currey Ltd. East African Educational Publishers and Heinemann, 1997.

Nyamnjoh, Francis B. *Married but Available*, Mankon-Bamenda: Langaa Research & Publishing CIG, 2009. Print.

Parker, Hershel. Ed. *The Norton Anthology of American Literature* Vol. B. (6th edition), New York: Norton, (1979) 2003. Print

Chapter 9

Gardens of Blooming Secrets, Silences, and Betrayals: Emmanuel Fru Doh's *The Fire Within* and Francis B. Nyamnjoh's *A Nose for Money*

Bill F. Ndi

Flowers would transform a forest of thorns into a beautiful landscape and a rugged mountain into a paradise and of splendor that every heart would make of it its object of desire, with humans longing to caress and strode; in short, such would be an ideal lovers' phantasmagoric dream-bed. In this light, the lines that follow contend that the two Cameroonian authors, Emmanuel Fru Doh (EFD) and Francis B. Nyamnjoh (FBN) from a nation seemingly degenerated into a forest of thorns, strive to complement the lopsided and often porous official national history which oftentimes is a subjective narration of convoluted facts from the perspective of the victors while discarding buried secrets, burning issues that have been silenced, as well as all the backstabbing and double dealing. These two Anglophone-Cameroonian novelists, seemingly because of their common socio-political and cultural history and affinity, have served their readers with a buffet of such historical elements that in real life have been discarded, buried and hardly ever talked about. By so digging, they have come up with a landscape of disconcerting ugliness and horrific beauty which is nonetheless admirable as validated by Julia Kristeva's *The Power of Horror: An Essay on Abjection* as a statement of truth pure and simple. Among that which does not respect borders, positions, and rules, Kristeva asserts that

> the traitor, the liar, the criminal with a good conscience, the shameless rapist, the killer who claims he is a savior ... any crime because it draws attention to the fragility of the law, is abject, but

premeditated crime, cunning murder, hypocritical revenge are even more so because they heighten display of such fragility ... there can be grandeur in amorality, and even in crime that flaunts its disrespect for the law... (4)

Kristeva's affirmation as well as EFD's *The Fire Within* and FBN's *A Nose for Money* simply strengthen the case that in silencing and making secrets of the shameless acts that mushroom in our contemporary global world would be tantamount to betraying the course of human history and knowledge in general and most specifically the cause for which the Anglophone-Cameroonian writer fights and writes.

With all of the above stated claims, one is tempted to ask what makes these novels gardens. Besides, how do the secrets, silences, and betrayals blossom therein? Are these secrets, silences, and betrayals merely those of common folks or do they expose a greater evil plaguing the Cameroonian society which the authors, in their attempt to bring such existential dilemma of Cameroonians to the attention of the readers, cleverly use as tools to keep the reader from despairing like those trapped in the snare of such evil? Again, are they just buying into Stephen King's remarks substantiating "why we crave Horror Movies" that "people's appetites for terror seem insatiable?" (qtd. *in* Flachmann & Flachmann 415). Or could it be that they are just tapping from the modern day media frenzy, fear which has been transformed into a commodity for mass consumption? Thus, to address these questions, the historical background against which these authors write, their respective settings, storylines, style, characters, and thematic analyses would elucidate that "from their representations out of such daze [...] along with loathing, one word to crop up is fear. The phobic has no other object than the abject" (Kristeva 4).

Situating these two authors in context is more than just a mere case of examining the setting of the respective novels. Although it is a platitude that works of fiction differ from factions, creative nonfiction and historical accounts as well as sociological treatise, the sociological, political, cultural, historical and philosophical background of any work of art or author would illuminate and clarify the unfamiliar and even that which is defamiliarized in the work. It could further be asserted that writing about or critiquing any piece of Romantic literature or art without mention of the Industrial Revolution and without foregrounding it in Neo-classicism, against which the Romantics revolted, would leave the foundation of any such literary endeavor shaky. Consequently, the novels under study do not escape mention of the background information that anchors the work into the thematic concerns here examined.

Both authors, EFD and FBN translate personal, communal, societal, national and global secrets, silences, and betrayals into literary figures of speech with which their works are embellished. Both works are set within two national settings often linguistically opposed. The Cameroons, it must be recalled, is a French/English bilingual polity in which the majority French speaking Cameroonians are the drovers raining their goads on the minority Anglophone Cameroonians. This linguistic bipolarity is also marked in separate geographical settings of the country (i.e. the French speaking Cameroonians occupy the eastern part of the nation and the Anglophones, the Western part of the nation). Each of the settings raises issues of historical, national, and international concerns which are often kept silent or maintained as a secret. The relation between the two settings is always marked by backstabbing of the minority by the majority or also importantly, by some among the minority seeking fame, recognition, and position from the francophone majority. The international thrust here goes as far back as to the 1884 Berlin Conference, which in the words of Stephanie Newell, "provides a stark illustration of the power relations that are embedded in maps" (17). This could also be extended to the 1919 Treaty of Versailles in which the formerly arbitrarily carved out German *Kamerun* was then ceded to Britain and France as Trust territory. Upon acquiring the travesty of an independence in the 1960s, the French speaking majority Cameroonians, garbed as the new oppressors, since then have left the oppressed Anglophone minority with no choice. Any attempt to upset the applecart by the latter, is muzzled with long years of imprisonment or even death. It is against this background that Jimenez-Munoz, in discussing EFD's works as mirrors of Romanticism, highlights that,

> Despite both the French and English languages being official in the country, the Anglophones who form the minority in Cameroon have long denounced marginalization by the Francophone majority. They have claimed that their language, disfavored against French as the language of the administration, limits their participation in the decision-making of the country and also in the provinces where they live, which they believe are deliberately backward in socio-economic development compared to the rest of the country. (31)

From the above, it is not immediately evident that the establishment of this linguistic polity was set on a simulacrum of a foundation purported to have either French or English speaking Cameroonian feel always as equal to the other; and not inferior.

Yet, that the minority should find the progress of its socio-economic development slowed down, retarded, and even halted by the majority, is redolent of betrayal. Further, given that no one from the Francophone majority takes up the Anglophone cause is just an affirmation of a blanket of silence under which is shrouded the secrets of a tale of betrayal which EFD and FBN bring out to the fore and let flower in their works under study. These awe inspiring monstrosities and objects of horror are here transformed into pleasure machines driven by the sublime. These writers sublimate such as a result of the random censorship of literary works like theirs which are offensive to individuals in positions of power (Larson 121). It will be judicious to recall that Stephanie Newell highlights the fact that "the imperial map set in place administrative units that were inherited largely intact by West Africa's new governments in the

1960s" (18) and the two successive governments in Cameroon have held fast to their inheritance. As such the autocrats have had to oppress their fellow "compatriots" to impress. It is this ugly face of their spatial background—Cameroon under Ahidjo and Biya's corrupt administration, the identical twin of Pope's object of satire, "English society under Walpole's corrupt administration" (Alastair Fowler 155)—that EFD and FBN elevate to the heights of pleasure and the sublime. Consequently, confronting acts of betrayals, intended to be kept secret or silent, dictate conscientious choices to capture the settings in which the authors' craft, purpose, and intent are not betrayed, shielding them from the whims and caprices of repressive forces. Thus they communicate through their setting, in the words of Alastair Fowler, "a positive sense of liberation and excitement" (170).

To validate or go against Fowler's assertion above, examining settings in the present studies aims at establishing the historical, geographical and physical context as well as the cultural and socio-political context in which EFD and FBN shape and model the characters therein present, the authors' concerns and their approach to deconstructing and reconstructing the universe. These settings like "maps do not present neutral account of places. Rather, they are loaded with their own historical narratives, telling their own […] stories about local struggles and victories on the ground" (Appiah qtd. *in* Newell 17). They also determine the characters' drive and how they define the power structures. They draw attention and illumine the writers' major thematic concerns as well as they drive the plots. Here, one could evoke Appandurai's model which is a subtle reminder "of the different ways in which global ideas and identities are taken up in different historically specific settings" (qtd. *in* Newell 15). It is against this premise upon which this analysis of EFD and FBN's novelistic locales is predicated to warrant a careful appreciation of the characters' "current geographical location" (Appandurai qtd. *in* Newell15).

In a prior publication, alluding to EFD's setting in *The Fire Within*, Ndi views Caramenju—the novel's macro setting—as a fictional theatre in which EFD unfolds his world view (qtd. *in* Fishkin, Ankumah & Ndi 226) while quoting Eagleton that EFD's is a "medium/place where the truth of the world speaks itself..." (56). In short it is no place for secrecy, no rug under which evil is swept and kept secret, and nothing is ever heard of any perpetrated malice. It is rather, for EFD, a stage on which to showcase all of these unwanted and intended-to-be-hidden acts of betrayals. Thus, he situates Papa's residence at the Sunshine Chemist roundabout with its different roads sprawling out and transforming the micro setting into a spider web-like network to spell the disguise, the silence, and the spider's predatory act that webs in the betrayed, Adey/Papa, the Anglophone. Though Adey/Papa is not the protagonist of the novel, he takes the relay baton from Mungeu', the female protagonist and is foregrounded as the languishing memory of a departed betrayed by all: kin, friends, foes, and institutions alike. Through a well-known platitude of spiders preying on the weak, EFD takes the reader into the heart of an oppressive system. The spider builds its web silently and secretly, displays it as it awaits any inattentive prey to fall into its trap. In EFD's case, the narrative angled and fertilized with such ingredients leaves the survivor of such betrayal no choice but that of going insane. This symbolic narrative of the plight of many a betrayed Anglophone-Cameroonian such as Adey, vividly depicts where, when, and how Adey finds himself in the grip and center of this garden in which gloom blooms and become a compelling creative trope. In describing what is left of this setting after everything is said and done, EFD writes,

> In a way, the roundabout itself is in the heart of the town of Batemba, the capital of the Savannah Province. As he lay there, different roads leading out of the roundabout were like the network of a spider's web. He himself, in the centre[sic] of the roundabout, looked

like prey, the surrounding houses and people, spiders of different sizes and shapes, creeping threateningly towards him. (1-2)

Here above, attention is drawn to the setting, Batemba as capital of the Savannah Province. It is the writer's leitmotif to inject both a colonial and a political spin into the plight of his fellow Anglophone-Cameroonians against whom a predatory regime operates, in secrecy, reminiscent of a spider's, and would muzzle any who dares to break the silence in order to betray the secret. Again, the excerpt brings to mind a central question seeking to know why the narrator captures, puts to the forefront and insists on, "the surrounding houses and people" as "spiders… creeping threateningly towards him" (2). Is it a way for the author to allow the reader to draw a parallel between this bloom of gloom with the stalemate that is his people's lot day in day out?

In a twist to give a bigger picture of the unparalleled betrayal in Caramenju, the narrator takes the reader to the capital city Nayonde where the only psychiatric center in the country is. Nayonde's psychiatric "Centre[sic] Bonaparte" becomes a stage for EFD's theater of the absurd geared at exposing the senselessness and purposelessness of a union between East and West Caramenju that is much vaunted only to leave its citizens from West Caramenju betrayed by the very institutions that are intended to guarantee them all that which give meaning to human life. As such, it is no accident that the author through the character Yefon tells the reader what happens in that theater. Yefon's is an eyewitness account. She says,

His parents and I have been there with him four different times. First of all, nobody speaks English there and so we could barely communicate. They kept him there for about a month without any changes. A doctor saw him once in all that time. We had no choice but to bring him back. All his parents can do now is pray for him while I hoped you would someday see him during one of your visits back home. (3)

It is yet through another health institution that EFD allows reckless betrayals, secrets, and silences to blossom. A hospital, where patients are supposed to be treated, turns out to be the very place where they are left to die. When Mungeu' attempts her abortion and loses blood profusely, she is taken to the hospital where the nurses realizing it is an abortion attempt vow not to do anything if they are not told exactly what happened. Yefon informs Mungeu' of the nurses' declaration: "they said it is an abortion attempt, and if I didn't say exactly what happened then they weren't going to attend to you" (188). This withholding of patient information and the nurses' refusal to abide by the Nightingale Oath they had sworn exposes the gossip that these nurses are willing to hurry out and spread. This behavior transforms this narrative into an arena of double betrayal. On the one hand, Mungeu', who upon hearing Adey had been by her bedside exclaims, "Adey! Oh, My God, ..." (189) is fully aware of the gross act of betrayal that she has committed and in her dying minutes insists on the oath of silence. She requests Yefon be quiet: "[p]romise me to be quiet" (195). On the other hand, "all they [the nurses] were interested in was to see and then go out and make scandalous stories that would mystify their positions as nurses in the eyes of ignorant patients and visitors" (189). Thus, the setting becomes a real burial ground for the seeds of professional ethics around which will grow systematic gestures and acts of betrayals in those who arrogate themselves the power to backstab and go unharmed. No wonder the narrator points out, "strangely, the nurses had kept their promise not to attend to her until she confessed what she had done" (195).

Mungeu' is thus betrayed by the medical profession and its institutions as a result of her making an attempt to abort a pregnancy she wants to keep secret and is silent about when asked or required to vocalize what the matter is with her. This strange tale of betrayal which turns out to be an angle of a triangle made up of secrets, silences, and betrayals, exposes the duplicity of most of those caught in the web of backstabbing. With all purposes and intent, Mungeu' clears her name on her deathbed. She makes it clear, in her confession to Adey, that her attempt at aborting his baby without his knowledge could not have been an act of betrayal because she was simply doing what was in their interest. While weeping and begging Adey for forgiveness, Mungeu' emphasizes,

> Don't blame me Adey... I wanted to save us from all that people would have said, from the insults, and, above all, from the wrath of my family. They would never have understood, no matter what we could have said or done. I didn't want the memory of my mother tortured by unkind words which I'm sure my parents would have uttered. Anything can be said now and the strange customary squabbles about unmarried women chanted. I will not be there to receive the blows. In any case, I never suspected it would turn out to be like this, but let God's will be done. If I should die, then pray for my soul for I did all that I did with.... (194).

Mungeu' here above foresees her death as she tries to clear herself of any wrongdoing for her intentions were not glossed with ill-will. The ellipsis at the end is EFD's way to absolve her, for he leaves the reader to imagine the ellipsis could only be filled by the word "love". Nonetheless, an institution such as a hospital purported to save lives becomes the target for EFD's skillful articulation of the troubled spirit of the times in his Cameroon/Caramenju. Though EFD seems to express a deep sense of loss here, in this episode he establishes a critical deconstruction of institutional norms and practices as well as he leaves the possibilities and choices of reconstructing to the reader. He does what Alastair Fowler considers as a look "towards a new age of enlarged possibilities" (148). The episode also unfolds how institutions make certain norms and practices secrets and keep silent about them over others. And in doing so, they betray the same they are supposed to govern simply because they are mute in the face of repression.

On the other hand, like EFD's *The Fire Within* set against the ugly face of the Cameroons under the only two, and corrupt administrations so far, Ahidjo's and Biya's, FBN in *A Nose for Money* casts his action, characters and central thematic concerns in a metaphorical prison, a country called Mimboland, in which the oppressed and the oppressors suffer the same fate but in varying degrees. The secrets, silences, and betrayals in this space are sublimated and elevated to new heights of pleasurable splendor. It is this careful choice of setting that warrants FBN's protagonist's vertical, horizontal, and spatio-temporal movements, the scheming, machinations and exploitative machinery of the Mimboland government and its agents and operatives. First Mimboland is a polity constituted by East Mimboland and West Mimboland where French and English are spoken respectively. The binary of East and West, French and English underlies the unsaid, the backstabbing, and often occultist atmosphere prevalent in *A Nose for Money*.

It is through a vivid description of socially constructed space that FBN sets the tone for the muteness, treachery, and underhandedness that overwhelm Mimboland. FBN splits the settings into macro and micro settings: East and West Mimboland, The River Roungoum, the Donaperim bridge, the River Mourim, Sawang, bars and Chicken parlours(sic), the streets, the hospital, Old Belle, Minka, Bassangland, Victoria, Paris, Nyamandem, Elakgan, etc. The nature of the roads, the atmosphere around the bridge that links East and West Mimboland, the surrounding trees, the heavy traffic, and even the rumbling from the heavens, all turn out to be apparent and veiled metaphors for the splendor of the author's object of ugly beauty blossoming.

The division of Mimboland into Eastern and Western is the basis for a national conflict with inherited colonial origins. This colonial heritage highlights the fact that all the bases of the conflict within Mimboland are drawn from extraneous repertoire. This is a conflict which betrays the peace that might have reigned between these same parts of pre-colonial Mimboland. And worse still, both conflicting parties are silent on this facet of their past. They are both under the grip of a hegemonic cultural imposition. The narrator tells the reader:

> ...at Roungoum, the river that had marked the boundary between Western and Eastern Mimboland in colonial times, and that continued to impose attitude, language and behaviour(sic) codes drawn from the cultural repertoire of the English and the French as the respective former colonial masters. (32)

At the River Roungoum, a radical Anglophone movement fighting against unification chooses to erect a sign on which they express their dissatisfaction with a union that to them represents nothing but a hollow sham. They consider Eastern Mimbolanders as strangers. The sign reads,

> [t]o all foreigners: Thanks for visiting Western Mimboland. We hope you enjoyed our Anglo-Saxon hospitality and generosity. Wishing you well as you start your journey of a thousand dangers into La Répbulique. We can't protect you against their savagery, but we'll pray for you. Do come again if you survive the intrigues. (45)

This signals the colonial legacy in both sides of Mimboland. Eastern Mimboland or La République is, in plain terms, a land of a "thousand dangers" as opposed to the Movement's perception of Western Mimboland as the land of Anglo-Saxon hospitality and generosity. Here, one is tempted to wonder if Mimboland, Eastern or Western, was devoid of hospitality and generosity in its pre-colonial times. One could also quest how Eastern Mimbolanders perceive their compatriots from the West. The reader is given the opportunity to perceive Western Mimboland from the perspective of Eastern Mimbolanders when the honourable(sic) Matiba instructs Prospère on how to carry himself around Nyamandem. When he sees Prospère's Toyota Corolla, he is quick to warn Prospère must not be seen driving such a thing like that. He brings to the fore the geographic setting where Prospère now finds himself. He tells him, "for the sake of credibility… You are now in francophone territory, no longer West Mimboland… Here prestige counts for everything" (138).

In spite of Matiba's assertion of the superiority of the francophone territory to West Mimboland, Prospère's immediate thought upon meeting with the former to discuss business seems to contradict common knowledge. It is a jungle marked with greed, devoid of humanity and contrasts sharply with Sawang. When Matiba asks for half of the total amount Prospère wants to bank and or invest in business, the latter finds himself as W. Lawrence Hogue would have it when discussing Baldwin's *Another Country,* "in the midst of social forces, of suffering and pain, in the void of his unknown self, and within the web of ambiguity, darkness, and paradox" (3). FBN's narrator captures and paints a picture of the new setting in which Prospère finds himself. He says,

> What an urban jungle Nyamandem was, Prospère thought. All the civil servants he had met were like starving vultures, ready to pounce even on the living. It was a city of extreme greed, where there was an aversion in everyone to the smell of money in others. Among the women, the religious worship of dresses, shoes, creams, perfumes and everything European, was more than anything he had remarked in the ghettoes of Sawang. (132)

The above and the fact that civil servants come to the ministry in hope to see the minister and end up grumbling their way back home only confirms Prospère's qualification of Nyamandem as an urban jungle in which even authority figures, like rodents, are missing in the towering layers of acts corrupt practices.

From the perspective of micro setting, FBN carefully dedicates the first few paragraphs to describing the place of occurrence of the events in the story. Through this local trope, the author seems to bring to the readers' attention, the fact that it was the ideal place for any such happening and allows readers to anticipate the narrative trajectory. The narrator brings us to the Donaperim Bridge over the River Mourim. He quickly reminds the reader of the treacherous nature of the roads and how mindful any driver who would want to venture to travel to Victoria in West Mimboland should be. The treacherousness of the roads, their overcrowded nature and the dastardly dealings between drivers and policemen fertilize the plot in the same way the ominous "rain clouds circling the sun" (3) betray the hopes and aspirations of those who like Prospère had forecast a bright afternoon. It also made traveling a nightmare as the narrator arrests the readers' attention in these words:

> The roads were very bad at this time of the year, and he knew it was no use trying to drive to Victoria without boots and a spade, if it was going to rain along the way… the roads were muddy and slippery, and drivers were often forced to dig, and ask others to help pull and push their vehicles. It was a nightmare. (3)

With just this snapshot of the state of the road, one is tempted to ask whose responsibility it is to fix the roads or why everybody is silent about it and doing nothing to that regard. The writer skillfully serves the reader a platter of an instance of betrayal from the state which should be there to look after the interest of the people. It is no wonder that the narrator brings in the unethical practice of a policeman who with some cab driver exchanges papers and money with neither fear nor reprisals. The ordinary Mimbolander that Prospère is can only fume and the narrator tells us, "[h]e worked very hard for his money, and didn't like the thought of passing it over to law enforcement agents for nothing other than the right to go home" (3). The narrator's use of "law enforcement agents" is nothing short of an antinomy of the practices of these agents who in reality are "corruption enforcement agents".

The bloom of acts of betrayals coloring FBN's novelistic scape is not limited to open spaces like the above mentioned. When FBN brings the reader into Tonton Bar, one of the hotspots in Sawang, he gives the reader the opportunity to feast on the ugly side of secrets, silences, and betrayals. This bar gains it notoriety not from the wonderful things happening there but, as the narrator hints, from "the strange things that happened there at the sinister hours of darkness" (58). This setting bespeaks of the woes of Mimboland. The bar is owned and operated by "an experienced prostitute" (58). It is where Prospère pulls to a stop upon his return from West Mimboland. There, he was sure of meeting civil servants who had come to get a drink or two before going back to their offices. And he was also sure of getting more news to satisfy his curiosity as to whether his involvement in the Mamawese's deal gone bad had been detected. He is curious to know what is in the newspapers from these civil servants who can read. The mix of "people from all walks of life" (58) in this place and the activities taking place there leave no doubt that this is the place where the dirty national linens are given a shine. The narrator tells the readers of those who were the most present and the most feared. The young unemployed, i.e. the dregs of Mimboland society, were here not only to drown the woes in drunken stupor but to smoke cannabis in quest for happiness; the happiness of which they have been robbed. This quest for happiness could conceal the desire for revenge on those who have so betrayed and left them in this state of hapless joblessness. No wonder, as soon as they smell money from someone's socks, they resort to cutting off the leg. The narrator is clear on this: "when a man went behind the bar to urinate, his leg was chopped off by thieves who must have been attracted by the smell of money from his socks" (58). In short, it is FBN's social and spatial construction of a central stage for violent crimes, mostly in the heart of the night.

Much more could be said of this place of dishonor with its stifling temperatures reminiscent of the pressures under which the corrupt Mimboland government puts its citizens; "[t]he temperature was very high and he [Prospère] felt hot, humid and exhausted. ...the bar was not sufficiently ventilated" (58). This example of unventilated bars constitutes a recipe for people to desire drinks insatiably. The narrator seizes the opportunity to chastise it as a ploy by politicians who allow local brews with very high levels of alcohol to be served at exceedingly low prices. A few people complain about the levels of alcohol and the cheap prices as the narrator informs:

> [p]erhaps politicians had a secret; maybe they saw alcohol as necessary for the attainment of their objectives. After all, who wanted a clear - and critical-minded populace? A sober population is a recipe for political nightmares and headaches. (59)

The narrator's rhetorical question above betrays the intent and purpose of the rulers who set up and or authorize places like these to flourish in Mimboland and in spite of the heinous crimes committed there. This echoes strongly Paul Valery's views on politics when he contends that, "[p]olitics is the art of preventing people from busying themselves with what is their own business" (qtd. in William B. Whitman 14). It is no surprise then, that, just a short while after a man's leg was hacked off here; this place of disrepute is once again granted authorization to reopen its doors to business. This authorization is predicated upon a mere promise, and one made by a prostitute whose every word everybody knows would never be kept.

Towards the end of the novel, FBN takes the reader through the Narrator to Elakgan where Prospère hopes to find answers as to why his third wife, Monique, died. The scatological details of the environment, behind Ngek's house where the policemen go looking for Prospère, are enough to depict the mess in which Mimboland finds herself. One reads, "[t]hey scrambled behind the house and into the bush, where dry and fresh excrement was scattered all over like cow dung. The stench almost sent them off the trail…" (201). It is also in this setting that FBN reminds the reader of the Mimboland civil service maxim, "[a] goat can only eat where it is tethered" (201). Over and above it is in a gory setting, in a hut, that FBN closes his tale of a life of deceit, secrecy, backstabbing, silences, and debauchery as if to take Prospère back to Minka where he originally came from. Further still, the final setting echoes strongly, the biblical adage, "you are dust and to dust you shall return." The kind of setting Prospère thought he might have left behind him is ironically the very same kind in which his life is ended.

From the foregoing one would surmise, without overstating, that these two Anglophone-Cameroonian authors have grounded the setting of the works in totally deconstructed spaces with macro settings identical to that of the bilingual polity that is Caramenju and Mimboland, viz. The Cameroons. Their deconstructed spaces spew the buried secrets, silences, and betrayals that flower in that country like a volcanic eruption. It is worthwhile then to follow the events as they unfold in these respective settings.

EFD's novel follows a pattern of investigative exposition of ills and evils in the Caramenju society. EFD's is a simple storyline. It is the story of a girl, Mungeu', orphaned at birth. Her mother dies soon after she is born. In this event Bill F. Ndi sees a parallel with the colonial and postcolonial situation of the writer's clime (qtd. *in Fears, doubts, and Joys of not Belonging* 234). She is brought up by a stepmother and a father who both, but most especially the stepmother, seem determined to crush any ray of hope in her. Unrelenting in her determination, Mungeu', the orphaned girl, chooses to volunteer her services in partial payment for her education at Holy Rosary Home Craft Centre (HRHCC). After graduation she establishes her own business. There she is paid predatory visits by her former economics teacher at the HRHCC, Fon. He ends up having his way and leaves the poor, innocent Mungeu' pregnant. Oblivious to her pregnancy, it is her stepsister, Mabel, who informs her that her morning sickness might be due to pregnancy. Having established Mungeu' pregnant, they both try to handle this delicate and thorny issue with the utmost care viz. secretly. However, Mabel leaves for a nearby village market at Bansei and never comes back as was scheduled. She is involved in an accident which has her evacuated abroad. With her only support system in a critical state and unconscious, Mungeu' now has to deal with the overbearing mistreatment society inflicts upon any unmarried woman who happens to be pregnant. She is unable to stand this oppression and chooses to leave for Njunki where she reestablishes herself as a businesswoman. With her business thriving, she soon begins to travel back to Batemba to buy products that she would sell in Njunki. It is during one of her business trips that she meets and falls in love with Adey.

The pair at an untimely moment gives in to their passion and Mungeu' becomes pregnant yet again. Having had firsthand experience of the oppression to be handled as a woman pregnant out of wedlock, she is bent on getting rid of the child in spite of Adey's dissuasions. She goes ahead to venturing with the abortion with the sole desire of keeping both pregnancy and abortion secret and quiet. She opts for a quack practitioner and then, in the process, it becomes apparent that she must seek proper medical attention. She is then rushed to the hospital where the nurses as well as the doctors insist on her voicing what they understand to be a secret she is determined to be silent about. With her persistent silence, she is left to die. The ensuing funeral arrangement, burial, and aftermath are all EFD's way to exhibit the burgeoning of flowers of gloom engendered by secrets, silences, and betrayals.

Structurally, the prologue turns out to be the epilogue of this story and warrants the assertion that to untangle the storyline, Mungeu's "representation seems to stem from a logic following a process of reasoning akin to the workings of the mind of an observer and critic and not just a spontaneous, irregular firsthand character creation" (Ndi in *Fears, Doubts, & Joys of not Belonging* 218). In short, EFD's prose, albeit a postmodernist deconstruction of post-colonial Africa, conforms to Pater's definition of imaginative prose as, "the special and opportune art of the [post]modern world" (qtd. *in* Buckler xvii-xviii).

In terms of plot, FBN like EFD trails Prospère, the protagonist in a pattern that betrays the writer's intent to paint a sordid tableau of acts akin to secrets, silences, and betrayals for both reader and the culprit to revel in. These ills transform Mimboland into a macabre laughing stock. FBN weaves his plot intricately in a style analogous to Henry James' art of subduing the "plot to his secret design," a point that Fowler emphasizes about James' writing, stating that, "…the same strength underlay his firm architectural structures, with their intricate plans of framing arrangements" (314). FBN in his trailing of Prospère unfolds his narrative with the latter caught in the midst of his work as a driver for Mimboland Brewery Company (MBC), driving back from Victoria in West Mimboland. The nature of his job and the dense traffic condition become the first elements of conflict as the Narrator intimates that, "[i]t kept him away from his precious Rose for longer than he would have liked. No man likes to stay away from the woman he has just married…" (4). This brewing conflict is just a matter of time before it drives the protagonist to the next phase of his folly. The narrator reminds us that "their decision to get married had been swift, and together they had worked to overcome the rigorous scrutiny of her demanding parents" (5). Besides, the reason advanced for his getting involved in a marriage is none but the fact that she was beautiful. The events in this relationship lead to a feud when Rose is caught cheating on Prospère with a soldier. This paralyzing act of betrayal leaves Prospère mute. Rose, overwhelmed with a sense of guilt and expecting the worst, receives no reaction from Prospère and finally frustrated by such silence where the worst is expected, she leaves.

After Rose's departure, many a colleague of Prospère's at work take interest in his tale and feed him with many tales about women being "she-devils" and all his quest for understanding why men remained married to their wives was that "women are a necessary evil" (17). Thus he endeavors to make amends and have Rose back with him after several trips to Rose's parents'. The failure of these attempts to regain his lost love propels Prospère to new heights of debauchery.

He settles for low level prostitutes and becomes a regular, knowing exactly what part of town these kinds of prostitutes hung out. It is through this phase of his life that he acquaints himself with sexually transmitted diseases. His visits to the doctors and the treatment meted on patience with such diseases turn out, in his eyes, to be a show of public disgrace; one to which he would not want to submit himself. Nonetheless, he continues his work for MBC until he meets two Mamawese fraudsters, Jean-Claude and Jean-Marie on his way from West Mimboland. This meeting with the Mamawese will stir the course of Prospère's life in a dramatic way and direction. His fortunes make a 180 degrees turn. The fraudsters, having befriended Prospère and using his home as their hideout, are killed. They leave him a booty in his house. This leaves Prospère conflicted as he does not know whether to return the booty to the police or to keep it. He settles for the latter as this is a way for him to advance himself and better his financial situation.

Now in possession of a huge sum of money from the Mamawese's scam, Prospère makes plans to relocate to the capital city Nyamandem. But before he relocates, he has to seek counsel from Seng, a diviner in Minka, his village of birth. At Minka, he impersonates a friend of Prospère's, Dieudonné. Dieudonné has been sent to Seng by Prospère to come and consult. Oblivious to the impostor, Seng warns Prospère via Dieudonné to "be careful with women" (84). Obstinacy yielding an upper hand, Prospère assures himself that, "that won't be a problem" (84). He simply dismisses Seng's fears as unfounded and inconsequential. It is a paradox in itself because Prospère had come to Seng to seek his opinion not only because of his clairvoyance and renown but, above all, for the fact that "he is aware of things that are normally hidden from others" (68). When he revisits Minka before his departure to Nyamandem, Seng gives him further warning, still presuming he is Dieudonné. Seng, in a bid to show the grievousness of the warning, uses a simile directly comparing Prospère's foolishness to a moth's. In his words, "your friend is as foolish as the moth that dances to the flame it mistakes for a friend" (90). Overpowered by the idea of resigning and relocating to Nyamandem, Prospère dreams of meeting a kinsman from Bassangland, "the honourable[sic] Matiba" who is a government minister. Matiba, according to Prospère, would help him bank and or invest "his money." Upon arriving Nyamandem, he struggles and finally meets Matiba with the help of Marie-Claire, Matiba's secretary and girlfriend, and with whom Prospère has a brief romance.

The rest of FBN's plot is centered on Prospère's meeting with Matiba and the agreement he brokers to help Prospère achieve his investment goals. He becomes a prosperous businessman and takes two wives who bear children he presumes are his. His third wife, unable to conceive, dies of psychological distress and Prospère embarks on a truth seeking mission as he thinks his two other wives conspired and killed the third. The above and the ensuing *coup de canon* ending of the novel are all articulated around and colored with secrets, silences, and betrayals. Thus the blossoms of such flowers transform Prospère's garden of a *wholesome life* into a nightmare when he, in the end, finds out that he has silently been living a secret life of betraying and being betrayed. A life not worth living as Prospère cannot stand the fact that anyone could beat him at his own game. His third wife has died of an unexplained illness; his first and second wives have double-crossed him all through their marriage and have only been compelled to tell the truth by Ngek, the diviner. With the bitter truth spewed out, Prospère cannot stomach it. One can only imagine Prospère's feelings at this time. His recalls Lizette's betrayal by Theodore which the narrator tells the reader, "the discovery of betrayal by Theodore, whom she had trusted completely, felt worse than lying on a bed of needles" (131). This is certainly the kind of feeling that leaves Prospère with only one option: put a bullet into his own head. He thus leaves behind his wallet which becomes an object of contention between the two police officers who had accompanied him in his truth seeking mission. This act of fighting over a dead man's wallet by these police officers, though coming across as a show of law enforcement's insensitivity in the face of tragedy, is as a matter of fact, the author's dramatization of the endemic corruption in his home country. This dramatization vividly brings to mind, Chaucer's rhetorico-poetic question concerning gold and iron: "if gold rust, what will iron do?"

Both EFD's and FBN's plots unravel the tragic and are seemingly centered on personal tragedy which masks a greater national tragedy. And even if the former's is marked by a solemn and sober reflection as denouement and the latter's ending is a dramatic *coup de canon* denouement, it becomes evident that both authors are preoccupied with the predicament of the oppressed in their respective constructed novelistic spaces wherein the tight knit structures underscored by the settings offer further useful strategies to appreciate the completeness and fullness of life, politics, culture, and individual liberties as spices to the writers' style, cast of characters, and central concerns.

The importance of exploring style in any analysis of this scope has been underscored by scholars. William E Buckler in his introduction to *Prose of the Victorian Period* states that, "when style is relegated to a parenthetical position, it is troublesome because, from one point of view at least, style is the very thing we should be thinking about" (xiv). He further cites John Henry Newman's mention of the written page as, "the lucid mirror" of its author's "mind and life" on which he tries

> to give forth what he has within him; and from his earnestness it comes to pass that, whatever be the splendour[sic] of his diction or harmony of his periods, he has with him the charm of an incommunicable simplicity (xiv).

These definitions are given in relation to Victorian prose. And even if different literary periods have "very different intellectual needs" and therefore want "great modification in literary forms," (Buckler xvi) they all fit perfectly well with the prose practices of our Anglophone Cameroonian authors and validate Appiah's assertion on African literature that, "literature follows routes that may have been opened up by colonialism, but have subsequently developed along paths of their own" (qtd. *in* Newell 18).

On this significant note by Stephanie Newell of the identical path of the origins of African literature in general and Anglophone Cameroonian literature in particular, it is evidently clear that in discussing the mirror reflection of these authors' minds and lives expressed in words, one cannot avoid examining if not all, some of these key aspects of theirs: language use, humor, irony, allusion, dialogue, diction, suspense, rhetorical questions. This would help avoid falling into the trap of Eustace Palmer's virulent attack on earlier critics of African literature whose Criticisms he dismissed as "largely characterized by vague generalizations and misjudgements[sic], partly arising from hasty and superficial reading" (10). Having established that both novels are set in a bilingual polity, identical to modern day Cameroons where French and English are the main inherited colonial medium of expression, these two authors, whose novels are both symbolic socio-political and cultural ethnographies, branch off when it comes to expressing the antagonism between these two linguistic groups emanating from the blossom of secrets, silences, and betrayals in the writers' fictional universes.

In spite of the bilingual nature of the writers' setting, EFD seems to have opted for a complete or near complete abstinence from using expressions in the language of him that betrays and passes his betrayal as a secret or an issue to be silent about. This avoidance is not unconnected to his total reprove of the turn of event in a union that in his eyes should have been a blissful union between East and West Caramenju. EFD's total reprove is expressed through Adey/Pa-pa when he is thought struck and sets out like a soldier in parade. He remarks, "just let me get there, fools. I'll make them know their right from their left. I'll make them know how to guide and not dictate their foolish superstitious whims to others" (3). Here, EFD makes it clear that Adey's problem can be resolved but the act of betraying the Anglophone Cameroonian by his Francophone counterpart who would not speak any English at all, leaves the Anglophone bewildered and in a quandary. The Anglophone problem that is apparent on almost every page of this novel, virtually, becomes attributed to the francophone's obstinate refusal to make an effort to understand the Anglophone, to begin with, even his language.

There are a few other instances in which EFD makes use of the French language and we might ask to what effect? In describing a scene in which he shows his total disavowal of the French speaking/Francophone Caramenjuan's ways of proceeding, the word's *kalé-kalé* and *Gardien de la Paix* are the French expressions he uses. These two expressions seem to come in handy in describing the way in which the francophone has impressed him/herself upon the Anglophone brothers and sisters. The disgust with which the writer, like his characters, welcomes this is fully expressed in a highly ironically tinged dialogue between Pa Adey and Nsung when the latter, running away from the police, encounters the former and lets him know how much of outlaws Caramenju policemen have become. This is an instance of supreme irony for the French *Gardien de la Paix*, i.e. police constable, translated literally gives "Keeper of the peace". Yet, EFD has Nsung demonstrate the monstrous transformation into senseless brutalizers of those who are supposed to protect the citizens and make sure peace reigns in the country. Nsung tells Pa Adey,

> What a shame… it is that nonsense from Caramenju East they call *Kalé-kalé*…
>
> It is a notorious practice by which police officers, simply because they have the authority, invade citizens' homes at any time, but usually very early in the morning, while they are still asleep…. The truth is that this is a systematized intimidation and subjugation of English speaking Caramenjuans who are too rights conscious in an emerging nation that could care less about the rights of people. Officers use the opportunity to harass and extort money from civilians for phoney[sic] reasons. […] a stupid police constable, *Gardien de la Paix,* threatens to seize a couple's

radio… simple because they could no longer provide the receipt. In the process of this so-called *kalé-kalé,* policemen go so far as to beat up those who dare to resist or question their actions. Can you imagine that? (180)

This closing rhetorical question and the subsequent elucidation of a pretext that these thieves parading as policemen use this dubious *kalé-kalé* as a means to identify homes with valuables only to attack them later on with their gangs leave the author's lamentation and overt critic on the lips of Pa Adey who exclaims, "what a shame. Police my foot!" (180)

Also, in an attempt to free Mungeu' of letting others in the same trap others have set for her and in which she has fallen several times, EFD brings Adey to Mungeu' in her dying moments and she, through an emotional plea, endeavors to clear her good name. Her gesture is all but an act of betrayal. She might have undertaken it in secret and in silence but for all intents and purposes, she means well. In this moment of heightened pathos, the narrator shows the two lovers and tragic victims of social, cultural, familial, historical, and political betrayals, secrets, and silences locked in each other's embrace like orphans. During this encounter, Mungeu' requests not to be blamed, seeks forgiveness and explains her actions to the one she loves. She realizes were she given the opportunity to have a second chance she would certainly behave differently. Nothing but "my unlimited love…led me to this, but I will always love you and I'm happy you've loved me right through the end, so…" (196).

In discussing this narrative aspect of EFD's novel, one cannot help mentioning the dramatic opening of the prologue and many of the chapters. The examples of the prologue and the first chapter will elucidate and comfort this assertion. The opening of the prologue echoes the idea of a rejected offering and builds suspense on the very troublesome relationship between the two Caramenju/Cameroons. The first chapter also opens with Mungeu's troubling sickness not understood by Mabel who mistakes it for worms. Withholding this ailment from the reader until later on in the novel is for the author a means of letting the reader uncover the complex and nefarious foundation upon which the illness is caused as well as will stand.

FBN, in his novel set also in a bilingual Mimboland, resorts to making the linguistic bipolarity even more evident. Unlike EFD who only allows the reader to feel the pervasive dominance of the French when the action is moved to Nayonde, FBN makes subtle and efficient use of the French language in his novel to draw attention to the linguistic divide in Mimboland. He subverts the French language and makes it his weapon of satire and irony. In most instances, even beginning with the character names, when he uses this language, its worthlessness and meaninglessness to the author does not have him bother, in most cases, to translate them into the English language or simply explain what they actually represent. Again, and very often, they are antithetic representations of the apparent meanings and at times the French language is used to mark the deceitfulness of the language and also to exhibit the antagonism and continued backstabbing perpetrated by those from East Mimboland.

The French "Prospère," translated verbatim yields Prosper, and this name for the protagonist, is rather a joke for anyone who thrives. From the very opening of the novel this character seems to be content with the apparent meaning of his name that he takes his own desires for reality and would not heed any useful advice that could help him thrive, and this, notwithstanding that he has been warned against his recklessness in the streets of Sawang. It is these same tendencies that push him when he first gets to Nyamandem to venture his prospering game in his art of debauchery, deceitfulness, and backstabbing, all he cares for. The writer here uses this nomenclatural poetizing device to translate his disgust for the language of a trusted compatriot who unwittingly betrays fellow compatriots all in the name of *la fierté des français*. It is this piece of advice that is fed Prospère, upon his meeting Matiba, in order for him to fake his credibility and integrate Nyamandem business cycles. It is no surprise that the Mamawese fraudsters' dress style is French as the narrator informs the reader, "Jean-Claude and Jean-Marie had learnt to dress *comme les hommes d'affaires parisiens*. And so far, nothing had happened to make them think that they were wrong in adopting the French business suit as their dress style" (47). This rhetorical device helps the writer to bring out all that which disgusts him about French greed and their involvement in his imaginary universe, Mimboland. Using the French language once more with a dash of smothering irony, FBN hammers a nail into the coffin of French Greed and draws on the glaring example of Gaston Abanda who out of "Greed rather than love for *la patrie*" (56) i.e. *fatherland,* gets himself in real trouble which the corrupt judicial system equates with "dragging the President's name in the mud" (135).

FBN, in attempt to exonerate himself from "dragging the President's name in the mud" by actually doing so as a writer, introduces an epistolary technique through a letter supposedly written by some fraudsters. Resorting to nomenclatural poetization, to borrow from Ankumah's book title: *Nomenclatural Poetization and Globalization,* he names the President, "Longstai Moumou" (38). In this name is encrypted a deconstruction of the reproved political culture of Presidents' open secret of betraying their oath of office, not observing term limits and staying silent. His first name "Long + Stai" sums up his ambition as he would settle for nothing other than a "long stay" in office. His last name, "Moumou" is injected with the same ironic touch. To understand the treacherous nature of Mimboland President, there is need to explain this significant Cameroon Pidgin English lexis used as his last name. The word means someone who is speechless, so to speak, "dumb" or mute and doesn't hear, i.e. deaf. By remaining speechless, he creates an aura of secrecy and does betray his oath of office by not being a servant to the people but a silent witness and an unresponsive actor in the face of the pain and suffering of those he is supposed to cater for. He would not engage in any meaningful dialogue with those he oppresses, especially those from Western Mimboland. All he cares for is the deaf ear he pays them, his silence, and his interminable stay in office for life. By introducing the president by name only once in the entire novel, FBN creates and sustains a suitable atmosphere of mystery typical of most African dictators in general and that of Mimboland in particular. Blending character nomenclatural practice and the epistolary model transforms the novel into a veritable garden for the bloom of the obscure and the obscured.

Early on in the novel, the narrator points out how Prospère after having been stuck in traffic draws closer to home and how the bustling city center is curiously French: named "the Fontaine de L'Indépendance Modérée" (5). It is worthwhile drawing attention to this French expression which will translate "Fountain of Moderated or Regulated or Rationed Independence" (my translation). The significance of highlighting this very useful historical allusion and acerbic criticism to the French whose emblematic revolutionary slogan prides itself with "Liberty, Equality, Fraternity" is to bring to the fore FBN's understanding of how things ought to be and how they really are. It is certain that going by the French revolutionary slogan none would expect the French in FBN's Mimboland to be regulating, dosing, rationing, or moderating "Independence" cum freedom which should be total. The French, in Mimboland, therefore silently let down the same revolutionary principles which guarantee them their freedom. This ironic situation pushes the dagger of oppression deep into the Anglophone, the Francophone's open secret none talks about.

Besides, the only financial institutions mentioned in this work all go by French appellation: "Banque Française d'Outre Mer (BFOM)" (55) and "Banque Mimbolandaise de Développement Auto-centré (BMDA)" (136). If a critic were to venture and give these jaw breaking names a closer semantic look, the first BFOM would be translated as French Overseas Bank while the second, BMDA would give Mimboland Bank of Self-centered Development. These translations, in plain language, suggest that there is one bank that oversees French interest in Mimboland and the other bank caters for the abettors and lackeys of the French. This mention of the banks should ring a bell given that if one controls the purse string of another individual, the latter would be at his/her mercy. One needs to remember that Prospère, upon his arrival at the ministry in Nyamandem, requests to see the Minister and though a Francophone from East Mimboland, he is treated with condescension because he has mannerisms often attributed to Anglophones from Western Mimboland. In a bit to show how very poorly Anglophones are treated in Mimboland, FBN has Marie-Claire tell Prospère that, *"le ministre n'est pas n'importe qui, comme vous le savez"* (102) i.e "the minister is neither Tom nor Dick or Harry, as you may know" (my translation). One can only imagine what the response would sound like were Prospère an Anglophone requesting to see the minister in English. An anecdote in the Cameroons of today can elucidate the treatment an Anglophone would receive. The current Speaker of *La République du Cameroun* House of Parliament once ordered an Anglophone Member of Parliament not to speak in the House because he was not in Bamenda market, i.e. Bamenda, an Anglophone city reputed as a fertile ground and seat for everything that constitute obstinate political opposition in the Cameroons.

To further exhibit the linguistic duplicity in Mimboland, FBN takes us to the streets of Sawang with Prospère in search of loincloth for his wife. The salesmanship that had caught Prospère was *"venez me tromper ici. Je ne connais pas l'argent. Venez me tromper, ma sœur, mon frère. Je donne tout pour rien"* (8) and the salesman continues to attempt conning him with, *"c'est la vraie, vraie qualité, mon ami. Je jure. De Paris, de Cotonou, d'Abidjan..."* (9). The salesman's language and diction suddenly changes as Prospère is proving to be a hard to con customer. He starts by questioning why he does business like an Anglophone: *"comment vous faites le marché comme un Anglophone?"* (10) This language then becomes an insult depicted by the use of the word, « Anglo » and the expression, "comme ça tu n'achètes jamais rien pour la femme. Tu es chiche" (10) which in Cameroonian parlance must be recalled is an insult to any who does not conform to the French and francophone corrupt ways of doing things. It is through this exchange between Prospère and the salesman that FBN points out the hurt a francophone would feel when considered an Anglophone and also what the author sees as the fight for linguistic supremacy in Mimboland. The narrator exemplifies that, "…Prospère … though hurt by the remark and comparison" retorts with "I've told you I don't have money. That's the truth" (10). This response is "in the French that had beaten English hands down in the struggle for language supremacy in Mimboland" (10).

Again, Prospère's feeling of hurt upon being compared to an Anglophone should not come as a surprise because of his own supportive participation in the francophone fight for language superiority. Note must be taken that even in his humble profession as a beer delivery driver and in spite of his multiple trips to West Mimboland, Prospère, when in this part of the country, would insist only on using the French language if spoken to in English or Pidgin English, the lingua franca of West Mimboland. In an instance, when he stops at Wutengueneng during one of these trips to get himself a loaf of bread and a tin of sardines, the Mount Maleng shop lady recognizes him and addresses him in Pidgin English, he replies: *"Oui, comme d'habitude, madame"* (31). This is a response he could easily have substituted with a simple "yes" in English. But he dares not be heard speaking English because he is overburdened by his superiority complex. Over and above, the reader is informed that Prospère, a semi-literate "could tell an Anglophone from a francophone just by the French they spoke (33).

Another literary spice with which FBN punctuates his narrative of Prospère's betrayal by Rose is humor. Having betrayed the husband, Rose is expecting the worst which does not only delay in coming but it never comes at all. Though Prospère finds her behavior abominable, he is willing to forgive the woman he loves. Besides, he has been reliably informed by experienced hands at marriage that couples, in order to reaffirm their love and commitment to each other, had need for domestic rows and scandals. In the words of one of them, "[t]he tree of love must be watered from time to time with quarrels and confrontations in order to maintain its freshness" (17). This lesson is embedded in a paradox which transforms FBN's thorny bush of secrets, silences, and betrayals into a garden in which both the betrayed and the traitor delight in a despicable act as the real source of vitality.

The above examined narrative features embedded in the works of these two Anglophone-Cameroonian writers constitute for them the means by which to encode the contents of their minds regarding the conundrum of their fellow Anglophones in Caramenju and Mimboland. As such, they offer what Sartre contends to be "all the examples you want of meanness and ugliness" (126). This, to a greater extent, allows their prose to come across with both grace and force in Sartre's view as the authors are "sensitive to the materiality of the word and its irrational resistances" (121)

The novels under study come to life not only through the narrative techniques, settings, and background against which EFD and FBN as Anglophone Cameroonian writers write as already indicated above, but also through characters and the central thematic concerns raised by these authors to sustain the reader's interest. Talking of characters in his now classic *An Introduction to the African Novel,* Eustace Palmer reminds us that "[t]he characters are important not for what they are in themselves but for what they represent" (129). So, it is in representational deconstruction of these characters that EFD and FBN project their concerns with secrets, silences, and betrayals articulated around the tragic, history, society, politics, culture, etc. Accordingly, their novels adopt larger and universal themes in the tradition of David Hume's *Essays Moral and Political,* "of the dignity or meanness of Human Nature…" (qtd *in* Fowler 171). In them, man becomes man's backstabber who would display the meanness of his nature by ignoring the pain and suffering of another and letting the latter slowly moan to death.

EFD and FBN's protagonists—Mungeu' and Prospère respectively—are in and of themselves characters embodying the writers' major concern with the tragic. This assertion should also be extended to a greater extent to those characters through whom the reader has an aerial view of the bloom of secrets, silences, and betrayals, i.e. Adey in EFD's work and Monique in FBN's. Examining these characters in the light of the tragic, it would be appropriate to borrow from Eustace Palmer and qualify them as "tragic and ... enormously impressive hero[es] whose downfall is caused not only by the forces ranged against him [them], but also by [their] own weaknesses" (10). This argument is also highlighted by Jeannette King who talking of tragic responsibility points out that, though tragic characters "may be more sinned against than sinning, but, for [theirs] to be tragic, [they] must be at some stage actively involved in the course of events which initiates the disaster" (33). In the light of these claims, one wonders why these characters are at the origin of their own downfall. And one would further be tempted to question why these writers bring to life in their novelistic universe many a character who indubitably establishes a relationship between him/herself and his/her fate.

On the one hand, Mungeu's tragedy as the plot reveals is that of a character whose life from birth to death seems to be plagued by misfortune from the very early death of her mother shortly after giving birth to her till her own death. At the very beginning of her life, one would expect that in a world where good sense and rationale prevail, her father should instead dedicate himself to providing help and protection to his motherless child. He, nonetheless, is in a society within which the prevalent culture and thought warrant a man to be respected, not for how much he can pay attention to one wife but for how much he divides his love to many wives and leaves the children at their mercy. This is EFD's object of caustic criticism for, although he talks of and about polygamy in his novel, there is hardly any instance in which the reader finds anything positive relative to the marriage institution of polygamy. Also, the kind of education our protagonist, Mungeu', receives from a religious institution, yet again, spells doom for her. It is not an education that prepares its pupils to face the challenges of the real world. It rather evades topical issues and issues of concerns with which any young woman should be well versed while growing up. It is no doubt that when after an encounter with Fon, her former Economics teacher at HRHCC, the tragedy which she has all along endeavored to avoid becomes all too apparent. Once it is clear to her that she is pregnant and that she has lost the only source of support, her step-sister, Mabel, Mungeu' understands her life would be nothing short of a living hell on earth; she decides to move to a faraway land, Njunki where she can start life afresh. This is her attempt to avoid the worst. Up till this point, there is no gainsaying that the tragic looming over Mungeu' is not the result of Mungeu' sinning but from her being sinned against as her step sister Mabel aptly expresses through a number of rhetorical questions: "what grief is this? … How can a girl go on suffering all through her life and yet one cannot find what she has done wrong? Things just keep going wrong for her all the time?" (59)

Yet, Mungeu's decision to fall in love with Adey, and give in to her desires at an inopportune moment and moreover without forethought, seemingly the catalyst to the final disaster, are all her own responsibility. She is caught in the grip of the powerful feeling she and Adey express towards each other, the dilemma of making a choice between love and its repercussions, and especially the choice between life and death. Over and above, she makes the choice of a quack doctor over a hospital doctor and also she decides to stay mute when she could have opened her mouth and saved her own life. Even though these could be attributed to her, they seem to be the writer's approach to encrypting his greater historical, social, cultural, and political concerns. At the apogee of Mungeu's situation, the nurses are bent on not treating her until she speaks; a situation that the writer is bitter about and leaves the reader with the proverbial, "can two wrongs make a right?"

So, underneath Mungeu's tragedy is a greater national and international tragedy which is that of the oppressed Anglophone Cameroonian in *La République du Cameroun* greeted by silence from the international community. EFD fictionalizes this space and renames it Caramenju. In tracing the background against which Anglophone Cameroonian writers write, attention has been drawn on the underhand methods used to forcefully unite the Cameroons in an atmosphere of apparent peace. Law professor, Carlson Ayangwe's book, *Betrayal of Too Trusting a People. The UN, the UK and the Trust Territory of the Southern Cameroons,* is tellingly explicit of the traitors and betrayals of his people. Great Britain's hasty departure and the United Nations' imposition to British Southern Cameroons to achieve independence only by either joining Nigeria or by joining *La République du Cameroun* constitute an act of betrayal of British Southern Cameroons which later became West Cameroon, i.e. Anglophone Cameroon in the *La République du Cameroun* of today. This hasty departure like Mungeu's mother's hasty death before the child celebrates its first month of existence accounts for the tragic experience of Anglophone Cameroonians replicated in *The Fire Within* by the shared experiences of West Caramenjuans. EFD epitomizes this tragic circumstance in his prologue which in effect is the epilogue to his novel. When the United Nations left British Southern Cameroons in a dilemma, like EFD's Adey/Pa-pa at the crossroads, she chose to gain independence by joining East Cameroon in hope of finding reprieve in her sister. The depressed and insane Adey/Pa-pa who finds himself at a crossroads, the Sunshine Chemist Roundabout, symbolizes the Anglophone Cameroonian and the plight he shoulders since that betrayal. Let's not forget his only hope for treatment is the Centre [sic] Bonaparte situated in Nayonde, East Caramenju where no one speaks English and besides no one cared for him when he was taken there on at least two occasions. The challenges faced by the Anglophone in the Francophone territory in Caramenju leave the former completely helpless and Yefon expresses this situation when she tells her uncle that after all the frustration in Nayonde, due to lack of communication, "we had no choice but to bring him back. All his parents can do now is pray for him while I hoped you could someday see him during one of your visits back home" (3).

Before delving into the characters in FBN's work, it is worth stating that if Sandra Bertman views "[a]rtists [as] missionaries, shamans, magicians of the crafts, expressing, in many modes and in various media, the inexpressible", (203) then FBN fits well into this category of artists for he not only uses his protagonist, Prospère and his third wife, Monique, to portray the tragedy he weaves himself in but as a means to express the inexpressible in a context where exposing any silenced secret or acts of betrayal could determine whether or not one lives or dies. He thus allows such silenced secrets and acts of betrayals to flourish in his work while escaping the wrath of the oppressor.

Prospère's end is a reflection of the writer's encrypted philosophy which highlights the dangerous and deadly consequences of reckless past, ignominies, and errors that, in the words of the writer, "the future never forgives" (28). Pursuant to this, FBN in a Hardyan thrust has Prospère's sexual instincts, which have often been his guide, lead him into the hands of treacherous wives, the cause of his impending tragedy. Besides, he is so blinded by his own dishonesty and life of lies, desire for and pursuit of sexual and material fulfillment to the point that he fails to see how he is entangled in the very web he has overly displayed in his attempts to subjugate women and later on his wives. Propère's life has been constantly punctuated by lies, mystery, and duplicity from the very time he left Minka and found himself in Sawang. Prospère, like his wives who lead a double life that finally drives him to his ultimate suicide, is the product of the society from which they all hail, and if they are the embodiment of immorality and evil, it is simply because, as Baudrillard would have it, the evil "imagination is inherent in everyone" (qtd. in *Contemporary Sociological Thought* 253)

When Prospère is about to leave Sawang for Nyamandem, he makes a quick trip back to Minka, his village, as if he were conscious of the fact that he still had scores to settle with his own fate. He goes to seek the help of a diviner, Seng. Yet, true to himself, he continues his life of lies; he passes for "a friend" of Prospère's, Dieudonné.

Even though he is warned through the impersonator himself, he does not heed the counsel of the old sage who clearly intimates him that he has a problem with women and must be careful with them. He misconstrues the nature of the problem with women; assuming that he could control his relationship with them. Again, in spite of the fact that the diviner insists to "Dieudonné" that Prospère must come and see him, he still discards this clarion call to help the desperate man that he is. He heads out to Nyamandem, settles and when things seems to be spiraling out of hands with his two first wives, he settles for a third, Monique. In Prospère's calculation, just like in the case of his second marriage, the goal is to keep the first in check; this fails woefully. And Monique, brought in to play this role (of keeping the first and second wives in check,), comes with the loyalty of a dutiful, trusting, and faithful wife whose only hopes are to bear and raise children for the man she loves. The failure to do so leads her into an early death. Monique's death spells the tragic for Prospère, and, at the same time, evokes the author's concern with society, culture, politics, and to an extent, history.

Prospère, while embodying the tragic, is also the totality of everything wrong with the Mimboland society: its cultural, social, and political practices. And through him, his earlier profession as a beer delivery driver to West Mimboland, the reader has a bird's eye view of all that which the oppressors work really hard to silence and make secret. It is on his way back from one of his trips after Gaston Abanda has been defrauded by the Mamawese that he, for no apparent reason, chooses to listen to the 1:00 p.m. news. The signature tune for the 1:00 p.m. news, to which Prospère listens, echoes the socio-political stalemate in a country overwhelmed by divisive politics. The songwriter in it expresses the wishes, desires, and thoughts of the masses. However, the masses misconstrue him for panegyrist or griot in West African parlance. It is in talking about this tune that the writer skillfully takes a swipe at Mimboland's president's divisive politics. The narrator informs the reader that this song was written by a "patriotic musician" who urged "the President to unite rather than divide" (54). It is in his explanation of the signature tune for the one o'clock news bulletin that the narrator seizes the opportunity to expose Mimboland, a country ruled by "a disciple of the antichrist: determined to put asunder what God has put together" (p. 54). Even if the narrator claims this information is from the *radio trottoir*, i.e. a rumor mill, he explains the mysteries and secrets surrounding the president's approach to ruling his fellow Mimbolanders disguised as one to undertake national development. His explanation simply betrays the secret and silent machination of the ruling party with its deceitful slogan "the Party of the People and of Development" (55) that has transformed all in Mimboland into zombies. The narrator tells us that in these words:

> [H]is approach to national development was like that of someone ordained to make zombies of his fellow Mimbolanders for personal profit. Yet the newspapers and radio, funded by all but owned by the clique in power according to *radio trottoir*, were overflowing with praises for the President and curses for his enemies, both real and imaginary. (54)

The dealings between Gaston Abanda and the Mamawese fraudsters give Prospère a push to realizing his dream. The deal is actually frowned upon by the journalist who reports the news and concludes: "greed, not love of *la patrie* had pushed Gaston to report himself to the police" (56). In Nyamandem the same motivates Matiba to cancel all appointments under the guise of having important matters at hand. The national sport of secrets, silences, and betrayals comes to light when Matiba instructs Marie-Claire to do the above and ask her to meet him later at "Monte Carlo". "Marie-Claire brightened up and winked at Prospère, who winked back. That alone was enough for both to recall all that had transpired between them, which they had mutually agreed to keep a secret" (137). FBN's treatment of this love (love affair between Marie-Claire and Prospere) demonstrates utmost sensitivity. It is a love affair built along the lines of Baudrillard's argument on simulations and simulacra wherein "simulations are representations of real events, and simulations lead to simulacra, the reproduction of objects or events that no longer correspond to an original form" (qtd. in *Contemporary Sociological Thought* 252). The above mentioned love affair equally foreshadows the deceitful kind of love Prospère will eventually find in this "jungle" as he calls it himself. FBN's is therefore a garden with such secrets and backstabbing all mushrooming in a nation reminiscent of a tomb with lifeless content and only the beautiful, yet thorny and spiky flowers in bloom decorating it.

In short, every step of the way in FBN's universe, like in EFD's, characters' secrets, their desire to be mute and silent as well as their practice of backstabbing each other are all welded to those of the characters' tragedy, society, culture, politics, and history of Mimboland and Caramenju. These are EFD's and FBN's central thematic concerns. All of these facets of their novels proliferate within the nation and translate into national desire that exceeds the bounds and limits of the ordinary and as such become that which governs Mimboland and Caramenju. This situation sickens these writers whose only choice is to use these disgusting by-products of the occult at the origin of the political quagmire and its pollutants, to paint a tableau that fascinates and inspires awe as would a beautiful predator in the like of a tiger in William Blake's poem "Tyger".

The novelists, EFD and FBN broach ideas of secrets, silences, and betrayals. The abundance of their examples strongly echoes the element of game highlighted by Fowler. He holds that, "in the multiplication of these there is a noticeable element of game..." (148). Their deconstructive powers, serving as motifs, point to the futility of any endeavor, in a system skilled at letting down its own citizens, by planting anything meaningful in the garden wherein only secrets, silences, and betrayals are permitted to blossom. These novels become for our authors under study, a site where to unearth and warrant the bloom of secret, silences, and betrayals like flowers decorating tombs. Anglophone Cameroonian authors are therefore left with only the choice evoked by Samuel Beckett when he posits that "one writes not in order to be published; one writes to breathe" (Beckett qtd. *in* Lattanzi-Licht and Kenneth J. Doka 208). And adding my voice to Beckett's I would say, they write to maintain their sanity. EFD and FBN demonstrate a keen understanding of a society immersed in a culture of corruption, treachery, and debauchery buried in a cloud of silence. Their works, though—centered on the local, have a global thrust on the effects of deceptive international friendliness which push nations, just like the individuals in Caramenju and Mimboland, to think of nothing but their self-interest and consequently turn a blind eye to the atrocious abominations of so-called "friendly nations". If not, how could others not care for the misery of others? The painstaking and illuminating deconstructive analyses of "post-independent East and West Cameroons" brought forth by these authors warranting the blossoming of secrets, silences, and betrayals are embittered by the prevailing adulterated conditions in the Cameroons informed by the writers' commitment, resentment, and disappointment in the face of global silence; all of which bring to mind Paul Valery's famous statement that,

> Latent in every man is a venom of amazing bitterness, a black resentment; something that curses and loathes life, a feeling of being trapped, of having trusted and been fooled, of being helpless prey to impotent rage, blind surrender, the victim of a savage, ruthless power that gives and takes away, enlists a man, drops him, promises and betrays, and -crowning injury- inflicts on him the humiliation of feeling sorry for himself. (Web.).

It is in this light that their works offer insights, judgments and exemplary values for the understanding of power shifts in the Cameroons from its pre-colonial days through the colonial to the post-colonial or even the "colonial" in the post-independence era which otherwise would remain hidden or buried in the bones of the oppressed. With the authors digging up these while refusing to submit to the inflicted humiliation and feeling sorry for themselves, their novels, thus, become in DeQuincey's words, both "literature of Power and the literature of knowledge" (qtd. in Buckler xvi).

Works Cited

Ankumah, Adaku T. *Nomenclatural Poetization and Globalization* Mankon: Langaa-RPCIG, 2014. Print.

Ayangwe, Carlson. *Betrayal of Too Trusting a People. The UN, the UK and the Trust Territory of the Southern Cameroons*, Mankon-Bamenda, Langaa-RPCIG, 2009. Print.

Bertman, Sandra. "Public Tragedy and the Art" *in* Lattanzi-Licht and Kenneth J. Doka, eds. *Living with Grief Coping with Public Tragedy*. New York, Brunner-Routledge, 2003. Print.

Buckler, William E. ed. *Prose of the Victorian Period*. Cambridge: Riverside, 1958. Print.

Doh, Emmanuel Fru. *The Fire Within*. Mankon: Langaa-RPCIG, 2008. Print.

Eagleton, Terry. *Literary Theory: an Introduction*. Minnesota, the U. of Minnesota P. 1998. Print.

Fishkin, Benjamin Hart, Ankumah Adaku T. & Ndi, Bill F. *Fears, Doubts, and Joys of not Belonging*. Mankon: Langaa-RPCIG, 2013. Print.

Flachmann K. & Flachmann M. *The Prose Reader,* New York: Pearson, 2014. Print.

Fowler, Alastair. *A History of English Literature*. Cambridge: Harvard University Press, 1991. Print.

Guerin, Wilfred L. *Handbook of Critical Approaches to Literature*. 3rd ed. Oxford, Oxford U.P. 1992. Print.

Hier, Sean P. ed. *Contemporary Sociological Thought: Themes and Theories*. Toronto, Ontario, Canadian Scholars Press, 2005. Print.

Hogue, W. Lawrence. "The Blues, Individuated Subjectivity, and James Baldwin's *Another Country*" in *CLA Journal* 56.1 (September 2012): 1-29. Print.

King, Jeannette. *Tragedy in the Victorian Novels: Theory and Practice in the Novels of George Eliot, Thomas Hardy, and Henry James.* Cambridge, CUP, 1978. Print.

Kristeva, Julia. *The Power of Horror: An Essay on Abjection.* New York, Columbia U.P. 1982. Print.

Larson, Charles R. *The Ordeal of the African Writer.* New York: Zed, 2001. Print.

Lattanzi-Licht and Kenneth J. Doka, eds. *Coping With Public Tragedy (Living With Grief),* New York, Brunner-Routledge, 2003. Print.

Newell, Stephanie. *West African Literature: Ways of Reading,* Oxford: OUP, 2006. Print.

Nyamnjoh, Francis B. *A Nose for Money.* Nairobi: East African Educational Publishers, 2006. Print.

Palmer, Eustace. *An Introduction to the African Novel,* New York, APC. 1972. Print.

Sartre, J.P. *What is Literature?* (Frechtman, Bernard: trans.), New York, Philosophical Library, 1947. Print.

Valery, Paul. Quotes "thinkexist.com" web. Accessed 12/7/14

Whitman, William B. *Quotable Politicians,* Guilford, CT. Lyons Press, 2003. Print.

INDEX

A

Acholonu, Catherine Obianju. .. 116, 120, 127
Adeleke, Tunde 41, 46
Aeschylus 143
African Experience 21, 23, 193
African governments 22, 46, 181
Ahidjo, Amadou................ 199, 204
Ahluwalia 36, 46
Ainsworth 53, 54, 55, 64, 65
Akamba.. 39
Akan 126
American Experience 34, 35, 42
Ankumah, Adaku T.200, 222, 235, 236
Appandurai 200
Arnaud-Lindet.....132, 135, 146, 151
Aro 126
Asante.. 28
Asante, Molefi K. 38, 46
Atieno-Odhiambo 37, 46
Augustus 144
Axum... 28
Ayangwe, Carlson.............. 229, 235

B

Babylon............................. 144, 149
Backsheider, Paula. 174
Bakhtin, Mikhail. 143, 151
Balandier 24, 25, 46
Baldwin, James 206, 236
Bale & Sang................................. 39
Bale, John 39, 46
Ball, Edward 102
Bately 146, 147, 151
Baudrillard........................ 231, 233
Beck, Ulrich....................... 184, 185
Beckett, Samuel 234
Bede 130, 151
Behdad, Ali. 157, 161, 166
Bendix 25, 43, 46, 47
Berlin Conference................ 39, 198
Beye 142, 143, 144, 151
Bismarck, Otto von 185
Biya, Paul........................... 199, 204
Black Private Education 66
Blassingame, John W. 101
Blehar 53, 64
Bonaparte 201, 229
Bourdieu, Pierre. 179, 180, 193
Bowlby 52, 53, 64
Bozeman, Terry. 119, 127
British Empire 153, 171
British Southern Cameroons 229
Bronzeville 77
Brooksley Born........................... 19
Brown v. Board 68, 73, 82
Buckler, William E.212, 216, 217, 235, 236
Butler, Octavia........................... 110

C

Caedmon 130
Caldwell, Tanya. 115, 119, 127
Cameroon 49, 175, 181, 182, 186, 198, 199, 204, 222, 229
Cameroons 197, 204, 211, 217, 220, 224, 229, 234, 235
Canton-Thompson, Getrude 28
Carretta, Vincent. 115
Carthage 144
Carthaginian 28
Casella, leanor Conlin 153, 172
Cassidy, J. 64, 65
Cayton, Horace 71, 73, 81
Channock 26, 27, 47
Charlotte Stratton 69, 70
Charter school 80
Chaucer, Geoffrey. 175, 216
Chesnut, Mary 102
Chicago 32, 47, 48, 49, 51, 64, 65, 66, 67, 68, 69, 71, 72, 73, 74, 75, 76, 77, 78, 79, 80, 81, 82, 83
Chicago Defender 72, 75, 83
ChildAid 34
Chisholm, Hugh 30, 47
Christianity 24, 40, 46, 131, 139, 144, 164
Cibulka, James 78, 80
Clarke, Duncan 102
Cliff, Michelle. 153, 154, 164, 165, 167, 171
Clinton, Catherine 101, 102
Clough, Marshall S 37, 47

Coetzee, J.M. 153, 154, 159, 160, 171
Cohen, David William 38, 47
Collins, Janelle 113, 118, 127
Colonialism 40, 156, 171, 172, 182, 184
Colonization 22, 46
Conrad, Joseph 31, 45, 47
Corr, Kendra 28, 47
Croesus 142, 143
Cryptonymy 19
Culkin, John C. 71, 80
Cunningham, Albert E. 74, 77
Cyrus 133, 134, 138, 141, 143, 145, 148, 149

D

Dahomey 28, 49
Danns, Dionne 69, 80
Dar es Salaam 42, 49
dark continent 24, 31, 32
Davis, David Brion 72, 101
Defoe, Daniel. 115, 173, 174, 178, 192, 193
Denniss, Richard 174, 175
DeQuincey 235
Dickens, Charles. 178, 193
Doh, Emmanuel Fru 195, 236
Doka, Kenneth J. 234, 236
Doris Allen Anderson 69, 74, 75, 76
Dow Jones 181
Dowden, Richard 181, 193
Dr. Harvey 21
Drake, St. Claire 71, 73, 81

Drayton, Julien D. 77
Duiker, William J. 35, 47

E

Eagleton, Terry 200, 236
Ebola 183
Edwards, Paul 120, 127
EFD (Emmanuel Fru Doh) 195, 196, 197, 198, 199, 200, 201, 202, 204, 212, 213, 216, 218, 219, 220, 226, 227, 229, 233, 234
Egeland 53, 65
Egypt 24, 28, 31
Elshtain, Jean Bethke 19
Emmanuel Fru Doh 200, 211
England 48, 113, 114, 122, 123, 124, 125, 126, 130, 147, 159
Ennius 141
Epistemology 23, 41
Equiano, Olaudah 113, 114, 115, 116, 117, 118, 119, 120, 121, 122, 123, 124, 125, 126, 127, 128
Erickson, Donald A. 74, 81
Eroticism 153
Ethiopia 35, 40
Europe 28, 32, 33, 40, 116, 117, 119, 155, 164, 181, 184
Evans, E.W. 47, 151
Evans, Richard 129

F

Fanon, Frantz. 97, 111
Faulkner, William. 103

FBN (Francis B. Nyamnjoh) 195, 196, 197, 199, 200, 204, 205, 207, 208, 209, 210, 213, 215, 216, 220, 221, 222, 223, 224, 225, 226, 227, 230, 233, 234
Ferguson, Moira 166
Ferguson, Niall 33, 47, 171
Field, Emily Donaldson. 120, 121, 128
Fishkin, Benjamin Hart. 173, 200, 236
Flachmann & Flachmann 196
Fornero, George 79, 81
Foster 67, 81
Foucault, Michel. 157, 171, 185, 193
Fowler, Alastair 199, 204, 213, 226, 234, 236
France 180, 198
Franklin, Benjamin 110
Franklin, John Hope 101
FRELIMO 36
Funada-Classen 36, 48
Fyle, C. Magbaily 24, 48

G

Garton, Stephen 166, 171
Genovese, Eugene D 101
Ghana 28
Gilgamesh 43
Gilroy, Paul. 116, 117, 118, 126, 128
Greece 139, 144, 145
Greg, Thomas 158, 167, 171, 172
Grossman, James 68, 81
Grossmann 57, 65
Guinea 184

Gwendolyn Brooks 72

H

Hall, Jennifer 120
Hall, Martin 28, 48, 128
Hamilton, Clive. 174, 175
Hampton University 21
Hardin, William 31, 48
Hazlitt, William 19
Hegel, Georg 24
Hegemony 157
Heidegger, Martin 19
Hellenic 28, 143
Hennick 45, 48
Herodotus 131, 132, 133, 134, 136, 137, 138, 139, 141, 142, 143, 144, 145, 149, 150, 151
Herrick, Mary 68, 74, 81
Hesse, E 57, 63, 64
Heteroglossia 140, 141, 143, 149
Hier, Sean P. 184, 193, 236
Hirsch 68, 71, 136, 137, 138, 151
Hirsch, Arnold 81
Hogue, W. Lawrence 206, 236
Holland 123
Holme, Jellison 66, 82
Homel, Michael 68, 81
Homer 43, 115, 140
Howalton 66, 67, 69, 70, 71, 72, 73, 74, 75, 76, 77, 78, 79, 81, 83
Hume, David 24, 226
Hyam, Ronald. 153, 157, 158, 164, 171
Hybris. 142, 143, 145, 146, 149, 150

Hyden, Goran 35, 48

I

Igbo 114, 115, 116, 117, 119, 120, 124, 126
IMF 181
Industrial Revolution, the 197
Irele, Abiola 41, 48, 186, 193
Irons, Peter 67, 81
Irvine, Jordan 67, 81

J

Jacobvitz 61, 63, 64
Jacqz, Jane Wilder 35, 48
Jaros, Peter. 115, 128
Jeyifo 41, 48
Jimenez-Munoz 198
Jones, Edward P. 110
JUGERA law 27
June Howe Currin 69, 72

K

Kelleter, Frank ... 118, 119, 121, 128
Kemble, Frances Anne 102
Kenneth Smith 75
Kenya 37, 38, 39, 46, 49
Kenyatta, Jomo 37, 40
Kikuyus 38, 39
Kilwa 28
Kimathi, Dedan 37
King Alfred 147, 149, 151
King, Jeannette 227, 236

King, Robert. 114
King, Stephen............................ 196
Kitigawa, Evelyn M. 81
Kluger..................................... 67, 82
Knupfer, Anne Meis.............. 72, 82
Kolchin, Peter. 101
Kristeva, Julia 195, 196, 236
Kuhn, Thomas 32, 33, 48
Kush 28

L

Lanaghan, Frances. 166
Larson, Charles R. 199
Lattanzi-Licht.................... 234, 236
Law, Robin........................ 29, 47, 48
Lefevere, Andre.. 129, 131, 139, 151
Lewis.. 141
Lewis, Robert . 75, 76, 151, 156, 171
Liberia....................................... 184
Livingstone, David 45
Loomba, Ania.................... 158, 171
Lopez, Alejandra 66, 82
Louis XIV 45
Lugard, Frederick 26, 45, 49
Lyons-Ruth 61, 63, 64

M

M'Baye, Babacar. 120, 128
Macedon 144
Machel, Samora 36
Magna Carta 45
Main & Solomon.................. 61, 63
Maina, Ephalina A. 39, 49

Makong'o, Julius 39, 49
Mali 28
Margaret Walker 72, 110
Martin Luther King Jr 68
Marva Collins Preparatory School 79
Masai 38, 39
Mau Mau 37, 47
McClintock, Anne...... 155, 156, 171
McCoy, Fleetwood M. 74, 77
McCutcheon, Marc. 102
McNeill, William H. 30, 49
Metcalfe, Ralph 72
Mimboland173, 175, 176, 178, 179,
182, 184, 185, 188, 191, 204, 205,
206, 207, 208, 209, 210, 211, 213,
214, 220, 221, 222, 223, 224, 225,
226, 231, 233, 234
mission civilisatrice 170
Mitchell, Margaret.............. 102, 110
modernity 24, 45, 109
Moeller, Wendy 28, 47
Mombasa..................................... 28
Mondlane, Eduardo 36
Monroe, J. Cameron 28, 42, 49
Morgan, Philip D. 78, 101
Morrison, Toni 98, 110
Motley, Susan 72, 82
Mozambique.......................... 40, 48
Murphy, Geraldine. 119, 128
Mwakikagile, Godfrey 35, 40, 49

'

'Mwalimu................................... 40

N

Nabudere, D. Wadada. 42, 49
Ndaloh, Agumba 39, 49
Ndi, Bill F. ...195, 200, 211, 212, 236
Ndlovu-Gatsheni, Sabelo 31, 49
Neo-classicism 197
New World 100, 113, 120
Newell, Stephanie198, 199, 200, 217, 237
Newman, John Henry 216
Ngomba-Roth, Rose 35, 49
Nigeria 38, 114, 116, 229
North Africa 28, 29, 30, 50
Nunez, Elizabeth.153, 154, 167, 168, 172
Nyamnjoh 19
Nyamnjoh, Francis B.173, 174, 175, 176, 177, 178, 179, 180, 181, 182, 183, 184, 185, 187, 188, 189, 190, 191, 192, 193, 195, 237
Nyerere, Julius 39, 40

O

O'Brien, Michael. 102
Oates, Joyce Carol 108
OAU, Organization of African Unity35, 39, 40
Oboka, Wycliffe A. 39, 49
Ochieng, William Robert 46
Ogot, Bethwell A. 46
Okoth, Assah 39, 49
Old English129, 130, 131, 140, 145, 146, 147, 148, 149, 151
Oppong 37, 49

Orosius129, 131, 132, 133, 134, 136, 137, 138, 139, 141, 144, 145, 146, 147, 149, 151

P

Palmer, Collin A. 102
Palmer, Eustace . 217, 226, 227, 237
Pattillo-McCoy 75, 78, 82
PBS, Public Broadcasting Service 20, 34, 49
Pemba 28
Pennycock, Alastair. 155, 167
Pharaohs 45
Phillips, Rodney 19
Philpott 71, 82
Pincham, R. Eugene 78
Pope, Alexander 173, 199
Pyramids 45

Q

Quaker 126
Queen Anne 174

R

Renaissance 32, 72, 82
Richard Wright 72
Richardson, David 47
Robert Cole 70
Rodney, Walter 41, 42
Roebuck 123
Roig-Franzia, Manuel 19
Roman 28, 30, 144, 149

Rome 27, 144

S

Sabino, Robin. 120, 128
Sanders............................69, 78, 82
Sang, Joe 46
Sarkin-Hughes, Jeremy 33, 50
Sartre, J.P. 226, 237
Scotland 50, 123
Scott, James C. 19, 27, 50
Senegambian 126
Seven Years War 114, 123
Shakespeare, Willaim. 115, 167
Shaver, P.R. 64, 65
Shaw, Rosalind. 120, 127
Shillington, Kevin.................. 36, 50
Sierra Leone 50, 184
Sizemore, Barbara....................... 75
Slaughter 67, 80, 82
Slave Coast 42
Slavery...............101, 102, 113, 127
Socrates 45
Sollors, Werner.................. 127, 128
Somalia 35, 40
Songhai 28
South Dakota 179
Southern Rhodesia 40
Spangler 56, 65
Spielvoge, Jackson 35, 47
Sroufe 53, 65
Stambouli, F. 29, 50
Stanley, H.M............31, 45, 50, 151
Stevenson, Brenda E. 101, 178
Stewart, James 31, 50

Stock 31, 33, 50
Strange Situation54, 55, 56, 57, 59, 60, 61, 62, 63, 64, 65
Stulberg 67, 82
Sudan 28
Sumerian-Akkadian.................... 139
Swahili 42
Swift, Jonathan. 102, 115, 173

T

T. M. Thomas 33, 45
Tanzania 36, 38, 40, 42, 44, 49
Teachers Union 66
The Royal George...................... 124
Thoreau, Henry David. 183
Torok.. 19
Trans-Atlantic trade 45
Translatability 130
Treadwell............................. 72, 78
Treadwell, Jimmie 83
Treaty of Versailles 198
Twain, Mark. 173

U

UHURU 37
United Nations 229
Urban Gateways 75
Urban League 68, 75

V

Valery, Paul 210, 235, 237

Victorian153, 154, 159, 185, 216, 217, 236
Voltaire 173
Voss, Barbara L. 153, 172

W

wa Thiong'o, Ngugi188, 189, 190, 193
Wai, Zubairu 41, 50
Washington Post, The 19
Waters 53, 64
Weinfield 53, 55, 65
Wells, Amy Stuart......................... 82
Wells, Stuart 66, 82
Wellstown 68
Western civilization 129
Westphalian......................24, 40, 44
Wheatfall, Robert......................... 75
White, Deborah Gray. 102
White, Frances .33, 51, 97, 101, 102
Whitelock 144, 147, 151

Whitman, William B............ 210, 237
Wiese, Andrew........................ 78, 83
Williams, William Julius................. 83
Wilson, William Julius 77, 83
World Bank 181
World War II 67, 68

X

Xerxes 142, 143

Y

Yaccino, A. 66, 83

Z

Zanzibar 28
Zghal, A................................. 29, 50
Zimmerman, Andrew 33, 51

www.ingramcontent.com/pod-product-compliance
Lightning Source LLC
Chambersburg PA
CBHW070828300426
44111CB00014B/2486